Endorsements for *T*  *Held*

It is the children the world a... ...old in your hands the story of on... ...eemed an unimportant, second-rate mandate, terrible things can happen—neglect, abandonment, and abuse of every kind. Dianne's story is all of that, plus the amazing power of courage, resilience, and redemption. I know this because her story is also my story—I lived part of it with her as childhood friends and survivors. Through reading this book, may you be encouraged and inspired to trust God's amazing grace with every aspect of your own story.

Dr. Wess Stafford
President Emeritus, Compassion International
Author of *Too Small to Ignore: Why Children Are the Next Big Thing*
And *Just a Minute: In the Heart of a Child, One Moment Can Last Forever*

Resurrecting a "maelstrom of memories," Dianne Couts brings her missionary kid upbringing to life in this poignant memoir spanning continents and generations. It's a story with much beauty but also one in which the saving of African souls often took priority over the suffering of children.

Christa Brown
Author *This Little Light: Beyond a Baptist Preacher Predator and His Gang*

Deep-hearted thanks to my heart sister Dianne for this unforgettable memoir, made beautiful by courage and honesty in the telling of her story. Often deeply painful, sometimes sweetly whimsical, it is ultimately anchored in hope and has been repurposed in her life as a strong voice of advocacy for other missionary kids, now adults, whose traumatic memories continue to haunt and hinder. May we all find the healing and hope that Dianne has, and may that center of grace continue to hold for all of us who have similar stories.

Margi Timyan McCombs, PhD
Director, Children/Teen Trauma Healing
American Bible Society

Don't read this book if you don't want to mess up your perception that all has been well and wonderful in the evangelical mission world. However, if you want to know the sad reality some have experienced growing up in the mission community, this is your book. Dianne's story is not unique. Too often, I have heard horrendous stories like Dianne's in my counseling office. As a missionary kid, I also heard stories like hers whispered among my peers. In this memoir, Dianne bravely shares how her deep faith held true and strong in the midst of sin and cover up by those who proclaimed to be followers of God. This is a topic that must be openly discussed in order to heal old trauma and prevent further harm of the most vulnerable among us, our children, and future generations. Thank you, Dianne, for your courage and candor.

Lois J. Bushong, M.S.
Licensed Marriage & Family Therapist
Owner of Quiet Streams Counseling and International Speaker
Author of *Belonging Everywhere & Nowhere:*
Insights into Counseling the Globally Mobile

In her memoir, Dianne Darr Couts recounts an enduring lesson learned from the choices her father made which affected his standing within an extended missionary and church community, and thus had implications for his family, including young Dianne and her siblings: "…standing for the truth may cost you, but ultimately people will respect you for holding your ground." Dianne is a truth-teller and truth-enactor whose integrity is rooted in faith and sustained by a deep courage. She deserves our full respect and attention. This personal and family narrative reveals the hidden phenomena of the sexual abuse of children whose parents were serving as missionaries from the U.S.A. in First World settings. That the abuse was perpetrated from within the insular cohort on which her family depended is a betrayal which intensifies the adverse consequences she experienced. This disarmingly honest narrative also reveals the resilience which bore her during trials and tribulation: a family's intergeneration love, the commitment to do what is right, and God's abiding grace. While deepening our understanding of the horrific nature of sexual abuse in faith communities, Dianne Darr Couts entrusts us with a legacy of hope. May her memoir inspire us to risk being truthful witnesses.

Rev. James S. Evinger
Minister, Presbyterian Church (U.S.A.)
and consultant, FaithTrust Institute, Seattle, WA

Things Fell Apart, but the Center Held

Dianne Darr Couts

Published by Dianne Darr Couts
April 2020

Cover designed by Chuck Jarrell
Edited by Sally Rushmore

ISBN 978-0-578-65456-0

Printed by Kindle Direct Publishing, an Amazon.com company

For my parents, Dick and Anne Darr,
who loved and defended me fiercely;

For my husband, Bud,
who loves me in spite of it all;

For my brothers, David, John and Rich,
who understand because they lived it too;

For my children, Robert, Jeanette and Janelle,
who crown my heart with gladness; and

For my grandchildren,
so that they will know.

Table of Contents

Acknowledgements 11

Author's Note 13

Prologue – First Impressions Last 15

Part I – I Barely Came and We Went Away 19

    Chapter 1 – Before I Came Together (1881–1944) 21

        My Mother's Story 21

        My Father's Story 24

        Stories Told, Facts Revealed, Memories Made 27

    Chapter 2 – How I Came and Why We Went Away (1944–50) 29

        Love and War 29

        Marriage and Me 31

        Doctrine, Destiny and My Baby Brother David 33

    Chapter 3 – My World Takes Shape (1950–54) 37

    Chapter 4 – Forces That Shaped the Whole (1954–55) 43

Part II – France – Where I Could Have Stayed Forever 49

    Chapter 5 – Once Upon a Time (Fall and Winter 1955) 51

    Chapter 6 – Far Away in France (Spring and Early Summer 1956) 61

    Chapter 7 – There Lived a Little Girl (Summer, Fall, Winter 1956) 69

Part III – Trauma and the Terror That Followed 75

    Chapter 8 – When Night Came in Africa (Spring 1957) 77

    Chapter 9 – Darkness Under the Bright African Sun (Summer 1957) 83

    Chapter 10 – Alarm and Kindness in Kayes (Fall 1957–Spring 1958) ... 87

    Chapter 11 – A Seismic Shift in My World (Apr 1958–Aug 1958) 97

    Chapter 12 – My World Explodes (Fall 1958–Dec 1959) 103

    Chapter 13 – Rough Seas and New Landscapes (Dec 1959–Mar 1960) ... 113

Part IV – Mamou Academy – A Maelstrom of Memories........................ 119

Chapter 14 – The Minefields of Mamou (Spring–Fall 1960 – Grade 6) .. 121

Chapter 15 – Sirakoro: Sad and Sweet (Dec 1960–Mar 1961) 131

Chapter 16 – Nightmares and Pleasant Dreams at Mamou (Spring–Fall 1961 – Grade 7) 135

Chapter 17 – Nonkon: Lessons Learned (Dec 1961–Mar 1962)......... 143

Chapter 18 – Deviations from Normal at Mamou (Spring–Fall 1962 – Grade 8) 149

Chapter 19 – Last Days at Mamou (Spring 1963 – Grade 9).............. 159

Part V – The Girl Survived but the Body Remembered 163

Chapter 20 – Mamou Girl in America (Summer 1963–Summer 1964 – Grade 10) 165

Chapter 21 – Studies and Survival on the Savanna (Summer 1964 – Summer 1965 – Grade 11)... 175

Chapter 22 – The Last Year I Called Africa Home (Summer 1965– Summer 1966 – Grade 12)... 187

Chapter 23 – The Old World Haunts Me in My New World (Sept 1966– June, 1967_Toc36718858 – Freshman Year of College in Greenville) 195

Part VI – Weathering the Aftershocks 205

Chapter 24 – Mountains High and Valleys Low (1967–1973 – College in Akron, Marriage, Motherhood, Moving Away) 207

Chapter 25 – Tropical Paradise and Stormy Seas (1973–1979 – Teaching in the Bahamas, Childbirth Trauma Again).................................... 217

Chapter 26 – Full Circles, Lasting Ripples (1979–1986 – Furlough, Third Childbirth, Medical Problems Escalate) 223

Chapter 27 – All My Worlds (1986–2020) 231

Family Matters 231

Advocacy for Missionary Kids 232

Repercussions of a Vow Fulfilled.. 234

Hope for the Future... 235

Epilogue..237

Resources...239
    Websites about and for MKs and TCKs...239
    Books about MKs and TCKs...239
    Documentary about Abuse at Dianne's MK Boarding School.......239
    Books Explaining the Lifelong Effects of Childhood Abuse..........239
    Books about Preventing and Responding to Abuse.......................240
    Organizations Focused on Preventing and Responding to Abuse..240

About the Author...241

Acknowledgements

I am grateful to the many people who read, edited, critiqued, and corrected my manuscript. Their insights and encouragement kept me going on the long road between writing and publishing. I've listed them here in the order they read my book: Julie Rine, published writer and English teacher extraordinaire; Katie Sams, avid reader and social worker who understands what trauma does to humans; Lois Bushong, expert on TCKs and MKs and wise counselor; Christa Brown, fierce advocate for survivors of clergy abuse; Wess Stafford and Margi Timyan McCombs, fellow Mamou survivors and world changers for children in need around the globe; James Evinger, scholar and advocate for change in regard to abuse in religious settings; Shary Hauber, fellow GMU missionary kid, Mamou survivor and dedicated MK Safety Net board member; Sarah Klingler, passionate MK Safety Net partner; Peter Janci, attorney and faithful friend of MKs; Stan Burns, Lynn Miley and Susan Douglas Fultz whose stories are part of mine; Cousins Barbara and Barry Dunaway, extended family I trusted to read and understand; my brothers, David, John and Rich who could correct me because they were there; my children, Rob, Jennie and Janelle who know their mother better now.

Without the documents my parents saved, it would be impossible to prove my tale. I am thankful that, unlike the thinking of many, they did not believe that remembering was a sin.

Thanks to my brother Rich for having the foresight to interview our parents. Their voices, telling their stories, are a treasure and provided me with many details for the early chapters of my memoir.

A special thanks to my Aunt Peggy Bandy who has known and loved me longer than anyone else I know. She not only encouraged me to tell my story but verified my memories and provided dates and details that otherwise I could not have included.

A special thanks to my husband, Bud. His understanding during the three-year journey that it took me to create this book was a gift. Beyond that, his fine editing skills found almost 100 errors that my other superbly educated, highly gifted readers missed! Because of that, when my manuscript went off to my editor, it was nearly perfect.

To my editor, Sally Rushmore, thank you for navigating the publishing aspects of this book for me. Without you, it would be dead in the water!

Thank you, Chuck Jarrell, for getting the cover just right and for restoring some pictures that bring my story to life.

And, to you my readers, thank you for wanting to read my story. If it resonates with you, or if it helps in some small way to heal places that may have fallen apart on your journey, I would love to hear from you.

Author's Note

The people and the places I describe in my memoir are real and are presented as I remember them. The dialogue between characters was recreated from what I remember of real conversations. Where noted, names and situations have been changed to insulate those who are far removed from the events that happened to me long ago.

My aim in writing my story was not to air dirty laundry nor to solicit pity or praise. I simply wanted to tell what happened to me, to explain how those experiences impacted my life and to show my gratitude for those whose love and courage kept my world together, allowing me, in spite of it all, to thrive.

Beyond that, if what I wrote helps people understand that abuse is not a one-time event whose effects can simply be forgotten, forgiven and prayed away or helps them realize that unflinching love in action makes all the difference in the life of a child, then the candid telling of my tale will not have been in vain.

Prologue

First Impressions Last

My first recollections of the world, and of myself in it, are these:

- I flush the toilet but the water keeps rising, rising, rising. I am so afraid I can't move. The water spills over the top of the bowl and splashes around my shoes. I start to cry and mommy comes running in.

- I am lying on the living room floor, a coloring book in front of me and a crayon in my hand. Suddenly David is behind me, pulling my hair, laughing. I yell, and keep yelling, but he doesn't stop.

- Nurses roll me in a sheet and a doctor stands over me and stitches up my forehead. I am screaming. Next, Daddy is carrying me down the hill to our house and Mommy and David are waiting for me. I smile.

- Headlights flash over the top of a hill and as soon as the car zooms past, I am dashing across a dark street holding an older girl's hand. With my other hand, I clutch tightly to my bag of candy.

- Mommy is talking to Daddy about the little girl upstairs. I ask what urine is. "It's pee, honey. She smells like pee." Mommy is upset with the little girl's mother.

- I am looking out the window at a 15-foot wide crater in the middle of the yard. It looks like a huge, grass-lined bowl with big brown cracks. I can tell that Mommy, standing behind me holding David, is afraid.

- I see a splatter of bright red blood on the kitchen floor. Someone is holding on to mommy and they are walking away from me, out the door.

I became curious about these memories when I was in my teens. One day, when my mother was at the ironing board and I was standing by with the hangers, ready to catch Dad's freshly ironed shirts as soon as she flipped them, crisp and warm off the board, I asked her about them.

"I remember the first place we lived in when we moved to Greenville."

"Really?" she said, not even looking up. "You were just a toddler when we moved there."

"A little girl lived upstairs," I continued, "and you were upset because she smelled like urine."

At that, there was a slight pause in the rhythmic passing of the iron as Mom glanced over at me. "I'm surprised you remember that. She used to come down every morning to play with David and you. I was so disgusted with her mother. Couldn't she smell? Maybe she didn't care."

"Was that the girl who took me trick-or-treating?" and then I added, "By October I would have been two and a half," hoping that making myself a little older would help her believe I really did remember these things.

"No. That was an older girl who lived next door. I told her to go just to the houses on our street but, when you came back with all that candy, I knew she had taken you farther. I was so mad. You were too little to cross that busy road, especially at night."

"I remember that we lived downstairs and the yard sloped downhill. Did the yard cave in, or am I imagining that?" I asked.

"The yard did cave in where a well had been. I'm just glad it happened at night and not when you and David were out there playing." I could tell it scared her, even then, just thinking about it.

"I remember blood on the kitchen floor. What was that all about?"

"That's when I had my miscarriage," Mom explained, matter-of-factly. "At the bottom of the yard, the clothesline was too high for me to reach so I stood on a chair to hang the clothes. One day the chair tipped and I fell, really hard, and it caused my miscarriage."

Like pushpins on a map, what happened in my early childhood would move with me across the globe, puncturing my world in ways that rang familiar and true: scary things happen, people are not always good, there is blood and pain, and even the very earth can give way. But just as true was this: I was never alone, I was loved and cared for, and somehow, together, we all survived.

Dianne, David, neighbor girl and the clothesline where Mom fell

Part I

I Barely Came and We Went Away

"Stories have to be told or they die, and when they die,
we can't remember who we are or why we're here."
Sue Monk Kid, *The Secret Life of Bees*

Chapter 1

Before I Came Together
1881–1944

I always knew that my beginning was more than the facts on my birth certificate. For as long as I can remember, I was told:

"Your Great-Grandpa Koehl left Germany because he did not want his sons fighting for the Kaiser."

"Your Grandma Koehl was a scullery maid in England before she came to America when she was 18 years old."

"Your Grandma Darr learned English because she was the first child in her family to go to school."

"Your Grandpa Darr became an orphan because his parents died in a fire when he was a little boy."

As a little girl, I had no idea where Germany was, or who the Kaiser was, or why only some children got to go to school, or what a scullery maid was, or what it meant to be an orphan. But this I always knew: my beginning involved the lives of more people than just my parents and Akron was where I was born, but it definitely was not the only place I was from.

My Mother's Story

"We grew up on the wrong side of *two* sets of tracks," my mother's youngest sister Shelly would say, with an emphasis on the word *two*. The quip was funny, but it was also literally and figuratively true. The eight Koehl girls grew up in a small house on a little ridge next to the Beltline railroad tracks that linked the small city of Barberton, Ohio to the eight sets of tracks bisecting the city of Akron where trains clicked and clacked night and day bringing rubber and coal into, and taking tires of all sizes out of, the Rubber Capital of the World.

The Koehl family was poor and not just-because-of-the-Depression poor. Frank Koehl's German immigrant family was staunch Catholic and his

21

family tree was dotted with successful farmers in the Old Country and with priests, nuns and architects in the New. But although Frank's ten years of schooling made him better educated than most young men in the late 1900s, he had wanderlust and, when he wasn't on an adventure to the West Coast, he preferred working with his hands. When he did decide to settle down in his mid-thirties, he married my grandmother, a recent immigrant from Wales who was thirteen years his junior. Annie Richards was poor, Protestant and of the working class. The Koehl family was not amused and refused to welcome her into the family.

When my grandmother was barely sixteen, her hostler father beat her when her employer brought her home pregnant at the hands of his son. Two years later, her father was kicked in the head by a horse and died. The insurance money from that tragedy allowed the family to book passage to America. Grandma's little boy came to America too, but died as a toddler in Philadelphia before the Richards family settled in Akron.

I learned about my grandma's little boy when I was a teenager, but imagine my consternation when, sorting through my mother's things in 2014, I learned the child's name and date of birth. On the back of a picture of a little boy I read: *Robert Arthur Richards, December 19, 1910*. Had my grandmother winced when I named our firstborn Robert or when our little girl was born on December 19, 1974? She never said a word about Rob's name nor about Jennie's birthdate, but I can only hope they were gentle reminders of her sweet boy who left her far too soon.

Frank Koehl and Annie Richards were married on Columbus Day, October 12, 1916. Nine months and one day later their baby girl Betty was born and two years later Grandpa bought property at 2515 Seventh Street on the southern edge of Kenmore, Ohio, a town that was later annexed by the city of Akron. The property included a little house, another tiny house and a small barn. Over the next fifteen years, seven more sisters would be born in that house: Sue, Mary, Barb, Annie, Katie, Peggy and Shelly. Those weren't necessarily their real names, of course. At the end of Seventh Street, what appeared real was not necessarily the same thing as the facts.

Frank Koehl picked cherries every summer on the Fourth of July. But in 1926, the year of a very warm spring, he was up on a ladder in the cherry tree on June 24th. It was as good a place to be as any other while the doctor was in the house helping his wife deliver their fifth child, my mother. Grandma got to deliver the babies, but Grandpa got to name them—mostly after his sisters who never accepted his wife. My mother was named Anna Marie after his sister, whose name as a nun was Sister Mary Perbora, one of the Sisters of Notre Dame. But the baby was simply called Annie, like her mother, and Annie-with-no-middle-name was the only name my mother knew at home and at school. It wasn't until she was seventeen years old, standing incredulous in the courthouse in downtown Akron, staring at her birth certificate, that she learned her legal name was Anna Marie Koehl. It was a shock to realize that she had a different identity than the one she had left home with that morning.

Years before that, as a little girl, Annie developed a serious medical condition called rectal prolapse. The doctor came to the house, did what he could, but told Annie's parents that this was a serious condition and she could die. That evening, with the shadows hiding him, Frank Koehl went behind the house, leaned on the wall and sobbed, asking God to spare his little girl. Annie, lying wide-eyed in the bedroom near the open window, heard it all. For a little girl who was a middle child, one of many, it made an impression on her tender little heart that she never forgot. And, even though he had stopped attending Mass long ago, that night Frank's humble, broken-hearted prayer was heard.

As the fifth child of eight, Annie was lost somewhere in the middle, wedged between her sister Barb, who was so smart she skipped two grades, and her sister Katie, who was valedictorian of her class. Barb, also stuck in the middle between Mary, Grandpa's favorite, and Annie, Grandma's favorite, vented her frustrations on her sisters and especially delighted in tormenting Annie about her crooked teeth.

But, when Annie was in Grade 7, Miss Inez Cole chose her to be her helper after school, something Mom always recounted with pride. When school closed for Christmas that year, Miss Cole gave Annie the classroom Christmas tree. She dragged it home over the ice-covered swamp behind the school, across the Beltline tracks, and up the ridge to her house where her big sisters somehow stuffed it into their tiny living room. It was 1938, just before the end of the Depression. On the day before Christmas, packages arrived to go under the tree—gifts bought by the teachers at Rimer School for the poorest children they knew.

The Koehl girls may have been the poorest kids on their street, but they had one feather in their cap: their mother spoke English. Their neighborhood between the two sets of tracks was called the Russian Cell because most of the families living there were Eastern European with last names like Onesko, Prachter, Schentenberger, and Olynek. Another woman who spoke English on Seventh Street was Mrs. Jones and she noticed that the little girls living at the end of the street never attended church. She not only invited them to church, she picked them up in her car and took them. The kind members of Goss Memorial Evangelical Reformed Church welcomed the little girls who lived on the other side of the tracks, and it was there that the girls learned about God and about Jesus, who loved them.

In the fall of 1940, Annie became a freshman at Kenmore High School where her teachers and classmates started calling her Anne. She enjoyed her classes, especially art, typing and shorthand. She played on the softball team, marched as a majorette, was voted onto the May Court twice and was crowned Hi-Y queen her senior year. She and her friends also attended the Kenmore Cardinal football and basketball games.

After one of those basketball games, on December 19,1941, Anne was in an accident that almost took her life. She and her friends—sisters Delores and Ann Hensley, Fay Walsh, Aileen Dunn and Irene Buck—were walking in the street because the sidewalks were covered with snow. They were wearing long, dark winter coats, typical of the time. A fellow in a car pulled up to the girls, talked to them, sped away, turned around and came back, but the lights of an oncoming car blinded him and he plowed right into the girls. Delores Hensley was killed. The other girls were hospitalized with serious injuries, including Anne who was knocked unconscious and remained in a coma for two days.

Several articles were published in the *Akron Beacon Journal* about the tragedy[1] and the first one included a picture of Anne, recovering in the hospital. It is no surprise that Frank Koehl's family, who had shunned his bride, had little to do with his children. However, like everyone else in the 1940s, they got the newspaper and there, a few days before Christmas, was their fifteen-year-old niece staring off the page at them from a hospital bed. They showed up with warm wishes and lovely gifts—more than likely relieved that this was less awkward for them than it would have been to show up for her funeral. After that, they made more of an effort to keep in touch with the family. And thus, while she recovered, Anne learned once again that when your body is broken, people love you.

My Father's Story

Two generations after Johann Lorenz Linder had immigrated to Ohio from Ungstein, Germany, his descendants were still worshiping in German in a Lutheran Church and speaking German in their homes. But one of his granddaughters, Dorothea (Dora) Linder, my father's mother, got a break. With two older brothers to help on the farm and an older sister to help in the

---

[1] Auto Plows into Kenmore High School Victory Promenade, Injures Six Girls. (1941, December 20). *Akron Beacon Journal*.

house, she was allowed to go to school, making her the first person in her family to learn English.

The lovely portraits we have of Dora as a young girl would indicate that her family was not poor. We know little else about her childhood, but we do know that, instead of getting married in her late teens as other young women did in the early 1900s, Dora worked as a housekeeper, reputedly in the home of the Fisher Body family in Norwalk, Ohio. It was in that town that she met my grandfather, Frederick Darr. Their marriage certificate, dated August 28, 1916, lists Dorothea's age as 26 and Fred's as 27. Fred gives his occupation as a rubber worker which explains their move to Kenmore, Ohio. Over the next 14 years, they had four children including my father, Dick Linder Darr, who was born on January 21, 1926.

Dad had very few memories of his father because, in the wee hours of March 13, 1933, four years into the Great Depression, Fred Darr hung himself on a tree just a block away from where his family lay sleeping. Johnnie was fifteen, Mary Jane was eleven, my father had just turned seven and Jimmy had just turned three. Uncle Johnnie, who was older when his dad died, wouldn't tell me much about his dad either except that Fred was from somewhere in New York, his parents had died in a fire and, because he was an orphan, no one could find out anything about him. Eventually it came out that Fred had been sick a long time and couldn't work and, in the days before he hung himself, he had been caught pirating electricity from the neighbor's power line.

What Fred Darr never told his children, his grandchildren learned. Before he was born, Fred's father, John G. Dörr, had served time in the Auburn Prison in New York for nearly killing a man in a fight. After serving his time, John married and returned to Olean, NY where his son, John Frederick Dörr, my grandfather, was born in 1888. He did indeed become an orphan. When he was about ten, his mother Josephine dropped dead in front of the children in their home. In 1910, the year John Frederick turned twelve, his father died from the burns he suffered while attempting to rescue him from their burning home.

Although the orphaned children had older, married sisters living in Olean, John G. Dorr's brother Frank from Bowling Green, Ohio became my grandfather and his younger sisters' legal guardian. Frank not only moved the children to another state, he also changed the spelling of their last name to Darr and inverted my grandfather's first and middle names which explains why information about his early life remained elusive for so long.

Skirting the truth and hiding these stories was less painful for Fred, I suppose, than explaining them to his children who had no reason to know. But, eighty years after my Grandpa Darr died, when I learned the truth about his life, it helped me understand his death. Trauma in Fred Darr's life did not start with the Great Depression. It had piled up, one stigma and tragedy at a time, for as long as he could remember. When I think of him now, I no longer picture him swinging from a tree. I picture him as a little boy and my heart aches for what he endured and I marvel at the things he did overcome until he could take no more.

Fred Darr's death did not stop the trucks from barreling past my seven-year-old father's front door at 983 W. Waterloo Road, zipping their way across the state of Ohio on what had recently become U.S. Route 224. It did not stop the trains as they carried coal and steel, rubber and tires, and sounded their whistles night and day on the eight sets of tracks a half mile north of his house. Neither did it stop his mother.

With Fred's insurance money, Dora kept the house. With grit and determination, she kept the family together. People may have talked about Fred Darr, but his widow stood tall and went to work taking "baby cases"— moving in with families to care for the newborn and the mother and to help around the house for a week or two after a woman gave birth. People may have whispered about Fred's death, but Dora held her head high when visiting ministers who came to preach at Hope Evangelical United Brethren Church sat at her table for one of her renowned meals. During the spring and summer, flowers from her impressive garden decorated the altar at church and all year round, when hobos riding the rails needed a cup of coffee and a plate of food, they knew Dora Darr would never turn them away.

In the absence of a father in the home, Dick's older brother Johnnie quit school, got a job and handled the manly jobs in and around the house. Handling Dora was left up to Dick because he had a way of cheering her up when she was down and smoothing things over when she was upset. Dick's tender heart, along with his affable, light-hearted personality, made him perfect for the role.

My father, in spite of what life handed him, thrived.[2] That was in part because, once he turned 12, he left Akron every summer to live on his Uncle Fred Linder's prosperous dairy farm in Fremont, Ohio. Uncle Fred read from the German Bible at breakfast every morning and, every afternoon, as Dick and his cousins lounged around the living room for a break from the noonday heat, his Aunt Stella read to them from a Lutheran devotional book. Dick accompanied his cousin Lloyd every day on his route delivering milk and cream to the businesses in town. In the afternoons, he helped his cousins with

---

[2] *"If you take away a mother or father, you cause suffering and despair. But one time in ten, out of that despair arises an indomitable force."*
Gladwell, Malcolm. Chapter Nine: André Trocmé, Part 3, *David and Goliath: Underdogs, Misfits, and the Art of Battling Giants* (Little, Brown and Company, New York, 2013), Kindle Edition.

work in the fields. Living as part of that family and working hard to contribute to their successful business taught my dad valuable lessons that shaped him into the man, father and leader he would become.

Another factor was sports. Dad played basketball at Highland Park School and, during his Grade 8 year, they won the league title. At Kenmore High School, he excelled in football. As a JV player, he helped the Kenmore Cardinals to an undefeated season and, in Grade 11, he was a key player that led the Cardinals to an Akron City Championship. Being coached by Milo Ratkovich and playing on that team meant a lot to Dick, but he also joked that football was important to him for another reason: his senior year there was a beautiful majorette named Anne who had caught his eye!

Although he was an avid reader, academics were not important to Dick Darr and his rank near the bottom of his class was proof. But, to his credit, in the spring of 1944 when the graduation rate in the nation was only 42%, Dick finished his senior year and left Kenmore High School with a diploma in his hand. Unfortunately, the odds of him being drafted into World War II were 100%. A year and a half earlier, Congress had lowered the age of the draft from 21 to 18 and, in the summer of 1944, Dick knew that he would be leaving Akron—and it would not be to his Uncle Fred's farm.

Stories Told, Facts Revealed, Memories Made

As a child, I absorbed the stories I was told about my parents and grandparents. As an adult, I wove other facts into those stories as they were revealed. How the traces of trauma and the threads of resilience in my ancestors' lives have impacted me, I'll leave to the scientists to debate.[3] But this I do know: the strands of their lives intertwine with mine and to ignore that would be denying a part of who I am.

---

[3] Carey, Benedict. (December 10, 2018). Can we really inherit trauma? *New York Times*.

Chapter 2

How I Came and Why We Went Away
1944–1950

Love and War

Dick and Anne's first date was a double date in February of their senior year with Anne's friend Helen Kovatz and Dick's friend Paul Edwards who was home on leave from the Army. Dick and Anne continued to date during the spring of 1944 and went to their Senior Prom together.

A short time after graduating, Dick boarded a bus full of other 18-year-old boys and traveled to the Federal Building in Cleveland, Ohio. Once there, the young men were lined up in two rows down a long hall. When a CEO with six golden hash marks on his shoulder came out and asked who wanted to join the Navy, hands shot up on both sides of the hall but only two men were chosen: Dick Darr from one side and his childhood friend, Bernie Foutz, from the other. The rest were drafted into the Army and, after 90 days of training, were sent straight to the battle fields of Europe. By December, some of them had perished in the Battle of the Bulge.

Retouched by Chuck Jarrell

Dick went to basic training in Camp Perry, Virginia, and on to Class A Gunner's Mate School in Bainbridge, Massachusetts, in the fall. Dick and Anne kept in touch by letter while he was in training and were happy to be reunited in December when Dick was given a short leave. They posed for pictures on Seventh Street and also in Washington D.C. where Anne, Dick's sister Mary Jane and her friend Sara Washnock went to visit him the weekend of December 9, 1944. Perhaps it was during that time that Dick proposed and Annie accepted. However, before he sailed off to the Pacific in the spring, she returned the ring. Years later, when she told me about it, she said, "I loved him, but I did not want to be engaged to someone who might never return."

On April 9, 1945—three years to the day before I was born—Dick deployed from Philadelphia on the *SS Oklahoma City* to join the Third Fleet in the Okinawa Campaign against the Japanese in the Pacific. At one point, he did not see land for 72 straight days. That changed in the early morning hours of July 18, 1945 when, under the cover of darkness, his ship and three others slipped silently into the waters of Tokyo Bay and bombarded the radar installations there. That was the only combat mission the *USS Oklahoma City* performed during the war and it was its last.

On a sunny morning, less than three weeks later, an atomic bomb fell on Hiroshima followed three days later by another one on Nagasaki. The war in the Pacific was over.

Most of the battleships in the Third Fleet returned home after the peace treaty with Japan was signed on September 2, 1945. However, since the *USS Oklahoma City* had been in the Pacific for only a few months, she was assigned to the Fifth Fleet for patrol duty around Japan. During the months that the ship sailed those waters, she dropped anchor from time to time and the sailors were allowed on shore. When I was old enough to realize how significant that was, I asked Dad to tell me about it. He began to describe what he saw where the bombs fell and then said abruptly, "I don't want to talk about it."

On January 30, 1946, Dad's ship began its voyage east across the Pacific and docked in San Francisco on February 14, 1946.

In July, 1946, the boy Anne loved did come home and they began dating again. In the summer of 1946, when Dick proposed the second time, she did not respond right away. They were in the little living room of Anne's home and she recalled him nervously moving from one end of the couch to the other and back and forth to the arm chair while he pled his case. She finally said, "Oh, all right!" Anne's mother was in the kitchen and when Dick called her into the living room to tell her the news, she started to cry and went back to the kitchen.[4] When her mother's sniffling stopped, Anne called her back into the living room to go over their plans. "We've looked at the calendar," she told her mother, "and we'd like to get married on October 12, your 30th wedding anniversary."

It was a simple wedding at Goss Memorial Church on a Saturday evening, October 12, 1946, with Rev. William Troup officiating. Anne's sister Betty was the maid of honor and Dick's brother Johnnie was the best man. Betty and her husband Steve had a simple reception for the couple at their home at 2448 Conrad Avenue and they honeymooned in Pennsylvania at the Summit Inn. Sadly, we have no pictures of the wedding because Anne could not afford a photographer. However, Dick and his best friend Paul Edwards had matching dark brown suits made by the same tailor for their weddings and we know that Anne wore a beautiful white dress that fell just

---

[4] Darr, Anne. Interview by her son Richard Darr, Autobiography, Akron, OH. (April 23–25, 2001).

below the knee. We have a picture of the two couples posing in front of Grandma Darr's house wearing clothes that match those descriptions. The picture is in a sequence with those of their honeymoon and it is nice to think that it is of Dick and Anne on their wedding day.

Marriage and Me

The young couple moved in with Dick's mother and Anne continued working at the B.F. Goodrich Tire and Rubber Company where she had been hired right after high school. She worked in an office on one of the factory floors where the workers' time records were kept. She was punctual, smart and honest and not afraid to do what was right—even if it meant reporting a secretary who repeatedly took long lunch breaks and then lied about it on her time card.

Dick worked at several jobs before he found his niche as a Coca-Cola® salesman, delivering wooden cases of 6" bottles of Coke® to businesses in Akron. The ropes he had learned delivering milk from his uncle's dairy to the businesses in Fremont helped and, by 1950, Dick had the best route in town, delivering Coke to businesses on East Market Street, Howard Street, the north end of Main Street, and on West Market Street all the way out to Fairlawn.

Restaurants, nightclubs, grocery stores and business offices all sold Coca-Cola. Dick loved interacting with a diverse group of customers from Greeks and Italians to people from the hills of Kentucky. He also delivered Coke to Our Lady of the Elms, a Catholic girls' school on West Exchange Street. One day, as he pulled around the delivery driveway at the back of the school, he caught the nuns roller skating, their black habits and veils streaming behind them as they sailed across the parking lot.

Unfortunately, living with her mother-in-law on Waterloo Road, was anything but smooth sailing for Anne. Dora snooped in Anne's things in their bedroom and she was snippy with Anne. At Thanksgiving dinner that fall, she addressed Anne as "you little snit" right in front of her parents who had been invited for the meal. It came to a head on Christmas morning. Anne and her sister-in-law, John's wife Fern, had gone together to buy new kitchen curtains for their mother-in-law. Anne's share of the cost was more than what she had spent on her gift for her own mother. When Dora opened the present, her reaction was an outburst of criticism and disdain, "Curtains! What kind of a Christmas present are curtains?"

Anne's childhood home may have been little more than a shack, but it was clean and orderly. Her parents were soft spoken and kind and never meddled in their adult children's lives. Life on Waterloo Road was not what

Anne was used to and neither was it her style to confront. Dick's role as mother tamer was suddenly in direct conflict with his wife's happiness and in January of 1947 they rented an apartment and moved out. But they were gone for only one year. By July, Anne was pregnant and when she quit working in early 1948, they moved back to Dora's house on Waterloo Road to make ends meet.

I was born on April 9, 1948 and was named Dianne, a combination of my parents' first names. When I asked Mom about her labor and delivery, she said matter-of-factly, "They knocked you out back then," and refused to elaborate. But she did tell me that she was happy she got her wish for a daughter and she nursed me even though bottle feeding was the rage at the time. When I came home from the hospital it was to a bassinet in my parents' bedroom at Grandma Darr's house. Mom appreciated Dora's experience taking care of babies, but living there was not ideal, so by August our little family of three moved into an apartment in The Projects, the housing units Goodyear had built for their war employees and which were now available to veterans as well.

Up to that point in my life I was no different from the Baby Boomer babies all over the City of Akron. I was the grandchild of immigrants whose parents had lived through the Great Depression, whose father had served in WW II, and whose parents were building the American dream in a booming economy. However, when I was four months old, my father decided to go to church with my mother and, because of that, my roots would never grow deep into the Rubber Capital of the World.

32

Doctrine, Destiny and My Baby Brother David

Although they had grown up going to church, Dick and Anne Darr did not attend services regularly after they got married. But when I was born, Mom took the advice of Mrs. Werner, one of her childhood Sunday School teachers, to start going to church again for my sake. Dad was not very keen about attending so, most Sunday mornings, he stayed home and took care of me.

One Sunday, in August of 1948, Dad decided to attend a service with Mom at Goss. Rev. Troup's sermon that day was from Ephesians 2:8–9, about being saved by faith and not by works. At the end of the service, a man named Matsy Smith tapped Dad on the shoulder and asked him if he was saved. Dad politely brushed him off and even joked about the incident that night. However, a few weeks later Dad went back to Goss for a Saturday evening musical presentation by a team from Bob Jones University. After the concert, the director, a Mr. Howard, closed with a short message urging people to follow Christ.

In later years, Dad summarized his conversion experience like this: "I had been raised in the church all my life but I began to understand—I guess it was the Holy Spirit—the doctrine of being saved by grace and not of works. That was a big thing. So then, that night, I accepted the Lord as my personal Savior in the middle of the night."[5]

In the context of Akron, Ohio, in the late 1940s, Dad's conversion was nothing unusual. At the time, if you were in Akron and didn't know where it was on the map, you would have thought it was in the middle of the Bible Belt. The city's nickname at the time was "The Capital of West Virginia" because two decades earlier, while the mining industry there was waning, the rubber industry in Akron was waxing and the city flooded with families from south of the Ohio River looking for work. It was a time when churches were suspect of the liberalism creeping into the mainline denominations. Independent Baptist and Bible churches sprang up and some, like the Akron Baptist Temple, drew crowds in the thousands. Fundamentalist Bible Colleges like Bob Jones University, Tennessee Temple, Wheaton College and Moody Bible Institute taught the preachers who filled their pulpits. One of their tenets was that Christ would return when every tribe on earth had heard the Gospel and it was their job to make that happen.

Goss Memorial took the command of Jesus to "Go into all the world and preach the Gospel" very seriously as evidenced by the huge world map hanging in the front of the sanctuary showing where its missionaries were

---

[5] Darr, Dick. Interview by his son, Richard Darr, Autobiography, Akron, OH. (April 23–25, 2001).

serving around the globe. During the winter of 1948 and into the spring of 1949, Dad felt a gradual desire to join their ranks. Approaching Rev. Troup (who had an honorary doctorate from Wheaton College and who preached in tux and tails from behind a large, imposing pulpit) was daunting to Dick Darr, a 23-year-old Coca-Cola truck driver who, less than a year earlier, had rarely darkened the door of the church and whose high school transcript was less than stellar. But Dad made an appointment, met with Dr. Troup and started following his advice on how to reach that goal.

Mom, like young wives of the day, wouldn't have thought to question her husband's call. Besides, she had grown up at Goss where choosing a path like that was admired. During the summer and fall of 1949, while Dick drove his Coca-Cola route and focused on his goal of becoming a missionary, Anne was busy and happy being a full-time mother and awaiting the birth of her second child. In preparation for that, we moved into a bigger apartment in The Projects at 780 Donald Avenue.

My brother David was born on October 20, 1949 and this time it was my Grandma Koehl who helped when mother and baby came home from the hospital, even though it meant riding two different bus routes for her to get there. Heaven knows Mom needed the help. I was just 18 months old, Mom was nursing David, and Dad worked all day and was gone every time the church doors opened or a ministry opportunity called.

During the summer of 1950, with Dr. Hamilton from Goss helping with the application process and with the G.I. Bill paying his tuition, Dad was enrolled at Bob Jones University. In late August of 1950, Dick and Anne Darr left Akron with their little girl Dianne Louise, who was two, and their baby boy David Edward, who was ten months old, and drove south through the Smoky Mountains to settle in Greenville, South Carolina. It would be our home for the next four years.

I have never known how rooted feels. My haven was not a house with a street address in a town where everyone knew my name. The only constant in my life was the people who sailed away with me again and again to drop anchor in yet another harbor. When our little family pulled away from Akron, I was way too little to know that my childhood journey was now on a path less traveled, one that would eventually take me to places most people in Akron had never heard of—across oceans and seas, down dusty roads and over wild rivers, through savannas and into rainforests—far, far away.

Chapter 3

My World Takes Shape
1950–1954

In September of 1951, we moved out of the apartment where the yard caved in to a trailer park for BJU married students and settled into our own house— a 20-foot by 16-foot box[6] with a roof. Unlike the isolated snapshots of what happened during my first year in Greenville, my memories of that place include the big picture of our tiny home, of my neighborhood and of my relationships with the people who loved me.

Dad in front of our tiny house, BJU trailer park, Greenville, S.C

The front door of our house opened into 10-foot by 16-foot room that comprised a living room, kitchen and dining area. Beside it was a 10-foot by 12-foot bedroom with a double bed for Mom and Dad on one wall and a twin bed for David and me on the other. At the back of the bedroom there was a

---

[6] Ibid.

10-foot by 4-foot closet and storage area but no bathroom, making the chamber pot a part of my childhood. Mom carried it up the sidewalk every morning to empty it in the public restroom where there were rows of toilets, showers, cement wash tubs and a few wringer washing machines.

During the week, David and I were washed off at the kitchen sink but on Saturday afternoons Mom took us up to the wash house, filled a wash tub with warm water, had us strip naked and climb in. While she scrubbed us from head to toe, we splashed each other and our playmates who were also being scrubbed by their mothers in the tubs beside us.

I was a preschooler, unaware that our house was minuscule and that most Baby Boomers lived in homes that had a toilet. My mother took these things in stride because living in a tiny house with a chamber pot and no bathtub had been part of her childhood too. Luckily for David and me, our mother followed her mother's example of making do with little and keeping a clean, orderly home. Mom had weekly and daily routines for managing our household but life in our home was far from rigid. Mom was warm, openly affectionate and interactive with David and me, something she told me she had to cultivate.

"The first time I held you on my lap and read you a *Little Golden Book*, I was embarrassed to hear my own voice reading out loud."

"Really?" I responded. "How old was I?"

"Oh, about nine months, I suppose."

"You were embarrassed to read to a baby?" I laughed. "Did you think I would critique you?"

"I don't know," she said. "I had never seen anyone read to a baby before, but I did it because I wanted you and David to be confident and smart."

She not only read to David and me, she sang to us, she taught us nursery rhymes and she encouraged us to learn. I remember lying on the floor, writing the letters of the alphabet on a chalk board propped up against the wall. That must have been on a Tuesday because that was the day Mom ironed and I remember the ironing board above me and Mom glancing over it to praise my efforts. But her sweet mothering style did not mean that David and I were coddled.

My first memory of Mother meaning business took place at an Easter Egg Hunt in the trailer park. I remember walking up the sidewalk with Mom, wearing my pretty dress and carrying my Easter basket. But, when the egg hunt began, I was too shy to run around and pick up the eggs. At the same time, I was upset when I saw other children put eggs in their baskets and I had none. Mom knelt down, encouraged me several times to try and then, when I kept throwing my little fit, she marched me straight back home.

Besides being a full-time student, Dad also worked to support his family. His jobs included delivering newspapers, selling Fuller Brush® products door to door and being a salesman in the men's department at Sears®. During our first year in the trailer park, the 1951-1952 school year, Mom also worked for a firm that did accounting for the big cotton mills in Greenville. Mom and Dad needed her income to pay back the money Grandma Darr had loaned them to buy our little house. While she worked, David and I went to a Lutheran preschool where my only specific memory is of lunch on the first day. That incident stuck because, even though I was full, the teachers made me finish all the crackers and cheese in my lunch box while they stood behind me criticizing my mother for packing too many. I didn't like what they were saying. I didn't like watching the other children play while I sat alone at the table. I didn't like the feeling that somehow something was wrong with me.

Mom didn't work the second year we were in the trailer park because, on February 28, 1953, our baby brother was born. It was a happy day when David and I saw Dad pull up to our house, walk around to the passenger side of the car and open the door. As we ran up to the car from the neighbor's house, Mom swung her legs out the door and there on her lap was our new baby brother, John Andrew. I was not quite five, David was not even three and a half and now there was a newborn added to the mix. Grandma Darr flew down from Akron to the rescue and Mom was thankful for her help.

One day while Grandma Darr was there I came running down the sidewalk from the wash house, tripped and slid across the pavement on my face. It took skin off my nose, above my lip and across my left cheek. When it scabbed over and I saw myself in the mirror, I refused to leave the house even when Dad asked me to go with him to the grocery store, something I never turned down because that errand usually involved a candy treat. Eventually he persuaded me to come and, at the checkout counter, the clerk asked Dad what had happened to me. After he explained, she turned to me and said, "It's okay honey, those scabs will come off and you'll be as pretty as ever." That day I learned something important: feeling like a freak did not make you one and even strangers can be kind.

Another memory with my Dad involved the new shoes we never wore. Mom and Dad had saved for months to buy David and me new shoes but, when Sunday morning came around, they were gone. After searching every corner of the house, Mom wondered if they had accidentally been thrown out. Dad, David and I walked to the end of the street to the place where everyone burned their trash. Leather would not have burned up very easily but, after poking around in the ashes, Dad didn't see anything that looked like little shoes. He walked home heavy hearted and they started saving again.

My Aunt Peggy, one of mom's younger sisters, also lived in Greenville because her husband Julian was on the music faculty at the school. One spring day, Mom and Peggy sat me on a chair outside our house, draped me in a plastic cape and gave me a permanent. I was all excited before it started, but not so much when the chemicals burned my scalp and the fumes stung my eyes. I cried and begged them to stop, but they made me endure to the curly, beautiful end.

Our last summer in Greenville, the summer of 1953, I was five and I recall it well because I was old enough to go to Vacation Bible School. I remember the teacher telling us that we had all sinned, which included things like disobeying our parents, and that sinners went to hell, but that Jesus died on the cross so we could go to heaven—which was, of course, where I wanted to go. So, along with a dozen other kids, I raised my hand and asked Jesus into my heart. Fortunately, while this glimpse at God's wrath and damnation made a distinct impression on me, it did not dominate my idea of God because it was not reinforced at home. Jesus loved us, this I knew, and we went to church, said grace before meals and heard Bible stories before we went to bed because we loved him. It was as sweet and simple as that.

Later that year, when Johnny was old enough to be outside, David and I played with him like he was our real, live baby doll. One terrifying day we almost lost him. He choked on a piece of hard candy and mom couldn't get it out. He was turning blue when she picked him up and ran screaming into the street. A man came out of nowhere, grabbed him by the heels, swung him upside down, hit him hard in the middle of his back and the candy flew out. When he handed John to Mom, she collapsed to the ground where she rocked back and forth on her knees, sobbing, cradling her screaming baby in her arms.

As Dad's college days were coming to an end, he received a shock. His tuition payments from the GI Bill had stopped in April because he had been enlisted a few weeks short of two years. It would be impossible to earn that kind of money before graduation. Dad wrote Goss Church, explained his predicament and asked if they could help. Thankfully, the church sent a check for $240 dollars, allowing Dad to finish his degree in Education Administration on time. Grandma Darr and Dad's sister Mary Jane flew down for his graduation and Mom, who was seven months pregnant, flew back with Johnny and Mary Jane. Grandma Darr stayed to drive back to Akron with Dad, David and me.

Before leaving, Mom had packed up a little trailer with their bed, the crib, a dresser and other household items. Dad hitched it to his 1946 four-door Plymouth and with Grandma Darr in the front seat and David and me in the back, we set off for Ohio. Because of the trailer, Dad took the long way around on Rt. 11, through the Shenandoah Valley up to the Pennsylvania Turnpike driving straight through with just some short stops to sleep along the way. "Mother was good that way," Dad would later recall. "She was crabby and had her faults, like everyone else, but she tried to help her kids."

After getting back to Akron, Dad learned firsthand from a church member that the highly esteemed pastor of Goss Church had openly questioned sending Dad the money to help him graduate on time. Dad's telling of it ends with this: "The pastor did more than enough to help us through the years, but the man was not perfect."[7] In the years ahead, the lesson that men on pedestals are just as human as everyone else would prove to be just as valuable to Dick Linder Darr as his hard-earned college diploma.

---

[7] Darr, Dick. Interview

Chapter 4

Forces That Shaped the Whole
1954–1955

Our return to Akron landed me back at my Grandma Darr's house where my life had begun. Right after we moved in, Mom told David and me never to ask Grandma about our Grandpa Darr. She explained that he had killed himself when our dad was a little boy and that talking about it would upset her.

A few days later, while watching Grandma Darr prepare supper at the kitchen counter, she paused, turned slightly toward me and told me about my Grandpa Darr's death: the suicide note, the men finding him hanging, the location of the tree. When she finished, she looked directly at me and told me not to tell my parents that I knew about this because it would upset them. And then she calmly turned back to her task. In my peripheral vision, I could see her arms and hands moving across the counter beside me while I stood still, staring straight ahead at the wall between the counter and the cupboard above, not saying a word, confused at the story and overwhelmed by the burden of carrying two secrets that I, as a six-year-old child, didn't really understand.

Two other memories from Grandma Darr's house during that time are significant. One involves my grandmother pushing me face down in the empty bathtub with one hand and lifting a bright red enema bag over me while my mother, all but hidden by the doorway to the hall, watched and ignored my screams. Constipation and its opposite would plague me my entire life, especially during times of transition or stress, and my mother's reaction to conflict or crisis by retreating powerlessly into the shadows would be a recurring theme as well.

The other memory is not being able to fall asleep. After we were tucked in bed, David and I would whisper awhile as Johnny, snuggled safely between us, would fall asleep. David would eventually turn toward the wall and drift off too, leaving me wide awake and alone. When that happened, I would get up, put my pillow next to Johnnie to keep him from rolling out of bed, tiptoe across the bedroom floor and down the hall, hugging the wall to minimize the creaking of the floor, and carefully, silently sit down at the top of the stairs. From my little perch above the landing I could see the staircase lit softly by the living room lamp below and I could hear the muffled voices of my parents and grandmother visiting in the kitchen in the back of the house. I was not afraid. I just didn't want to lie in bed, wide awake.

On August 25, 1954 our baby brother, Richard Stephen, was born. While Mom was in the hospital, David and I stayed with our Aunt Mary Jane and Uncle Bill and our cousins Billie James, Herb and Ed. On the day we came home, I remember tiptoeing into the dining room and peeking over the edge of a bassinet and there was our newest little brother, sound asleep. Like our father, my brother David and me, Dr. Hamilton had delivered him and he advised Mom not to nurse him. "You have a toddler and two young children. You need to gain back your strength to take care of them," he advised.

Earlier that summer, Mom and Dad were accepted as missionary candidates by the Mission Endeavor International (name changed to protect identity), a non-denominational faith mission agency that required its missionaries to raise their own support. In the fall of 1954, our parents started making the rounds at fall missions conferences in churches near and far, explaining their call to Africa and explaining what their missionary work would involve.

While they started raising support, I started first grade at Highland Park, the same school my father and his siblings had attended before me. However, I wasn't there long. Dad's deputation travels took him away for weeks at a time and Grandma Darr was often away caring for elderly persons in their homes. It was a blessing when Goss Church arranged for us to move into a house on Kenmore Boulevard close to a grocery store, a dairy, a bakery, a butcher shop and a Woolworth's Five and Dime®. The owner of the home, Mrs. Carlisle, was a member of the church and lived upstairs and, best of all, the house was right around the corner from Goss Church and Heminger School where I finished first grade.

Like the other Baby Boomers in first grade in the mid-1950s, I learned to read from the *Dick and Jane* books, how to print with a pencil and how to add and subtract. I went home every day for a lunch of soup and crackers, or toasted cheese or lunch meat sandwiches, or my favorite, "Goldenrod." I liked waiting for the toaster to pop and then watching Mom ladle my piece with chunks of hardboiled egg whites in white sauce. Then she'd stand behind me saying, "Lean to the side, honey. I don't want this getting in your hair." Over my shoulder a little sieve would appear with an egg yolk rolling around inside it and, with the press of the back of a spoon, bright yellow dust showered over the sauce. It was as pretty to look at as it was delicious to eat.

I marvel now at how Mom did it. Richie was an infant, John was not quite two, David had just turned five and I was six. However, being alone with the children wasn't much different from what Mom had always known. Between going to school and working, Dad had not been home much for the past four years. I have six specific memories of him during my first six years of life: taking me to get stitches in my forehead, taking me to the store with my scabby face, telling me never to stare at Negroes because they were people just like us only with dark skin, visiting him once at the men's department at Sears, opening the car door so we could see our baby brother John, and looking in the burning trash for our shoes. That's it. In comparison, there are dozens of overlapping memories of my mother's presence tenderly caring for us day after day. The fact that our change in location, once again, didn't trouble me, I attribute to her loving, steady presence.

One memorable Sunday, Dad was scheduled to preach at a little country church close enough for all of us to attend. Our family sat about three pews from the front with Richie on Mom's lap, Johnny on her left and David and me on her right. Part way through our father's sermon, David and I started whispering and wiggling around in the pew until our father barked from the pulpit, "Anne, control those children!" I jerked to attention, pressed my back against the back of the pew and barely breathed until the benediction. In the car on the way home, Dad blamed Mom for not controlling us, scolded David and me for distracting him during his sermon and lectured us all about people being unwilling to send us to Africa to tell people about Jesus if the children in our family didn't know how to behave. The incident is funny on the one hand, but it makes me cringe on the other. How, as little children, was the Great Commission supposed to be our responsibility too?

By early summer of 1955, enough support was pledged that the mission board changed Mom and Dad's status from missionary recruit to missionary. Since their assigned field was the French Sudan in French West Africa, their first task would be to study French in Paris. Beyond applying for passports and booking tickets, there were two other loose ends to tie up before we left. One of them involved us four kids. None of us had been officially dedicated to the Lord, the equivalent of baby baptism in evangelical circles, and it was probably a good idea for our parents to do that before taking us off to the Dark Continent where perils of all sorts surely awaited us. One Sunday morning our little family stood at the front of the church and Pastor Troup prayed for us one by one by name. I still can feel the weight of his hand on my head and hear his voice above me, calling my name and asking God to bless and keep me.

The other thing involved our whole family posing for a picture which would be sent to all our supporters as a reminder to pray for us. It may have been taken on the morning of Mom and Dad's commissioning service because Dad has a flower in his lapel. Gene Baldensberger, a member of Goss and the professional photographer for Goodyear, took the picture right next to the church sign which read *By Grace Are Ye Saved Through Faith* which was the same text that was preached six years before when Dad got saved.

And then we were off. Dozens of family members and church friends gathered at the Akron Canton Airport to send us off to New York City. Never one to be shy, I dashed ahead to be the first one up the steps and onto the plane. Flying in those days was a fancy affair and children were treated to gifts and a visit to the cockpit to watch the captain fly the plane. In New York City, we stayed overnight in a hotel where telegrams and a fruit basket arrived wishing us *Bon Voyage.*

I probably would not have remembered our hotel room on the 23rd floor if Johnny hadn't locked himself in the bathroom. Mom saw him walk in, heard the door close, went to open it but couldn't. It was a hot August day and she knew the window, just above the toilet, was wide open. Johnny was two and a half and a lively little boy. She turned to Dad and said, "I can't get in and the window is open. If he climbs up on the toilet ..." Dad immediately dialed the front desk and Mom knelt by the door, ashen faced, and calmly talked to Johnny through the key hole. "Stand right by the door, honey, where you can hear Mommy's voice, okay?" After an eternity, someone appeared with a key and there was our little brother, standing obediently just inside the door. Later Dad lifted David and me up and had us look down at the street far below. It was a lesson about safety that I never forgot.

Within a day or two, we boarded the *S.S. United States*, a new luxury liner that crossed the Atlantic faster than any other passenger ship. Our cabin was well below deck with three narrow bunks on each side. Mom and Dad had the lower ones, Rich and John slept above them, and David and I had the bunks on top.

Our steward gave David and me directions to the elaborate play room and assured Mom that he was there for anything she might need. Mom and Dad alternated having their meals with the younger boys in our cabin and with eating with David and me in the dining room. I'll never forget our first meal on the ship. My head and shoulders just cleared the large china place setting and my view of Dad across the table was blocked by a row of crystal glasses. The linen table cloth nearly touched my lap and on it were rows of spoons, forks and knives stretching out to the left, out to the right and above my plate. Dad ordered us chicken noodle soup and, when I had finished, I pushed my chair back to leave. Dad laughed, "That's just the first course, honey. Wait. There will be more."

Just nine years before, at the end of World War II, Dick Darr had sailed east across the Pacific and into San Francisco Bay. Now he was sailing east once again, but this time it was across the Atlantic and he was headed into a battle of a different sort. Christian hymns like *Onward Christian Soldiers, Am I a Soldier of the Cross*, and *Soldiers of Christ Arise* were rallying cries for the church to fight against the powers of darkness and to spread the light and truth of the Gospel. Dick had been called to that battle in 1950 and now, five years later, with a college degree, the endorsement of a mission board and the financial backing of a dozen churches and numerous individuals, he was on his way to that battle with his wife, children and all.

After five days at sea, the *S.S. United States* docked at Le Havre, France where our family boarded a train for Paris. From Paris, we traveled 13 miles south of the city on another train to the little village of Crosne which would be our home for the next year and a half. We never forgot the date, August 25, 1955, because it was Richie's birthday, the day he turned one.

Part II

France – Where I Could Have Stayed Forever

"Life itself is the most wonderful fairytale."
Hans Christian Anderson

Chapter 5

Once Upon a Time
Fall and Winter 1955

I have never doubted fairy tales. Little girls like Lucy Pevensie in the *Chronicles of Narnia* do get whisked away to lands where magical things happen and they are forever changed. I am no C.S. Lewis, but I will try my best to put into words how, once upon a time, a little American girl named Dianne lived in a little French village far, far away where she had all kinds of adventures and was very, very happy.

My new world did not start out feeling like magic. My first memory of France is in an attic—kind of like Cinderella—where I was helping my mother make the beds.

"I don't like it here," I snapped, yanking the sheet up to the top of the mattress and slamming a pillow on top of it. I was standing on the side of the bed, hunched under the sloping ceiling of the garret room where we were staying temporarily. "And," I continued, "we didn't have cereal for breakfast and I didn't see one thing I recognized in that tiny grocery store we went to yesterday."

"It will be better when we move into our side of the house. You'll get used to things. Give it time." Mom replied evenly.

"I don't even know why we're in Crosne," I snapped back.

"Dianne," she said firmly, "if you keep complaining, I'll give your brothers your share of the candy I bought at that store you didn't like. Now be quiet and help me make these beds."

I shut up; I made the beds; I had no choice but to give it time. And, before long, I was charmed by Crosne. I loved the poplars, standing tall against the sky, watching over us on our way home from the train station in Montgeron and the cobblestone street in front of our house, hemmed in by walls on both sides, sloping its way past the bakery, the tiny grocery shop, the butcher shops and the vegetable shop on its way to the town square. I loved the Yerres River, flowing deep and forbidden at the end of our huge, wooded yard and reappearing further downstream near the town square where we sometimes watched the women washing their laundry along its banks.

Street in Crosne, France

We lived in one end of a stately manor house built centuries before by aristocrats who had also been charmed by the Yerres and the rolling vineyards and farmland along its banks. Our side of the house had a large kitchen and a living room on the first floor, a bathroom and bedroom on the second floor for Mom, Dad and Richie, and a garret bedroom on the third floor for David, Johnny and me. On crisp, sunny mornings, Mom sometimes opened our little balcony window and would caution, "Be careful that Johnny and Richie never come over here alone," and then she'd flip our sheets and blankets over the railing to let them freshen up in the sunshine.

Every night, Dad crawled into bed with us and told us two stories, one about the woodland adventures of Gray Squirrel and Red Squirrel followed by a spell-binding episode of Tom and Jack, whose daring deeds during the time of the American revolution left us spellbound. I thought my dad was the best storyteller of all time until I read *The Last of the Mohicans* in college and found the plot and the characters strangely familiar. But I forgave him for the plagiarism because, better than the stories, was being snuggled up in the crook of his arm every night and knowing he loved us.

Our new world even had a fairy godmother, Mme Dusquesne, who was also our landlord's wife. Her magic powers were hospitality, empathy and kindness. She was the one who let our mother know that when school started, David and I would need a *tablier* to wear over our clothes. She communicated this by coming into our kitchen with one draped over her arm and with her ten-year old daughter, Marie-France, in tow as her mannequin. She pointed to David and me, took the little smock off her arm, put it on Marie-France and then pointed to David and me again. After this pantomime, Mom understood that her children would need *tabliers* too and Mme Duquesne offered to sew them for us once Mom picked out the fabric.

Retouched by Chuck Jarrell

A few days later I was standing in the little office of the School for Girls where the principal spoke very limited English. I stood amazed as two adults spoke simple, choppy sentences to each other and used lots of gestures to explain themselves. Dad showed her my report card from grade one in Akron and held up seven fingers to indicate my age. It was decided that since I spoke not one word of French, it would be best to put me in grade one again, which in France was called grade 12. Dad repeated this scenario with David at the School for Boys one block away, up a little hill. David wouldn't turn six until the end of October but he proved to be braver than me.

Even with a fairy godmother who knows how to clothe you and parents who love you, a little girl in a strange new world is sometimes afraid and not very brave. On the first day of school, when all the little girls went into the courtyard for a break, I nonchalantly worked my way along the stone wall toward the gate and, when no one was looking, I lifted the latch, opened it just wide enough to slip through, held my breath as it creaked shut behind me, and bolted. I ran all the way home—past the bath house, through the village square, past the string of little shops, past the bakery and arrived panting and sobbing at the wrought iron gate to our house. I pulled the bell cord and waited.

Dad's classes at the Alliance Française in Paris had not yet started, so he was home. When he came to the gate he was shocked to find me crying outside. "Dianne, honey, what's wrong?"

I flew into his arms, "I don't understand. I don't understand," I sobbed.

"I know, honey. I know. But you will." He took me inside where Mom hugged me and wiped my tears. And then Dad bent down so he was eye level with me and said, "Little girls have to go to school. Come on, I'll walk you back."

We walked together—my hand tight in his, my stomach tight in me—down the winding, narrow street through the village and back to school. This same scenario played out for four straight days before I gave up; and, magically, within weeks, my metamorphosis began.

By the time the poplar leaves turned color and David turned six, we were both understanding and speaking French. We spoke it to our teachers and our classmates and at the little shops where we translated for our mother. We spoke it each other at home and on our way to and from school with Marie-France, who had become our good friend.

It was not just the *tablier* I wore over my clothes and the language the teacher spoke that told me I wasn't in Ohio anymore. The playground had no swings, slides or monkey bars and the restrooms had no toilets. Marie-France had to show me how to back into the stall, plant my feet on the ceramic floor, tuck the hem of my skirt up under my chin, pull down my panties and squat over the hole at the back. One day my foot slipped and went into the hole, much to her amusement and my mortification. When I said I should ask the teacher to go home to change, Mary France laughed again. So, my soggy sock and shoe went back to class with me where it oozed till lunch. Mom kept me home that afternoon while the contaminated shoe sat first in soapy water and then in the sun to dry. "Soap and sunlight disinfect," Mom said matter-of-factly. The next morning, I learned something else: they also make for a very stiff shoe.

My classroom had windows along one wall and a blackboard at the front. The other two walls were bare. We sat two to a desk with a sloping top and two inkwells, one on each corner. Pencils were not allowed. The teacher showed us, one student at a time, how to write with a stylus: dip it into the middle of the ink, just to the top of the split in the stylus, drag it carefully across the lip of the inkwell to remove any excess ink, carefully bring it across the top of the desk to your little notebook, lower it gently onto the page, and start writing. If your motions were jerky at any juncture, ink would splatter and a drop of ink anywhere was inexcusable. Those who allowed it to happen were brought to the front of the class, berated and made to stand there holding their notebooks in front of them with the damning spot visible to all. I didn't understand what the teacher was saying, but I understood shame and I made sure it never happened to me.

School was for learning. Period. Within a few months we knew how to add and subtract numbers of all sizes. Multiplication and division followed in the spring. We perfected our penmanship by copying and applying the rules of French grammar which were tested by dictations the teacher read aloud and which we were expected to write down verbatim. The curriculum included geography and French history. For fun, we learned the traditional French children's songs and the dances that went with them.

Once a week the street through the village became an open-air market. On our way home for lunch, Marie-France, David and I dodged people between the stalls and, on our way back to school, we kicked big cabbage leaves, other vegetable scraps, and pieces of brown paper down the sidewalk. Mom bought our butter there every week, cut from a huge yellow mountain, placed on shiny brown paper and weighed on the vendor's scale. One day, after we had lived in Crosne for many months, Dad came bounding through the door with a brown paper bundle in his hands, "Anne, you won't believe it! I found salted butter in the open-air market in Montgeron." The bread tasted really, really good at supper that night.

I was often sent to buy the bread. On my way home, when I was hungry, I'd break off the crunchy end of the loaf and eat it. When Mom's disapproval escalated to scoldings, I had to adapt. I figured out that if I broke the end, but not all the way through, I could pull out the soft center and close it back so the loaf still looked whole. When I placed the loaf on the counter, with the sabotaged end on the left side, the loaf looked perfectly whole. Mom was right-handed, so she always cut the bread from right to left. I can still hear her reaction as she reached the end of the loaf and cut through the crust into nothing. "Something's wrong with this loaf of bread," she exclaimed, and then, half laughing and half scolding, "Dianne, I told you to stop eating the bread on your way home. That includes the middle!"

The *boulangerie* near us made just bread. The *boulangerie-pâtisserie* on the village square made bread and pastries. Marie-France often stopped there for her afternoon goûter, or snack, while David and I waited for her outside. On the rare occasion that Mom gave us a few coins to spend, I always chose a *pain-au-chocolat*, a flaky pastry with a stick of dark chocolate baked in the middle.

There was a small dairy not far from our house where we would ring a little bell and, through the top half of the door, we could buy cream, yogurt and sometimes milk. They didn't sell cheese, but we were never in short supply of it. Dad loved bringing home different varieties from all the regions of France and none of it tasted bad on top of that crispy, fresh-baked bread. A huge block of ice from the ice truck kept the dairy products cold in an icebox during the warm months and a box with screened sides, sitting outside on the back porch, kept them cold during the winter.

Not being able to buy milk proved to be a problem for Richie who was still on a bottle when we arrived in France. But that wasn't Richie's only problem. Even when there was milk, Johnny would steal his bottle and drink it. One evening when mom was complaining about this happening again, Dad put an end to it. "Are all the bottles clean?" he asked.

"Yes, they're there on the counter." Dad pushed a chair over to the counter, climbed up on it, opened a cupboard that was so high mom couldn't reach it, put the bottles inside and closed the door.

"When there's milk, Richie can drink from a cup and when there's no milk, give him yogurt."

One evening Mme Duquesne brought us a tureen of French onion soup for our supper. My parents thought it was wonderful, but I was not a fan. After washing the tureen, Mom sent me to return it to Mme Duquesne. When I got back to our side of the house, Dad asked me if I remembered to thank her. "Yes," I responded, "I thanked her, and when she asked me if I liked it, I told her I didn't." First Dad chuckled and then I got a lesson on being tactful.

Mme Duquesne was obviously not offended by my lack of manners because, when Mom had surgery for appendicitis in December and spent five days in the American hospital in Paris, Mme Duquesne helped take care of us. Each morning Dad got the four of us up and dressed, walked us over to the Duquesne's side of the house, hugged us good-bye and then headed straight for the train station in Montgeron. Then Mme Duquesne would welcome us at her door where we'd say good-morning to her and Marie-France with a kiss, kiss, once on each cheek in the proper Parisian way.

The first morning, when our little entourage entered the dining room, M. Duquesne was already seated at the head of the table reading the newspaper. He lowered it slightly to look at us, grunted a *Bonjour* and went back to reading. Mme Duquesne had David and me sit on either side of Marie-France on one side of the table and had Johnny and Richie sit on either side of her on the other side. While she was seating the boys, I noticed there was bread, butter and jam on the table and, in front of me, a large bowl. "Oatmeal too?" I thought and then, there was Mme Duquesne, pouring warm milk into my bowl followed by a stream of dark brown, piping hot coffee. David and I watched Marie-France take the sugar bowl and drop three lumps into her bowl of coffee. We followed suit. We watched her lather her piece of baguette with butter and dunk it in her coffee. We followed suit again and it was love at first, slurpy bite. After I finished my bread, I drank the entire bowl: the creamy brown coffee, floating with melted butter, my little head, tilted all the way back so all I could see was the ceiling, making sure I got the very last drop.

Mom was home before we knew it and, much to our disappointment, refused to serve us *café au lait* for breakfast. "But Daddy gives us *canards* all the time," I argued.

"A sugar cube dunked in coffee is not the same as an entire bowl of caffeine which will stunt your growth!" she shot back and I knew there was no use in arguing. I am not particular about many things but, to this day, bad coffee and weak coffee are two things that I cannot abide.

By mid-winter, life had settled into a routine at 3 Ave Jean-Jaurès, Crosne. Mom, with John and Rich in tow, could now navigate the butcher shops (the one for beef and the other for pork), the little grocery store and the fruit and vegetable shops. She knew which days the bakery made *pain de mie*, the closest thing to American bread we could buy. Dad had learned how to navigate the train and métro systems that got him back and forth to his classes in Paris.

One day he took me to class and, instead of listening to the teacher, the man sitting next to him sketched a picture of me. The metro was very crowded on our way home and I stood sardined between my dad and strangers, my little face against his side, holding on tight as the train rocked and jerked its way between stops on its way to the Gare de Lyon. We crossed the street into the train station where Dad looked up at the clock and said, "Run!" He grabbed my hand and we flew down the platform to the last open door of the train and jumped aboard.

For part of the time we lived in France, we owned a car. Dad continued to go back and forth to Paris on the train, but a car allowed us to go places as a family. "Kids," he'd shout, "look out your window! That's the Arc de Triomphe!" Or, "Look, Notre Dame!" Or, "There's the Eiffel Tower!" All I saw were cars, careening around the Place de l'Étoile or trees and sky as we flew by the places that meant nothing to me. The car also took us to a little store on a side street in Paris where we could buy things from America like peanut butter, powdered sugar, boxes of cereal and popcorn and it took us to Sunday morning church services in a big room where lots and lots of missionaries had church in English. All of them were in Paris to learn French so they could go to Africa and tell people about Jesus, just like us.

Other Sundays we drove to a Huguenot church in Villeneuve-Saint-Georges, the big town next to Crosne. There weren't very many people in that little Protestant congregation where everyone wore black and nobody smiled. But I did learn the Lord's Prayer and a pretty little song in Sunday School whose sweet lyrics and lilting tune are with me still. "No child is too small for the narrow road...Even the youngest heart can be a temple for the Savior."[8]

One cold winter morning our little car took us to Villeneuve-Saint-Georges for another reason: the town's large open-air market. We ended up in a stream of people moving in both directions and pushing their way to the stalls on the sides of the street. Because of the press of the crowd, Mom and Dad were carrying John and Rich and David and I were walking behind them. And then someone stepped in front of me and when I looked up, my family was gone. I don't remember what happened after that, but it must have involved tears and someone calling the police because what I remember next is sniffling and walking down the street holding the hand of a tall policeman who was speaking reassuringly to me, "It's okay, my little one. Don't cry. I am taking you to a safe place and then I will find your parents."

At the bottom of the street where the open-air market ended, he stopped at a little newspaper stall which was a wooden structure no bigger than a closet with a hinged shutter that opened over a little counter. I had stopped at similar ones in Paris where Dad would buy a newspaper or a copy of *Time* or *Life Magazine*. "Good morning, Madame," the policeman said. "I have a little American girl with me who needs a place to stay while I look for her parents. May she stay with you?" And then, a narrow door opened on the side of the stall, the lady stooped down to ask my name, placed a little footstool at her feet and told me to sit down. She handed me a comic book and went back to selling newspapers, her long wool coat brushing my shoulder every time she moved. People were curious, of course, about the little child below the counter and so I listened to my sad plight being explained over and over again.

"She's a little American girl who got lost. The *gendarme* is looking for her parents."

"An American girl? There was an American family at our market? C'est bizarre."

"I only know what the gendarme told me," she'd reply and every time I just stared at the comic book, trying to be as inconspicuous as possible.

---

[8] Mégroz-Cornaz, H. *Nul Enfant N'Est Trop Petit,* French Children's Hymn.

I was there for quite a while and then there was the tall policeman talking to the woman again and standing beside him was my father. As we walked back to the car he told me something very important, "If you get lost, stop and stay where you are. That way we can come right back and find you."

There was another time when I realized that I was, in the eyes of others, not really a little French girl even though I felt like one. Marie-France invited me to a girls' event hosted by the local nuns. I recognized the little girls around the table from school and didn't feel out of place at all.

While we were filling in a worksheet of some sort, one of the nuns bent down and spoke quietly to Marie-France. Then she walked over to the wall and stood next to another nun, close enough that I could see their black habits and white coifs out of the corner of my eye.

"Did you find out who she is?" the other nun asked.

"Yes. Her name is Dianne and she is the daughter of the Americans who live in the Duquesne's house."

I heard a slight gasp, "They're not Catholic, right? Should we allow her here?" I kept my head bent over my paper, but I felt my breath turn shallow and my heart start to pound.

After a pause came a firm reply, "She's a little girl and she is Marie-France's friend. She is welcome here." My shoulders relaxed and I glanced over at Marie-France and smiled.

Chapter 6

Far Away in France
Spring and Early Summer 1956

David also learned that speaking the language and wearing a *tablier* to school didn't make him a little French boy. On a field trip to the Loire valley near the end of the school year, the teacher told the bus full of boys, "We will stop once on our way to see the chateaux and once on our way back and you can order either a *limonade* or a *bière* to drink."

David decided one of each would be nice until he tasted the beer. He gagged on the first sip and put it down but the teacher made him drink it. When Mom and Dad met him after the trip, he started to sob, "I drank beer. I had to drink beer."

When he calmed down enough to tell them what had happened, they told him, "It's okay, honey. You didn't know what it was and it's not your fault."

While the little conflicts in David's and my worlds had happy endings, international conflicts were causing my parents alarm. The Algerian War in North Africa made regular headlines in the Paris newspapers. Would a conflict like that erupt in French West Africa where they were about to take their family? And then, on January 8, 1956, five missionary men were speared to death in Ecuador by the Auca Indians they were attempting to evangelize. I remember coming home from school and seeing Dad sitting at the table with mom looking over his shoulder at a newspaper article and I could feel their fear.

"Should we take our kids into Africa if this kind of thing can happen?" Mom wondered out loud. I peeked over Dad's shoulder and glimpsed a picture of a body, floating face down in a river.

"Missionaries have been in the French Sudan for decades and I've never heard of anything like this happening there." Dad replied. "We don't leave until summer and by then the mission will advise us, I'm sure."

It was not just international events that were disconcerting to them. When the president of the mission came to Paris to meet with the missionaries who were studying French, he pulled Dad aside and suggested that the Chevrolet Carryall® that Goss Memorial Church had purchased for our family be put in the name of the mission so all the missionaries could use it. When Dad politely refused, his dedication to the Lord was called into question, but he quietly held his ground and thought the matter was settled.

In reality, it was a foreshock of similar events to come, events that would shake our family to its core.

I was oblivious to that, of course, and was happily anticipating our trip to Holland later that spring. Dad studied his Michelin® map and plotted our course through Belgium so we would stop in Ghent on our way to Amsterdam and at Waterloo on our way home. I liked the Lion on the top of the hill in Waterloo way better than Gravensteen Castle in Ghent. The torture museum there, complete with a guillotine, was terrifying, but that was just a prequel to the horrors I would take in during the days and months ahead.

What Dad's Michelin map didn't tell him was that thousands of other people wanted to see the tulips the same week that we did. We got to Amsterdam at dusk and, although Dad ran into hotel lobby after hotel lobby, he'd return to the car each time with the same news: "They don't have room either." It was dark when he tried one more place and this time he came bounding down the steps to the car and jumped in all excited. "They don't have room either, but they had a list of homes that take in visitors during tulip season. Here," he continued as he handed mom a slip of paper and put the car in gear, "read me these directions. I think we head a few blocks down this street and then turn left at a main intersection. Keep your eyes peeled for the name of the street you see listed there."

In fifteen minutes, we were stopping in front of a row of houses, all joined together. The hotel had called ahead and when we pulled up to the curb, a light was on inside and our hosts were already waiting for us at an open door. Much to Dad's delight, the husband spoke rather good English, so while they got acquainted, Mom and our hostess took David and me up a steep, narrow staircase to a bedroom with twin beds. After we changed into our pajamas and brushed our teeth, we climbed into bed where I sank, up to my ears, into a feather mattress. David was soon asleep but my feeling of being smothered would not go away and I started to cry. Mom came in and tried to help me get comfortable but my crying turned to sobbing which brought our hostess to the bedroom door. I don't know how Mom communicated with her, but I was soon standing up, the feather bed was being removed, the bed was being remade and our hostess was still smiling. I stopped my crying, climbed under the covers and fell asleep.

Breakfast the next morning can only be described as glorious. David and I found ourselves carefully balancing large plates and walking around a table laden with fruit, breads, jams, cheeses, meats and pastries. "That's enough, Dianne," mom whispered over my shoulder. "You can always come back for more if you finish what's on your plate." I did and I did, several times.

By mid-morning we were back in the car, headed for the tulip fields with Dad driving and Mom navigating by means of the Michelin map folded on her lap. That evening Dad learned that our host was also a tour guide, and when dad asked if he'd be willing to show us his country, he accepted. The next two days he rode along in the front seat of the car, telling Dad where to go and explaining what we saw when we got there. Without him we would never have ventured north to the island of Marken where people still dressed in traditional Dutch clothing, nor out across the Zuiderzee on the Afsluitdijk Causeway where we stopped and got out of the car. Our host stooped down by David and me and pointed over our shoulders at the water on one side of the road, explaining to us that on that horizon was the North Sea. Then he had us turn around and explained that we were now looking toward Holland where, in years to come, the water would be replaced by land because of the huge dike we were standing on.

When we got back to the house, our hostess had dinner waiting and, after dessert, the conversation turned to the war. When Dad asked what that time was like in the Netherlands, our host stood up, "Dutch families hid their sons up there," he said, pointing at the ceiling. Then he planted his feet, grasped an imaginary rifle and started jabbing it toward the ceiling, "The Nazi soldiers would come in and hit the butts of their rifles on the ceiling like this to find them." He sat down, gazed past us at the wall and continued quietly, "If they found someone, they took the entire family—grandparents, parents and children—lined them up in front of the house and machine gunned them down."

The next day, on our way south through Amsterdam, he had Dad stop at Dam Square so we could see the newly built National Monument in the middle of the roundabout. "Look way up. See the woman and the child? Look down. See the people chained to the rock? Those are the Dutch people. Look carefully, everyone. See the wolves at their feet? Those are the Germans." I saw them and I have never forgotten them nor the story I heard the night before.

David at the National Monument, Dam Square, Amsterdam

The rest of the day was more fun. We ended up in Gouda where Dad posed with a red ball of cheese that makes me laugh every time I see it. In the picture, he is smiling from ear to ear (which he rarely did for the camera) and it reminds me that there was never a man who loved cheese more than our father.

A month later, Dad was not smiling. In May of 1956 he developed severe back pain that required surgery to remove a slipped disc. Mom took my brothers and me to visit him once in the American Hospital where he was lying face down on a bed with his face peeking out through a round opening facing the floor. Dad's French studies were suspended during his recovery and, because of that, it was decided he would finish out his courses the following fall.

In June, the school year ended for David and me. In Crosne, the closing ceremony was held in the park near the town square where our whole family found seats on the folding chairs set up in the grass. The mayor spoke from an outdoor stage followed by a speech by the principal of the Girls School who finished by calling the top three students from each grade up to the podium to receive that year's academic awards: books wrapped in pretty paper and tied with a bow. The first-place student got three books, the second-place student got two books and the third-place student got one.

I had often been the top student in my class. I knew this because of two things. First, when Mom took David and me over to Mme Duquesne's side of the house to have her interpret our first report cards, Mme Duquesne started jumping up and down and clapping her hands. The other reason was that my teacher kept moving me closer and closer to the front of the class until I was assigned the front desk of the left-hand row, which put me literally at the teacher's right hand. I had no idea what ranking meant, but it was obviously a pretty big deal in French education in those days.

At the ceremony, as three names were called from each class, the audience applauded while the children made their way to the front. When my name was called, a little murmur ran through the crowd instead, followed by a smattering of polite applause. I kept my head down all the way to the podium, staring at the grass and the tips of my brown shoes, and I barely lifted my eyes when I said, "Merci, Monsieur," as the mayor handed me my first-place prize. David was treated far worse. Although he had ranked first in his class seven of the nine grading periods, he received no award. His teacher, a card-carrying Communist, had routinely berated and demeaned the little American boy in her class and this was her final triumph over him.

When we got home, Mme Duquesne met us at her gate. She was furious at how we had been treated, especially David. "It's okay." Mom and Dad told her, "Your friendship is more important than what strangers did today."

And it was. Later that summer, after Dad was well enough to travel, Mom and Dad planned a trip to visit friends of theirs in Oviedo, Spain. Mme Duquesne offered to keep Richie for the ten days we would be gone, "Why take a toddler on a long trip like that? Let him stay with me. I insist!" And so, five of us loaded into our car and headed southwest across France.

We spent one night in Bordeaux, stopped long enough at Biarritz to look out over the beach, crossed the Pyrenees and headed west through the Cantabrian Mountains toward Oviedo. Unfortunately, the narrow, twisting mountain roads took longer to travel than what our journey looked like on the map and, when we got to Oviedo it was dark. Mom had the letter with directions from Oviedo to where their friends lived and so we kept driving. Everything was pitch black except for our headlights but coming around one corner we saw one house, above the road, with a light on. Mom and Dad were sure we had not come far enough and didn't remember their friends saying their house was that far off the road, so we kept driving. A half hour later they realized we had come too far and might never find the house in the dark.

"Anne," Dad said, "I think we should turn around and stop where we saw a light."

"But Dick, we are in the mountains of northern Spain where no one speaks English. I'm not sure it's safe for strangers to drive up to a house in the middle of nowhere at this hour."

"I'll be careful. If it's not their house, and no one there can give us directions, we'll drive back to Oviedo and see if we can find a place to stay." He turned the car around, we drove back, the light was still on and it was their friends who came out to meet us. The couple's daughter Yolanda was about David's age and our time with them was wonderful. Three memories have stayed with me all these years.

First, I am climbing a very steep hill through lush grass. Near the top we find a goatherd in his summer hut, looking out over his goats grazing on the hillside. He gave us some cheese made from their milk and, at our picnic lunch, it melted in our mouths.

Next, we are stopping along a rushing stream to look at a stone bridge with a huge cross hanging below it. "It's called the Roman Bridge of Cangas de Onis," our host explained. "A bridge was first built here by the Romans, almost two thousand years ago." The picture Dad took shows a bright blue sky and white clouds above the bridge and the Sella River cascading over the rocks below on its way to the Bay of Biscay.

The last memory is of the Shrine of Our Lady of Covadonga where we climbed up a long flight of stairs to see the shrine. On our way down, we went another way to see three crosses framed in the opening of a cave. "At this place," Dad explained, "the Spaniards had their first victory against the Moors who had taken over their land. The people who fought in that battle said that Mary, Jesus' mother, helped them win the battle. That's why they built that big church down there and this shrine."

I learned something else that day. I overheard Yolanda's father tell my parents, "Notice the people climbing the steps on their knees. When they reach the top, their knees are torn to shreds." The next day, on our drive back to France, I asked my parents why people did that.

"It's called penance and it's something people do to show God they are sorry. People think that if they hurt themselves, God will forgive them or answer their prayers. It's sad because we know God loves them whether they do those things or not, but you don't need to worry about it."

I didn't plan to worry about it. I just wanted to be sure I understood what I had heard before tucking a picture of bloody knees into the back of my mind right next to the images of a body floating in a river, a guillotine, soldiers shooting families to death and wolves howling at the feet of people chained to a rock.

Chapter 7

There Lived a Little Girl
Summer, Fall and Winter, 1956

Other than that trip to Spain, we spent the rest of the summer of 1956 in Crosne. David and I played with Marie-France and her grown-up sister's little girl, Béatrice who spent time in Crosne with her grandparents in the summer; we made up adventures in the little woods in the back yard; we rode our bikes; and we went to the park near the town square where there were swings, teeter-totters and a little merry-go-round. And, because we were kids, we got hurt.

David, John and Rich in our backyard in Crosne

One day Richie was running across the playground, tripped, fell, and split open his forehead. David and I rushed to pick him up but when I tried to carry him, blood gushed all over both of us. The only way I knew to stop the bleeding was to hold the skirt of my dress over the wound. David and Johnnie took off running to get Mom. Richie and I started walking, with me holding Richie close to my side with my right hand and holding my skirt over his face with my left. Halfway home I stepped inside the little grocery shop where we shopped almost every day and said, "My brother cut his forehead. Do you have something I can hold over it?"

"No," the owner replied, stone faced. "Take him to his mother."

By then my thin cotton skirt was soaked in blood and so was my hand.

"We're almost home, Richie. David and John are already there and Mommy will be coming." If we had been in America, Richie would have gone to Dr. Hamilton's office for stitches, but we didn't have a doctor in Crosne, so Mom treated it with mercurochrome, kept a Band-Aid® on it and his forehead healed, leaving a scar to this day.

Then I got hurt. David, Marie-France and I found a piece of clothesline about 15 feet long and decided to tie it between two little trees to make a swing. We wanted to put a seat on it, but nothing we tried worked. Then one of us sat on the line and found that if we grabbed the line as far out as we could reach, we could balance pretty well. We took turns doing that a few times and then someone said, "I'll push you," and the fun began. We took turns seeing who could swing and stay on the longest before tumbling forward or falling backward and being caught by the one doing the pushing.

On one of my turns, instead of pushing on my back, they each grabbed one side of the line next to my hands. I was laughing as I was swinging until I knew I was more than just a foot or so off the ground. My laugh turned to a scream for them to stop and then, at the highest point of my arc, I fell backward and hit the ground hard. We all laughed—until I couldn't move.

"Come on, Dianne, get up. No one can swing with you there on the ground."

"I can't move."

"Stop joking and get up!" Marie-France said.

"Yeah. Get up. It's my turn," chimed in David.

"I can't. Go get Mom and Dad."

They dashed off, leaving me lying there alone. I felt little pebbles under my bare arms, I saw patches of blue sky and white clouds drifting through the leaves rustling above me, and I heard the screen door slam shut, but I could not move. Who picked me up and how, I don't know but somehow, I ended up lying in the back seat of Mr. Duquesne's taxi, with my head on my mother's lap. When the car started down the winding street toward the town square I was instantly car sick because I couldn't see out. It helped when Dad, sitting in the front seat, started calling out the landmarks so that I could visualize getting closer and closer to Paris. I made it to the American Hospital without throwing up and then two orderlies put me on a stretcher and carried me into the hospital. A doctor came in to the examining room, asked what had happened and ordered an X-ray. While we waited for it to develop, my legs started feeling like they were part of my body again. By the time the doctor returned, I could move my feet and lift my knees a little bit. He reported that the X-ray showed no fractures and he watched me move my legs. "She needs to lie flat on her back a little longer. I'll be back in a bit."

When he returned, he braced my neck and upper back with his hand and slowly sat me up on the edge of the examining table. "Okay, Dianne," he said, "I want you to slide off the side of the table and once your feet are on the floor, just stand still." After a minute of standing there, he held on to me and had me walk slowly across the room.

"It looks like she will be okay," he said to my parents. "Watch her tonight for signs of concussion and keep her quiet for the next few days. Bring her back to the hospital right away if she can't move again." For the next few days, I had plenty of time to read the three books I had received at the school closing ceremony, but I hated listening to David, Marie-France and Béatrice playing outside. Little by little Mom let me be more active and, after a week, I was running and playing like nothing had happened.

David didn't end up being hurt that summer, but something happened to him after school started that terrified us nonetheless. Several days a week, David and I attended enrichment classes after school that ended at different times, so we walked home alone. One winter night, after the sun had set and it was time for dinner, David still wasn't home so Mom sent me down the street to look for him. I walked all the way to the bakery, which by now was closed, crossed the street so I could see around the curve, but he wasn't there. When I got back home without him, Dad grabbed a flashlight, told Mom to feed the boys, and we went looking together. First, we walked all the way to David's school which was locked up and dark. On our way home, we went up the hill past the Catholic church to a home where David and I had played a few times with one of my classmates. He wasn't there. At every gate, Dad stopped and called David's name over the top of the wall. On our way back home, we stopped to tell another missionary couple who lived near us and the husband took off searching while Dad knocked on the Duquesne's door and told them that David was lost.

Dad and I went out again, walking through parts of Crosne where I had never been. When we got home, Mme Duquesne and two men I didn't know were in our kitchen, talking to Mom. Dad stepped up to the group, thanked them and they left. Before Mom could tell Dad what the men had said, the little bell by our gate rang and there was David. On his way home from school, a boy in his class had invited him over to play. They were in the lower level of the boy's house where there were no windows and David had no idea that it was dark outside. The family invited him to supper, which in France is rarely served before 7:30, and he stayed.

David, who had just turned seven, was not punished, but he was told that what happened made a lot of trouble for a lot of people. Both of us were admonished to never go to a friend's house without asking first. Before I went up to bed, I asked Mom who the men were in our kitchen, "One was the constable and the other one was a fireman. They told Mme Duquesne that

71

they would dredge the river in the morning in case David had fallen in and drowned." That night we didn't need a *Tom and Jack* story when we went to bed. There had been suspense and high drama enough for one evening. As I turned over and snuggled under the covers, with David drifting off to sleep next to the wall and John already asleep between us, I was thankful that the three of us were there together, safe and warm.

Another memory about David involved the time I stole money from the counter of a little store in Montgeron. Mom had sent me to buy sliced ham and, when the lady went to the back of the store to get it, I saw coins lying on the counter. "I wonder if I can take them without her noticing," I said to myself. While she sliced the ham, I took one coin. While she weighed it, I took another. While she wrapped it in paper, I took the last one. "Ah, hah! I tricked her," I thought as I skipped out the door and walked home under the poplar trees, over the bridge that crossed the Yerres and home.

"Look, Mom." I said proudly. "I took these off the counter and the lady didn't even notice!"

Mom was shocked. "Dianne, that is called stealing. You have to take them back."

"I didn't know it was stealing. I just thought I was tricking her," I explained. "Please don't make me go back."

"You have to. You took them." I cried and then I wailed to no avail.

Finally, between sobs, I implored, "Please let David go with me. Please!"

She thought about that for a minute and finally said, "Okay. But he has to stay outside. You have to return the money alone."

I sobbed all the way to the store. David waited outside. I opened the door. The little bell tinkled my arrival. The lady came from the back. "I took these and I'm bringing them back," I blurted out as I put the coins on the counter. Before she could even process what I had said, I was out the door.

Then there was our Christmas holiday, a few more weeks of school in January and then it was time to leave. I don't remember saying good-bye to Mme Duquesne or Marie-France, the two people whose friendship and loving kindness were priceless gifts for us who had been strangers in their land.

David, Marie-France, Dianne, John

But I do remember Mom and Dad's missionary friends, all dressed in their Sunday best like us, coming out in force to send us off at the train station. Mom and Dad stood close to our luggage next to the train talking with their friends. Now and again someone would pat David and me on the head with a cheery, "Bon voyage," while Johnny and Richie chased each other around the platform. Mom either didn't notice them or, more than likely, she wanted them to burn off their energy before being cooped up in the train for the next twelve hours. And then there was a wail. Richie, running away from Johnny, came too close to the edge of the platform and fell beneath the train.

"He's crying, so that's good," I remember a woman saying. At eight, I was too little to realize she meant that he wasn't lying on the tracks unconscious or dead. I was afraid of something else. I had often seen the trains jostle a foot or two forward or backward without warning, and my little brother was down there, right next to the wheels.

In an instant, Dad was lying face down on the platform, the toes of his polished shoes scraping the cement, his arms stretched straight down toward the tracks and his head angled to one side, trying to see where Richie had landed. Richie was only two and a half and he was screaming, but somehow Dad got his attention, had him come over to where he could see his arms, and convinced him to reach his little hands up as far as he could. Dad grabbed his wrists, slowly got to his knees, his face and torso pressed against the train, and pulled Richie's hands up to the platform where two other men grabbed his wrists and hoisted him to safety.

Dad stood up, brushed the dirt of his clothes from neck to toe and then turned to me and snapped, "Why weren't you watching your little brother?"

I would not have been more stunned if he had slapped me. If I had known the word *scapegoat* it would have explained things perfectly: he chastised me to cover up his embarrassment. I turned and walked away. If he thought it was because I felt guilty, he was wrong. I didn't want the people gathered there to see the tears in my eyes—tears, not of remorse, but of anger for being publicly shamed and blamed for something that had nothing whatsoever to do with me. David saw me standing on the other side of the platform, my back to everyone gathered around Mom who was holding Richie. He came over, saw me crying and asked what was wrong. When I told him, he just stood there staring with me at the empty tracks below, a comfort that needed no words.

Unlike Lucy Pevensie and her brothers from C. S. Lewis's *The Chronicles of Narnia*, my brothers and I didn't die at that train station, even though Richie came close. And, unlike their sister Susan, who lived but quit believing, I never forgot the wonder of my childhood in France where a beautiful world opened, took me in, and left me forever changed. The sights, sounds, tastes and experiences of that time remain inside me as crisp and clear as the days I knew them. But, I have learned not to look back at them too closely or for too long lest my heart break from a longing so exquisite that I shatter to pieces and am no more.

Part III

Trauma and the Terror That Followed

"To abuse a child or adult is to alter the course of their life. The shape of
their life and their sense of self has significantly changed."
Diane Langberg, Ph.D.

Chapter 8

When Night Came in Africa
Spring 1957

A train ride at night from Paris to Marseille probably sounded like a good idea for a family traveling with young children, but the reality of the journey was a different story. Every time we were lulled to sleep by the rhythmic clickety clack of the wheels, the brakes would squeal, our car would sway, the whistle would blow, and people would start talking in the corridor outside our door and on the platform outside our window. And then the sequence would start all over again. I don't remember anything the day we got to Marseilles, probably because we checked into our hotel and slept.

The next day, Dad took us kids to a park. While David and I ran and played, Dad sat on a bench, and let Richie and Johnny play near him. At one point, the lady sitting on the other end of the bench turned to Dad and spoke, "I have been listening to your children. You are from Paris, correct?"

"No," Dad replied in French, "we are Americans but we lived near Paris and the children went to school there." It was the first time I knew that people could tell where you were from by your accent. Her comment somehow made me proud, and whenever I start to think that my attachment to France is something I've imagined, I remember her comment with a smile.

The next day we boarded the *Maréchal Lyautey* and sailed into the Mediterranean Sea. I had expected the ship to be like the *S.S. United States* we had sailed on two years earlier, but it was smaller and, to my great disappointment, did not have a play room. Everyone on the ship was either French or spoke the language well, but they weren't at all like Mme Duquesne. The ladies wore fancy clothes and high heels and stood around smoking and looking at us kids like we were trespassing. Many of them, I suppose, were the French élite, headed to the beaches of the Canary Islands or Morocco to escape the cold, dreary winter in France.

On the second day at sea, everyone crowded together on the upper deck to see the Rock of Gibraltar. Like the man in Holland, Dad stooped down and pointed over my shoulder across an expanse of water and said, "That's called the Rock of Gibraltar." I scanned the water for a rock and saw none.

"I don't see it," I said.

"It's right there. Look!" I never did see a rock, but I did see a high cliff, tall as a mountain, reaching to the sky.

In the Canary Islands, Dad hired a taxi to give us a little tour of the island while the ship docked. Our next stop was Casablanca, Morocco. Everyone on the ship was warned, "You are allowed to disembark but do not venture away from the ship on foot. Do not get into a taxi other than those waiting at the dock. They are safe and the cab drivers know how to get you back to the ship on time." I don't remember what we saw on our tour because, like the monuments in Paris and the Rock of Gibraltar, I didn't know what I was looking at. But I do remember Dad and the taxi driver discussing how the war between France and Algeria, Morocco's neighbor, made things in the country tense for everyone. We got back to the ship on time. The best part of these stops was running up and down the gangplank to and from the ship with my brothers. That was almost as fun as having a playroom.

We were met in Dakar by Robert, a Mission Endeavor International missionary who was studying tropical medicine at the university in Dakar. Robert, his wife and toddler were renting a house in a suburb of the city and our family stayed with them. It was the end of the dry season and there was nothing but dry, brown dirt everywhere around that house with not a blade of grass, not a shrub, not a tree anywhere. The inside of the house was usually dark because the shutters were often kept closed, keeping out the dust, the heat and, along with them, the light.

The first order of business was getting David and me back to school. Robert had arranged for us to attend l'École Primaire de La Rue Kléber where our classmates would be the children of French and African professionals who played important roles in that colonial port. On our first day, Dad, David and I were ushered into a co-ed classroom.

Dianne and David in front of their school in Dakar

The teacher stood at her desk to shake our hands and then sat back down to look over our report cards from Crosne. As she studied them, I saw her right eyebrow go up like an eyebrow does when one is suspect. "They were both in first place, I see," she said in a flat voice and then she handed the papers back to Dad, walked to the front of the class, had the children stand and reseat themselves, placing David and me in desks half way down the second row. When I was seated, she looked at me as if to say, "We shall see." In the months that followed, she did not make eye contact when she moved us closer and closer to the front of the class.

The Carryall that Mom and Dad's Sunday School class had bought for them, along with the barrels they had packed two years before in Akron, were waiting on the dock. Robert had signed the papers to get everything off the ship, but Dad had to clear them through customs. When Dad arrived at the dock, he was shocked that the paper work for the Carryall was filled out in the name of the mission, a direct contradiction to what Dad thought was settled in Paris. A heated argument ensued and ended only when the *dounier* demanded to know who could prove they owned the vehicle and who was going to pay the bill. When Dad produced proof that the Carryall belonged to him and pulled out cash for the import fee, the officer tore up the first papers and wrote out new ones in Dad's name.

As I remember it, Dad went inland on the train to Kénieba first with the Carryall and our barrels to get things settled before Mom, John and Rich would follow. I do not remember the day my mother and little brothers left, but David tells me that I cried and clung to Mom at the train station. At the last "All Aboard" he remembers Robert pulling me, screaming, away from her and then my falling to the ground in sobs.

Life in Dakar settled into a routine for David and me that mostly involved Robert. He drove us to school every morning on his way to the hospital. He brought us home and played with us. He took us swimming. He tucked us in at night. His wife obviously made the meals, washed our clothes and cared for us too, but I only remember a few things about her. She made a cake and wrapped presents for my ninth birthday. Each evening, after tidying up the kitchen, she would disappear with her child into the bedroom where they all slept. When we were invited to the beautiful home of a French doctor, high on a cliff overlooking the Atlantic, she sat so still by herself on the far side of the room that I kept glancing in her direction to make sure she was still breathing. There are several pictures of her in Mom and Dad's slides, but she is not smiling in any of them.

On our first outing to the beach with Robert, there was no way that I was going to take off my clothes and put on my bathing suit on the wide-open beach even if I was only eight years old. I can still remember pleading my case with Robert, and him finally relenting. "Here, I'll hold up the towel and you can change behind it." I wasn't thrilled with the idea, but it was better than stripping down with no covering at all. As I took off my clothes, I looked up to see him looking at me and chuckling like my dad did when one of us did something cute. But I wasn't being cute. I was serious. And, why was he looking at me without my clothes on when he knew it was upsetting to me? Later he led my brother David and me to the dock where we took turns jumping into the water and into his arms. When I turned to dog paddle back, eager to do it again, he pulled me close instead, treaded water and held me tight against him before letting me go.

Robert played with us at home too. I remember him grasping my hands and spinning me round and round above the ground. He also taught me his version of Skin the Cat. Instead of holding on to my hands and flipping me over in one quick motion, he'd stop my momentum when I was upside down, and then after a long pause, he'd flip me over to my feet. It was play to me, but I know now that it was a way for him, even in broad daylight, to have my body close to his and my little derrière right before his eyes.

In Dakar, David and I shared a room with twin beds where every night Robert tucked us in and kissed us goodnight. After Robert's wife and child went to bed and the house fell silent, I was often still awake but I knew Robert was up studying his medical text books into the wee hours of the morning. One night when sleep eluded me for an extra-long time, I got up and slipped silently across the living room and stood quietly outside the doorway of Robert's study. Like at Grandma Darr's house, I was just awake. I just wanted to stand there.

When he sensed my presence, he called me over and asked me what was wrong. Was I afraid? When I told him that I just couldn't sleep, he hugged me and then put me on his lap. He put my head on his shoulder and told me to relax. His hands ran all over my little body in light caresses that I know now were not meant so much to relax me as to arouse him.

One evening, not long after that, he asked me to help him bring some things in from the garage just outside the kitchen door. It was right after supper and almost dark. As we squeezed ourselves around the far side of the car, I suddenly found myself being picked up and placed on top of a steel drum, the kind that missionaries packed their supplies in to ship overseas. I was now eye level with Robert who started kissing me in a way that I did not understand which was not at all like the goodnight kisses he gave David and me every night. And then, leaning in close, he whispered in my ear, "I'm going to call you Sarah because it means princess and you are my princess. And, I want you to save this side of your mouth for me." And then he kissed me again—a long, lopsided, slobbery kiss on the right side of my lips. "Don't tell, okay? It's our secret." Then he lifted me down, we got what we had gone out for, and we walked blinking into the light of the kitchen where his wife was at the sink doing the supper dishes and David was at the table doing his homework.

Another night when I couldn't sleep, I ended up on his lap again but this time he leaned over and got something from his desk, and then tilted me backward across his left arm. I saw his right hand, holding something white, coming toward my face and then, nothing.

Another memory involves a hot, steamy tropical night when he rough housed with me in his office and we ended up drenched in sweat. I wanted to take a shower but I was afraid to be in the bathroom alone in the middle of the night. Robert laughed at my fear and then he ended up not just waiting for me outside the curtain, but came into the shower with me. I was too embarrassed to look at him naked but he made me. "See, this is how it looks when a man is excited about a woman. It's okay. You can look." As I dried off, I turned my back to him, my head bent low, my eyes never leaving the floor.

At the end of the school year, another missionary couple with the mission came to Dakar. Don and his wife got the room with the twin beds and David and I slept on blankets on the floor of Robert's study. The first night we slept there, Robert came in for our customary good night kisses. First, he kissed David and then, when he knelt down to kiss me, he started kissing me like he had in the garage. I turned away in protest. When I looked up, he was laughing like he had at the beach, like he thought my indignation was cute and it made me angry.

One day when the four adults were standing in front of the house talking. I went over to Don, turned around and asked him to flip me over. He looked confused but soon figured out what I meant. He flipped me quickly all the way around. I corrected him and said, "No. You don't do it like that. Stop before I go over all the way."

Don's reaction after doing it like that was startling. His face turned serious, he looked intently at me and then said, "Who taught you that?" When I told him it was Robert, he stood stock still, looked over at Robert and his eyes narrowed. In that moment, I might as well have been served up to Don on a silver platter.

David and I traveled inland on the train with Don and his wife after being separated from our parents and brothers for four months. Dad was waiting for us at the train station in Mahina and swooped us up in a suffocating bear hug. He had grown a beard, which made us laugh. From Mahina we traveled miles and miles in pitch darkness over a very rough road

81

and then there was a tiny light shining from the window of a thatched roofed hut where our mother and little brothers were waiting.

The memories of what happened to me in Dakar have been with me all my life and, since they are linked to not being able to fall sleep, they sometimes cross my mind when I go to bed. It is always the same: I see the incidents in my mind's eye exactly as they happened, I lie very still and I don't feel anything at all. However, when I remember my father's bear hug at the train station and the tiny flickering light of home, surrounded by total darkness, I cry.

Chapter 9

Darkness Under the Bright African Sun
Summer 1957

It was the middle of a dark, moonless night but Mom was waiting for us by the light of a kerosene lantern in a large, round hut. After a snack, we went to the bedroom hut where John and Rich were fast asleep under their mosquito net. Mom tucked David and me under another net and, when we woke in the morning, I remember looking up at the thatched roof and realizing I had arrived in a different world.

Kénieba was a small town with a post office; a bakery where we could buy French bread; two small shops where we could buy canned goods, sugar, flour and other necessities; an open-air market where we didn't buy much that I can remember; and a compound with a French Commandant de Cercle and his family. The Commandant's job was to be the administrator of that isolated part of the colony and to keep it in line.

The mission compound sat on the edge of the village. There was no electricity and the water that was pulled up from a well was carefully filtered before we drank it. Two large huts with thatched roofs, connected by a thatched-roof veranda, had been built for our family. One hut was the bedroom and the other one was the kitchen and living room. A few yards from the huts were two small structures made out of straw mats lashed to poles in the ground. One was the outhouse. The other was where we showered standing on a wooden pallet and pulling a chain to release water from a bucket hung from a pole, as seen in the picture on the previous page.

The compound also had two small houses, one where Don and his wife lived and one where Robert and his family would live when they moved inland. A partially built building sat to the right of Don's house and between his house and our huts there was a small hut that served as a workshop. Next to it, our African helper N'fali would sometimes kill a chicken for our dinner. He would gently lay it down on the workbench, slowly curve its head back, carefully slit its neck, and let the blood flow.

Dad would leave every morning after breakfast and drive ten miles to the Falame River where he and a crew of Africans mixed cement with sand from a large sand bar to make cement blocks, one at a time. Some of the blocks would be used to build the hospital that Robert would run and some would be used to build our house which was another project that had been funded by Goss Memorial Church and other supporters of our parents. Its foundation was already laid when David and I got there in June.

Dad took us with him down to the river at least once. The savanna of French West Africa was still full of game in the late 1950s, so it was quite an adventure. Every mile or so Dad would slow down or stop and yell, "Look!"

"Where?"

"Over there!"

"I see it now! Wow!"

I liked the warthogs best, but the antelope and monkeys were wonderful to see as well. And once we got to the river, there were the crocodiles, floating lazily in the stream, death machines that killed regularly on the banks of the rivers in Africa.

Any time we were outside, my brothers and I wore child-sized pith helmets to protect us from the tropical sun. We wore them with the leather straps down under our chins so they would catch around our necks when we took off running. When we were standing still, we sucked on the leather straps, salty from our sweat. To protect us from parasites in the dirt, we wore shoes at all times. To ward off malaria, we took Nivaquine tablets every day and slept under mosquito nets at night. The one precaution that wasn't enforced with me was the noon rest, which all foreigners were supposed to take to help them survive the brutal climate.

After lunch, during the extreme heat of the day, foreigners lie down until three o'clock. I'm not sure if I rested sometimes or not, but many days I remember roaming the compound by myself. One day I saw Don go into the empty house where Robert and his family eventually came to live. It was always closed up and I was curious about what it looked like inside, so I followed. I remember it being dark because the windows were shuttered. At first, he talked to me and then he sat down on the couch and asked me to sit beside him. At that point he stopped talking, reached for me and pulled me close beside him. He began to touch me and I didn't move.

Another time he found me playing in the empty building next to his house. He did not say a word but sat down on some building supplies, pulled me close and fondled me again. My clothes were back in place and I was sitting quietly on his lap when one of the African workers appeared in the doorway. I remember a funny look crossed his face but he quickly asked Don what he had come to find out and left.

The third time Don molested me, he appeared at our hut and said to my mom that he was going for a walk beyond the station to see the mine pits where gold had been mined years before. He thought it would be interesting for me to see too. We found several pits and he explained to me about Mali being a source of gold in the Middle Ages. On our way back, he sat down on a tree stump beside the path and put me in front of him, between his legs. This time his touch was rough and he took my hand, put it between his groin and the small of my back and pushed—hard.

Another afternoon I heard a noise in the workshop and found him there sitting on a bench, working on a project. I watched until he paused and then he pulled me close again, began what he usually did but stopped abruptly. He buried his hands in his face and started moaning, "What have I done? What have I done?" Then he paused and said, "I won't do it again. Please, promise you'll never tell." I backed out of the hut, startled and confused, and ran home.

My memories of Kénieba included several other things that stayed with me. One was getting to know a French couple who ran one of the little grocery shops in the village. Mom would send me there on my bike to get things she needed and the lady was fascinated by this little blond American girl who spoke perfect, Parisian French. I reminded her of her granddaughter back home and she liked having me around. Sometimes I spent the day with her in their little apartment behind the shop, taking noon rest on a little cot at the foot of their bed. Her husband was as taciturn as she was bubbly but I think he tolerated me because I made her happy.

The second thing that made an impression on me was getting to know the Commandant's family. When they learned that David and I had gone to school near Paris and spoke French, they invited us to come and play with their children. They had a lovely home and their oldest daughter was around my age.

One day the Commandant told my Dad that he needed to go to the Catholic mission some distance away. He was taking his daughter along and he wondered if I could go to keep her company. A few days later I found myself bumping along a bush road, jabbering with my little friend in the front of a Land Rover driven by the Commandant. When we got there, we played in the open area in front of the church while the men talked and then, before we left, the priest opened the church doors and led us inside.

At the front of the church, in front of the altar, was a crèche. The priest motioned for my friend to kneel in front of it, which she did, but not before she glanced at me. Since the priest had not beckoned to me, I knew better than to presume I was invited. However, when they recited the Lord's Prayer, my voice chimed in with hers, loud and clear. I may not have been Catholic, but I knew well enough that everyone was allowed to pray. At the end of the prayer I lifted my eyes and got a nod of approval from the priest but he did not look at the Commandant who had stood right behind me the whole time and had not repeated one word, not even "Amen."

Unfortunately, my friendship with this little girl came to an abrupt end the first time she came to play on our station where we had a lovely time until she had to go to the bathroom. She freaked out over the outdoor toilet with the straw mat walls. No amount of reasoning with her would change her mind. Dad took her home to pee and we never played together again.

Later that summer Robert and his family came inland to Kénieba. I have only two memories of him there. The first one was when my mother took me to see him to make sure the swelling under my right nipple was normal. I was just nine and she thought it was too early for me to be entering puberty.[9] If it was awkward for him to lift my shirt and touch my body in front of my mother, he didn't show it. But I did notice that his gaze avoided my eyes while he talked to my mother and did his doctorly thing.

The other memory involves my father, standing in the doorway of our living room hut and watching Robert walk across the compound toward Don's house. "Anne," he said to my mother, "there they go again. If they are going to run the show and leave me out, we will find another place to minister." In September, our family moved to Kayes.

In the years ahead, I lived in many other places in Mali but none so beautiful as Kénieba. To the east of the village, the dramatic Tambaoura Escarpment rises 800 feet straight up to the sky. When the darker memories of that place feel like they will swallow me whole, a memory comes to me of the sun rising behind that massive dark bluff, perfectly framed by an L-shaped notch in the cliff where the mountain met the sky.

---

[9] Noll, Tricket, et al. (January 2017). Childhood Sexual Abuse and Early Timing of Puberty. *Journal of Adolescent Health*.

Chapter 10

Alarm and Kindness in Kayes
Fall, 1957–Spring, 1958

Kayes was nothing at all like Kénieba. It was a bona fide town complete with electricity, a train station, paved roads and stores. Once the capital of the French Sudan, its location on the banks of the Senegal River made it an important commercial center on the railroad between the coastal port of Dakar and the inland capital city of Bamako. Kayes was famous for two things: Fort Médine, the historically significant French outpost located seven miles from town and its reputation as the hottest, continuously inhabited city in Africa.

Retouched by Chuck Jarrell

David and John on the banks of the Senegal River

Within weeks of our arrival in Kayes, we got news that Robert had been seriously burned in a gasoline explosion and the French military had life-flighted him out of Kénieba to the hospital in Bamako. Dad left the next day for Bamako on the train. The day after that, a young man from the post office came up the steps to the veranda of the apartment we had rented and handed Mom a telegram. It was from Dad, telling us that Robert had died.

She placed it on the table, walked to her room, threw herself on her bed and started sobbing.

I walked to the edge of the veranda, put my hands on the wall to steady myself and stared over the rooftops of Kayes. I had never betrayed the secret Robert had told me to keep and now he was dead. My mind remembered and while I stood there—unable to cry, still as stone—my mother's sobs and everything but my hands and the blue horizon of the African sky faded away.[10]

Decades later, in a rare moment when my dad and I were alone and out of earshot of my husband and children, Dad asked me, "Did you name Robbie for Robert?"

The question took me by surprise because I had never thought about that. "No, it was just a name we liked." I hesitated and then added quietly, "You know, he molested me too."

"I've always wondered," he said. "At Robert's funeral in Bamako, one of the missionaries who was with him before he died told me that Robert asked him to tell me that he was sorry." That could have meant a lot of things, given the history between them, but it was interesting that Dad had suspected it may have had something to do with me.

A happier memory from that apartment was the day Dad brought home two large boxes from the post office. They contained the third grade Calvert® education courses for David and the fourth grade courses for me. It soon became apparent that David couldn't read English and so, since I had learned to read English in the first grade in Akron, I was obviously the one qualified to teach him! We laughed at the math books and quickly set them aside because the fourth grade math book ended in division—something we had already learned in Crosne. For a variety of reasons, we never officially completed the courses, but David and I read through all the books in both boxes and, in the end, that would prove to be enough.

All that reading, however, gave me headaches. One day Dad intoned, "Anne, it is not normal for a nine-year-old girl to have headaches like this. We need to get her to Bamako to the eye doctor." After a long train ride, during which a Frenchman tried to hit on my mother, Lloyd and Margie McRostie met Mom and me at the train station and hosted us at the Gospel Missionary Union guesthouse. Bamako amazed me with its wide, tree-lined streets and nice stores. It was fun meeting three missionary kids who were

---

[10] *"The whole world may ... seem to be disappearing ... Dissociation born of trauma...serves to protect the traumatized individual from an experience that is too terrible to bear or experience."*
Handelman, Mark. Trauma and Dissociation. http://psychotherapy-nyc.com/blog/2012/09/04/trauma-and-dissociation

around my own age. I thought it was weird that Marcia, Judy and Nancy couldn't speak French and they thought it was weird that I couldn't speak Bambara. My eye appointment revealed nothing seriously wrong. The diagnosis was astigmatism and I have worn glasses ever since.

We got back to Kayes just as the Harmattan season began in late November. Over the next few months, when the northern horizon turned black in the middle of the day, Mom would close up all the doors and windows, but she would let us kids stand on the veranda and watch the sandstorm, dark as night, roaring in from the Sahara Desert. When the black wall was a few blocks away, we'd dash inside, close the door and wait for the howling to pass. Then the sun would come out as if nothing had happened, except that every single thing everywhere was covered in a thick layer of dust.

Toward the end of the year, Dad rented an entire building in the center of town with an apartment on the upper floor and a commercial space below where he opened a Christian book store and arranged a space to hold Sunday services. There were some African Protestants in Kayes as well as a Protestant Lebanese family which made a start for a congregation. Dad stocked the bookstore with Christian literature in French and so his new ministry began.

The apartment upstairs was much bigger than the first one we had rented and there was a walled-in yard behind the building where we children could play. Lined up in a row between two balconies there was a kitchen, a living room/dining room, two bedrooms and a bathroom. In each room, floor-to-ceiling louvered doors opened onto the balconies on each side which allowed air to flow through even when the doors were locked at night. Ceiling fans made the heat bearable. It was a very nice place to live, but we didn't know that it would hold terrible memories for my brother David. It was in that place that Don, who sometimes came to town on business, molested him.

Retouched by Chuck Jarrell

Shortly after moving there, Dad learned that a cook named Yuba needed a new place to work because his employer, a military officer, was returning to France. Unless Yuba found another *patron*, he would have to go back to Guinea, which people in the expatriate community said would be a shame because Yuba was not only an excellent cook but was also a faithful, dependable employee. The legal wage for a cook was less than $10 a month, something I remember my parents debating if they could afford, but in the end. they decided to hire him.

The first few mornings that Yuba came to work, he asked our mother what she would like him to prepare for lunch and dinner that day. Our meals had always been simple affairs and I could tell she didn't really know what to say. On the third day she said, "You decide," and that was the beginning of a beautiful thing. Every morning Yuba went to the open-air market and to the stores that sold European fare. When he returned, he carefully cleaned the vegetables, mixed permanganate solution in a big bowl and made sure the vegetables soaked a long time to kill any germs. Those pretty colored vegetables, bobbing in the dark purple permanganate, would have made a beautiful picture but, unfortunately, slide film was expensive and was never wasted on the mundane.

Gone were the bowls and plates of food placed in the center of the table to be passed around. Yuba would emerge from the kitchen and would serve us, one course at a time. I can still sense him, slightly behind my right shoulder, lowering a plate of food into my view, asking how he could serve me and then elegantly placing what I had asked for on my plate. We ate vegetables, potatoes, rice or pasta, meat cooked to perfection and ladled with exquisite sauces, fresh salads with tangy dressings and, at the end, a piece of fruit and a small slice of cheese. This was a gift at the time, but a curse thereafter, because for the rest of my days food like that was nothing my station in life could afford. Now and again, however, I am in a situation where my taste buds remember and I am thankful for what they know.

Once a week or so Yuba would call, "Come children, I'm ready!" At that, we would stop our play and David and I would push two chairs over to the stove, one for John and one for Rich. Once we were all situated close enough to see but far enough away to be safe, the show would start. As Yuba flipped crêpes high into the air and unfailingly caught them in the pan, our squeals of delight delighted him and our joy was more than the anticipation of a good meal. Another memory is watching in amazement as Yuba turned egg yolks into mayonnaise by whisking oil into them one tiny drop at a time for what seemed like forever. It is my own personal definition of patience.

Yuba had children in Guinea and I believe that he saw them in us. He was loving, warm and kind so why wouldn't Richie, who was three and a half, decide to climb up on his back for a piggy back ride one afternoon while Yuba said his prayers? We were playing in the courtyard when I looked up and saw what was the biggest crisis, to date, in my role as big sister. How do you get your little brother off the back of a devout Muslim who is in the process of saying his prayers? You start with a whisper, "Richie, get off" and, when that doesn't work, you add a threat and a deadline, "Richie, you're going to be in real trouble if you don't get off right now!" But Richie was enjoying going up and down too much to listen to me. I'm sure no one ever told Yuba the proper protocol for removing a small American child from his back during prayer, so he just kept going through the motions with Richie dangling down his back, his little arms wrapped tightly around his neck. I looked at Yuba. His eyes were closed but there was the hint of a smile at the edge of his lips. The next time he kneeled down to touch his head to the ground, I peeled Richie's arms from around his neck and marched him straight upstairs. Our parents were not amused. Dad apologized to Yuba, Richie got a spanking and the rest of us got a lecture about respecting Yuba's daily prayers.

During that time, a young man from another part of French West Africa appeared at the bookstore, claiming to be a believer. He attended Sunday services for several weeks and then, without warning, disappeared with Dad's bike. The police looked for him, but he had timed his theft with either the arrival and departure of the train or had taken a market truck out of town. It sobered Dad, who not only felt betrayed but a bit foolish as well for having trusted the young man so quickly just because he claimed to be a

Christian. When Dad reported the theft to the police, they warned him that thieves were everywhere and to be careful to lock things up, especially at night.

David and I also had bikes which we could ride in the courtyard and even in the streets when there was no traffic. One evening, after I had ridden as far as I was allowed to go and was turning my bike around, I sensed that I was being watched. I looked up and there, behind a fence and some shrubs, was the Commandant's daughter, the little French girl I had played with in Kénieba. Our eyes met and I held her gaze long enough to see that she knew who I was. I could tell that she watched me as I rode away, and I remember wondering what it would be like to live behind a fence like her and decided I would rather be outside, riding my bike like me. I know now that lack of plumbing in Kénieba and wrought iron fencing in Kayes didn't separate us as much as class and status did. But, as a child, I also felt a pang of sadness and a twinge of shame because I was somehow excluded from her world.

That bike also could have killed my brother John and me. Sometimes, in the early evening, our family would drive out of town on a short, paved road so that David and I could ride our bikes for a couple of miles. One such evening John, who had just turned five, was riding on the seat behind me. David was riding beside us and we were following the Carryall which was about 100 feet ahead of us. I had my eyes on the vehicle and, before I realized it, we were coasting down a steep, curving slope toward a bridge and I remembered that my hand brakes did not work. I looked at the sand on each side of the road and contemplated running the bike off the road, but I knew we'd crash. I also knew there was a big bump where the pavement met the bridge below and hitting it at the speed we were going would send us flying. I was terrified and kept screaming, "Hold on, Johnny, hold on." On the last curve I looked up, intending to aim the bike dead center into the bridge, as far as possible from the sides. But Dad had stopped the truck just before the bridge and was standing off to the side of the road, his legs braced and his arms straight out in front of him. I aimed the handle bars at his hands and we crashed into him, bike and bodies flying in all directions. Johnny and I were crying—more from terror than from the scratches and bruises we got from the ordeal. As we got up and Mom examined us for any serious damage, I looked up to see David cautiously braking his way down the hill. That night, when Mom tucked John in bed, he asked, "Did I die?" If Dad had not remembered that my brakes were broken, he very well could have.

That little bridge crossed a dry river bed, or a wadi, where water flowed to the Senegal River during the rainy season. When it and everything else in the savanna were bone dry, Kayes was a stopping place for Tuareg herders who pitched their dark blue tents near the river to water their herds.

Dad told us their other name was the "Blue People" because the faces of their men, who were always veiled, were blue from the dye they used in all their fabric. They were skilled herders, fierce warriors and the keepers of the Sahara who held an uneasy truce with the French who occupied their land.

One day we crossed the river and stopped the Carryall to have a closer look at their encampment of dark blue tents pitched in the sand. When a young man came by on his camel, Dad motioned for him to stop, took out his wallet, pointed to it and then at me and then at the camel. The man was puzzled for a moment but then understood. He had the camel kneel, I climbed on in front of him and away we went in a big loop near the road. From that height, I could see the river on one side, the tents and herds of sheep on the other, and beyond them, the dry savanna stretching north toward the Sahara. It was magical for me but I'm not so sure what the young Tuareg thought. For all he knew I was a little French girl, the child of the enemy, whose father could not be refused.

We returned to spend Christmas in Kénieba with the other missionaries. On Christmas Eve, some of us slept outside on cots. My mind, as usual, was racing instead of calming down and the stars above me were so spectacular that I couldn't stop chattering about them. And, like whistling in the dark, it may have been my way to keep thoughts about the lions and leopards up in the escarpment at bay. But eventually I fell asleep and woke up to my first African Christmas. My present must have been a doll, because I'm holding one in a picture of my brothers and of me, glasses and all, sitting on a thatched roof that was waiting to be lifted onto its circular home.

93

Our return to Kayes was delayed because Dad came down with hepatitis A. It is rarely fatal but it can become serious if the patient does not have adequate care and rest. When Dad was well enough to leave Kénieba, a Lebanese family in Mahina invited us for a meal while we waited for the train to Kayes. I watched as our hostess spooned macaroni in tomato sauce onto my mom's plate and proudly topped it off with the cooked head of a rooster. Mom gasped out loud and I saw Dad kick her under the table in response. I stared at the eyes of the thing and was glad it wasn't on my plate. Mom somehow managed to eat the macaroni. I hope our hostess wasn't offended that the delicacy she had offered went untouched.

We got back to Kayes in January, and in February Mom came down with hepatitis. She wasn't just sick, but was deathly ill. She lay in bed, barely able to move. Like my father with his mother, I could make my mother laugh, so Dad often summoned me to her bedside to cheer her up. This is why I remember Yuba appearing at her bedside several times a day to ask, with concern written all over his face, "What can I make for Madame?" He'd reappear later with something he'd made, she'd take a few bites and push it away.

Yuba's day off was Friday, the Muslim Holy Day, but the first Friday after Mom became so sick, he was waiting on the veranda when we got up. I was standing behind Dad, still in my pajamas, when Dad asked him why he was there. His response was a question, respectful but firm, "But, Mr. Darr, who will cook for the children?"

Despite our prayers and Yuba's loving care, Mom worsened by the day and eventually the French military doctor admitted her to the hospital at Fort Médine. Every morning in the days that followed, Dad and I would drive out to the military complex, wait for the guard to open the gate and then we'd walk up to her hospital room on the second floor of one of the buildings. Dad would get a quick update from mom and then leave to get back to my brothers who had been left in the care of N'fali and Yuba. At that time, children were not allowed in hospitals anywhere, much less in military hospitals, so my days included explaining myself to the French and African soldiers who came in and out of Mom's room for one reason or another. The hospital was for soldiers, so there were no frills and certainly no call buttons. My job was to keep Mom company, to help her as needed and, most importantly, to act as her interpreter.

When the doctor and his entourage appeared, I would slide off Mom's bed and stand as straight and tall as my nine-year-old self could stand. I can see myself, wearing a cotton sundress, looking up intently at the doctor dressed in his Foreign Legion khakis, my mother's face to my right on her pillow. There was a rhythm to listening, turning to her with the translation, turning back to the doctor to translate her response and starting it all over again. One day the doctor praised me to my father and they chuckled over my role as little nurse and interpreter. I had no idea at the time that it really was an extraordinary experience for a little girl and that it all took place in a fort of historic significance.[11]

With Mom in the hospital, Yuba's presence was a steadying, calming influence for us children, so Dad managed—until the night when the burglars came. The iron ore in the hills surrounding Kayes trap the heat like a pressure cooker, making the city like an oven around the clock. We sweated so much in our sleep that we always got up during the night for a drink of water. For some reason, one night while Mom was in the hospital, Dad left the doors open. When David, John and I woke for our usual drink, the light from a full moon was shining into our room and, like magic, it drew us onto the veranda, all the way to the railing. Everything in the courtyard below and the surrounding rooftops were silver in the moonlight, but we didn't stay long because it was still the middle of the night. A minute or two after we crawled back in bed, David and I saw them at the same time: two shadowy figures tiptoeing across the veranda toward our dad's bedroom. We froze in terror. When they came back into view, carrying Dad's khaki trousers, David screamed and I joined in. David thought Dad's pants were a large sack and the men were coming to kidnap us. At our screams, the men dropped the trousers and ran. Dad leaped out of bed and gave chase, but they were gone.

On top of having a very sick wife, Dad now had two children who were too afraid to sleep. He moved our bed to his room where all five of us slept, sweltering behind closed doors. I would eventually fall asleep every night, but David would stay awake until the first light of dawn filtered through the shuttered doors. Not having Mom there made it all the worse. At the end of March, it all came to an abrupt end with these words, "Mr. Darr, your wife will die if you stay here through the hot season." The doctor discharged her on strict orders to get her back to the U.S. as soon as possible.

This presented a problem for Dad, who was now the Field Director for the mission. The next month he was scheduled to represent the mission at a conference in Upper Volta for all the Christian mission organizations in West Africa. At that meeting, mission leaders would discuss the changes that were bound to come as the regions they worked in became independent countries. With assurances from the mission that someone would meet Mom when she landed in Boston and with assurances from family and Goss Church that they would help her once she got home, Dad decided to stay. He went with us on the train to Dakar where, on April 7, 1958, the day after Easter, he put his wife and four children on a Pan American® flight back to the U.S.

---

[11] Fort Médine. World Monuments Fund. https://www.wmf.org/project/médine-fort

When we settled into our seats on the plane, the stewardess came down the aisle with a tray of fruit. When David and I spoke to her in French, she gave us a puzzled look. Mom smiled and told us to speak in English and then laughed when David reached past the apples, oranges and pears that we had not seen in over a year and chose a banana.

As that flight lifted off from Dakar and headed west across the Atlantic, the first chapter of my childhood in Africa came to an end. During that short time, just 15 months, I experienced firsthand the last days of Colonialism and had my innocence ripped away. Over the next few years, the political and social landscape of French West Africa would change dramatically, but that was nothing compared to the upheaval my family and I would face in the months ahead, far from Kayes with no Yuba, steady and calm, lovingly looking after us as our world fell apart.

Chapter 11

A Seismic Shift in My World
April 1958–August 1958

The trip to America was long, with stops in Lisbon and the Azores for fuel. It amazes me that our mother, still weak from hepatitis, managed the trip with four young children in tow. As promised, a leader from the mission board was waiting for us at the airport in Boston. Once we settled into a hotel, he broke the news to Mom that Pastor William Troup had died in his study a week and a half earlier. I presume that Goss Church had not telegrammed this news to us in Africa, but waited instead to inform Dad by telegram once they knew Mom was home and she could be told in person.

The mission leader helped us get back to the airport the next day for our flight to Ohio. It was April 9, 1958, my tenth birthday. When we got off the plane, there were grandparents, aunts, uncles, cousins and many people from church waiting to welcome us home. It was the best birthday ever, especially when Grandma Darr handed me a card and inside was a ten-dollar bill, the entire amount just for me.

Our arrival back home was newsworthy. A few weeks after we returned, a reporter showed up to interview Mom about life in Africa and her reason for returning to Akron. Dad loved his work in Africa, but life there had not been easy for our mother. But now she was home, pampered by family and friends and affirmed by the entire city, all of which surely reinforced the lessons she had learned about frailty as a child.

At first, we all stayed at Aunt Fern and Uncle Johnny's house. Their boys were Fred, who was my age; Bob, who was a little younger than David; and Larry, who was around John and Rich's ages. Best of all, I got to share a room with my Cousin Susan who was not only beautiful, but who was sixteen and a high school cheerleader. Having never had a sister, I was in absolute heaven. For us cousins, it was a whole lot of fun all the time; however, for Aunt Fern, who worked full-time, it probably wasn't easy.

When Uncle Johnny and Aunt Fern saw how weak mom was, they suggested that David and I stay with them and attend school with their kids to make things easier for her. And so it was that David and I were enrolled at Rimer Elementary School, the same yellow brick school that our mother and all her sisters had attended. The principal didn't quite know what to do with us. David was eight and a half and should have been in the Grade 3, but he had completed only Grade 1 and 2 in French. I had just turned ten and should have been in Grade 4, but I had only completed Grade 1 in Akron and Grade 1 and 2 in French. She decided to put David in Grade 2 and me in Grade 4 to see what would happen. What happened was that David soon moved up to Grade 3 and I came down with hepatitis and moved into the hospital.

It happened like this: During our first weekend at Aunt Fern's house I knew I was sick when my urine was the color of amber. I started to cry and found her in the kitchen.

"I have hepatitis," I whimpered.

"No, you don't. You just want to get out of your chores. When we're all done, we are roasting hot dogs for lunch so you'd better get started." I did my chores, I ate the hotdog—about the worst thing you can do for your liver even on a good day—and I held back my tears. Later that afternoon, Aunt Fern took us over to spend Saturday night and Sunday with our mother and brothers. As soon as she left, I started to cry.

"Mommy, I have hepatitis and Aunt Fern made me work!" I added the last part because I knew if you didn't rest, hepatitis could kill you and I was worried that working that morning might make me drop over dead sooner rather than later. She took me over to the big bay window in the dining room, pulled down my lower eyelid, confirmed what I knew and said that I would be fine.

First thing on Monday morning, Aunt Fern showed up, apologized for not believing me, and drove us to Dr. Widemeyer's office. He sent me straight to Akron Children's Hospital where I was admitted. In the Midwest in 1958, hepatitis was an exotic tropical disease, so I created quite a stir. I was put in isolation. Doctors, nurses and visitors suited up in white garments from head to toe before entering my room. Doctors who weren't even treating me came to see the little girl from Africa with hepatitis.

"Let's have a look at you," they'd say and off would come my gown and I'd stand once again next to the window in nothing but my panties while they checked the color of my eyes, turned me around to see how yellow my body was, and then pressed all over my stomach. When they left and the door closed behind them, I was all alone for hours at a time. How ironic that a month earlier, at Fort Médine, the military officers had made an exception for a little girl to be with her mother, but when I was at Akron Children's

Hospital no one thought that maybe a sick little girl might need her mother for more than a short visit every day.[12]

I had seen the doctor draw blood from mother's arm in the hospital at Kayes so I took it in stride at first . . . until both of my arms were black, blue and sore. The next time the nurse came to draw blood, I fought her tooth and nail. Reinforcements had to suit up and come in to hold me down. When the nurse described my behavior to my mother in front of me, I was ashamed and promised to be braver next time. Not long after that I got to go home to my mom's house with a strict diet to follow and orders to rest for a month.

The house that Goss Memorial Church had provided for Mom to live in until Dad got home was just a few doors down from the church, right around the corner from Mrs. Carlisle's house where we had lived before going to France and right across the street from Heminger School where, eternities ago, I had finished first grade. While I recovered, I could see the children lining up to go into school and I could hear them playing on the playground. Fortunately, weakness kills desire so it did not upset me that I could not join them.

Needless to say, the principal at Rimer School was furious. "How can you bring a child in here from Africa and expose our whole school to hepatitis?" she snapped at Aunt Fern when she reported why I was absent. The school arranged for a teacher to come to my house with my lessons during the month I was ordered to rest. That recovery period happened to end on the next to the last day of the school year. I clearly remember sitting at the dining room table and the teacher going over my last set of assignments. She looked at my mother and me and said, "I am going to reluctantly pass Dianne into the fifth grade." That was a relief, but an even bigger relief was that the period of incubation had passed and no child in Akron had turned yellow.

The next morning, I was allowed to go outside. "Take it easy," Mom warned as I walked out the door. She needn't have worried. I crossed the street to the playground and sat on a swing. I looked at the monkey bars and the slide and decided I had better save them for another day. It was good enough to swing gently in the sunshine and to be free.

After putting us on the plane in Dakar, Dad had set off on a road trip with Yuba to Guinea, which had already gained its independence from France. After dropping Yuba near his village, he continued up into the Fouta

---

[12] *"If you were ill as a child, you may have been separated from your family and forced . . . to undergo invasive and painful procedures [you may be] at increased risk for depression and traumatic-stress reactions."*
Kendall-Tackett, Kathleen. The Long Shadow: Adult Survivors of Childhood Abuse. https://www.vetmed.wsu.edu/docs/librariesprovider16/default-document-library/the-long-shadow-adult-survivors-of-childhood-abuse.pdf?sfvrsn=0

Djallon Mountains where he saw the Christian & Missionary Alliance boarding school at Mamou and then continued his journey to Upper Volta for the conference. His return trip took him through Bamako and then back to Kayes. Once there he packed up our belongings, took them and the Carryall to Kénieba to be stored, took the train to Dakar and flew home to join us in May.

It was summer and, oh joy, David was home, I was allowed to play, and something else exciting happened! Aunt Fern had a sister named Joyce Simms who was the organist at Hope EUB Church where my Grandma Darr still attended. Joyce taught piano lessons in her home and agreed to teach me to play. She had a hilarious sense of humor, but it never manifested itself during my lessons. If my music theory assignments were not completed or my songs had not been learned, a berating was sure to follow. This made me nervous, but practicing was a different kind of intimidating. The church parsonage was a few doors down from ours and Mrs. Troup had agreed to let me practice on her piano. There were strict orders from my mother, "Ring the doorbell, say hello, thank her when you leave and be sure to close the door." And, an admonition from Joyce, "There is no reason for you to be banging on Mrs. Troup's piano. You can learn these songs playing them softly just as well as playing them loudly. Remember, she is doing you a big favor to let you practice at her house!"

At the scheduled time every day, I clutched my piano books to my chest and walked bravely down the street. The warnings had not been necessary. The house was dark, the carpets were dark, the furniture was dark and so was the piano. It was too spooky to do anything but tiptoe, speak softly and play pianissimo until Mrs. Troup told me my half hour was up. Widowed just several months before and undoubtedly in deep mourning, she welcomed me, a little child, into her home and listened while I played songs that can drive even the most devoted parents crazy. I couldn't fully appreciate it then, but Joyce and Mrs. Troup gave me a lifelong gift and I remember them with gratitude and joy.

And then, in mid-summer, the nightmares began. I started waking in the night with explicit dreams of Don doing things to my body that I did not understand. I didn't want to wake my parents, so I'd just lie in bed trying to understand the dream and trying to forget it all at the same time. And then something happened that pushed me over the edge. I was walking home from the playground one afternoon when a voice said, "Little girl, come over here." I turned to see who was talking to me, but no one was there. That side of the school was in the shade, and the stairway there, leading down to the basement of the school, was darker still. The voice spoke again, "Come here. I have something to show you." As my eyes adjusted to the shade, I could see the head and shoulders of a man standing at the bottom of the steps. I turned and ran as fast as I could along the side of the playground, across the street, up the steps and into the house.

I was textbook hysterical. I went into the bathroom and my mother followed. I sat on the side of the tub and was sobbing so hard I was gasping for air. Finally, it all came out: the man across the street, the bad dreams and what Don had done to me at Kénieba. She listened calmly and then called my dad inside and had me repeat what I had told her.

He asked me a few questions and then hugged me tightly, "It's okay, Dianne, it's okay. You don't have to cry. That man at the school can't get you. It's okay. You did the right thing to tell us."[13] When I went out of the bathroom, my crying had stopped, but my breath still came in big gulps. A few minutes later they called David in to talk to him. When he came out crying, I knew it had happened to him too. We stood there together, in the light of the big bay window, while behind us, behind the bathroom door, our parents held each other and wept.

My nightmares did not return and summer played out as it should for little boys and girls. David and I roller skated on the sidewalk, swung on the swings and hung from the monkey bars on the playground, walked to the corner store for candy, had picnics with our cousins and went to Vacation Bible School. What I did not know was that a storm was brewing inside me and clouds of conflict were building up between my parents and their mission board. At the end of summer, we moved into a little house in Castle Homes where David and I started school at Highland Park and John started kindergarten at Guinther. As we settled into the new school year, a maelstrom was looming and when it struck I believed it was all because of me.

---

[13] *"Your reaction to the disclosure will have a big effect on how your child deals with the trauma of sexual abuse. Children whose parents/caregivers are supportive heal more quickly from the abuse. Stay Calm. Believe. Protect."*
What to Do if your Child Discloses Sexual Abuse. The National Child Traumatic Stress Network. https://kids.delaware.gov/pdfs/dscyf_trauma_disclosure.pdf

Chapter 12

My World Explodes
Fall 1958–December 1959

We moved to a small ranch house on Winston Street in Castle Homes, not far from where Dad grew up. David and I walked up Cory Avenue, past Hope Church and down Waterloo Road to Highland Park School. John started kindergarten at Guinther, a Grade K–3 school in Castle Homes that had been built to educate the hundreds of Baby Boomer kids growing up in our neighborhood. Those children welcomed us, played with us and included us in the group that knew a shortcut for walking to and from school. We fit right in, at least outwardly. But David and I knew that, below the surface, there were things our peers would never know about us, much less understand.

Fall, in evangelical and fundamentalist circles, is Missions Conference season. At these week-long events, missionaries who are home from overseas report about their work to their supporting churches. In the 1950s, the highlights of those events were slide presentations depicting how the church's money and prayers were reaching people for the Lord in exotic, faraway lands. Dad traveled alone to the conferences that were out of Ohio, but we went as a family when they were closer to home. David and I played our part by reciting John 3:16 in French and wearing our authentic African costumes, made for us by Boubacar, the tailor in the market place of Kayes.

One nearby church was in Atwater, Ohio. The pastor, Jimmy Douglas, was a Bob Jones grad like Dad and we were the first missionaries the church had pledged to support. On the weekend we visited there, the pastor's daughter, Susan, David and I were in the same Sunday School class. When the teacher asked if anyone had a question for the missionary kids, a boy raised his hand and asked if we had seen Tarzan. I was dumbstruck at the absurdity of the question. However, being the good little missionary kid that I was, I answered politely with an emphatic "No" followed by a pointed explanation of the difference between fact and fiction.[14] Afterward, on our

---

[14] Experiences like these and those that David and I experienced in France are typical for missionary kids (MKs) and Third Culture Kids (TCKs), something that was not well understood until the publication of *Third Culture Kids: Growing Up Among Worlds* by David Pollock and Ruth Van Reken in 1999.

way to the sanctuary, boys around my age were laughing behind us and I sensed it was about me—and years later I would find out why.

David and I were actually the main attraction at one memorable event. The Cathedral of Tomorrow, the mega church led by televangelist Rex Humbard, asked Dad to speak at a youth rally. In case the youth of Northeast Ohio were not keen about world evangelism, entertainment would surely lure them in. The Cathedral hired an elephant and its trainer and David and I, dressed in our authentic African costumes, rode it down the aisle to the front of the church. The elephant was young and God only knows how experienced it was around crowds. The closeness of the aisles and the clapping and cheering in the packed auditorium spooked it on the way down and the trainer had a hard time controlling it. We stopped at the front while Dad was introduced from the stage and then the elephant carried us up another aisle without incident. This was wrong on so many levels that I can't even begin to explain or justify it. I'm just glad the newspaper article and picture promoting the event were not followed by one describing a disaster.

Unfortunately, throughout the fall of 1958, Mom and Dad were not just happily sharing their ministry opportunities in Africa with their supporters. Between conferences, they were in the middle of a conflict with their mission board. They had contacted the leadership of the mission immediately after

David and I had revealed that Don had molested us. Those men confronted Don and he admitted to touching me, wept remorsefully and swore it would never happen again. My parents were asked to forgive him and to move on. They, however, insisted that Don not be allowed to return to Africa where David and I would be in contact with him. And, while our parents held their ground, the mission board held theirs, accusing Mom and Dad of trying to ruin Don's ministry. It was turning into a nightmare.

I knew nothing of this conflict with David and me at the center, and from all outward appearances, I was doing fine—until Aunt Shelly came home to Akron and took Mom and us for a ride in her big, beautiful car. Shelly's husband, Ron Negray, was a major league baseball pitcher and she was beautiful. I was in awe of her and there I was, in the front seat of her car, amazed and impressed as we went gliding down the road. I wasn't paying attention to Mom and Shelly's conversation until I realized that, in couched tones and in veiled language, my mother was telling Shelly what had happened to me. I leaned forward slowly, pressed my hands on the dashboard, and stared at the road stretching out before me, still as stone.

I kept my composure until we got inside the house. "How could you tell Aunt Shelly that?" I screamed so fiercely that I thought my voice had ripped my throat open. She explained calmly that it was okay if family members knew. I screamed back, angrier than ever, that I didn't want anyone at all to know. And I did not stop. I kept screaming it over and over again. This was no tantrum. It was pure, sustained rage at everything that had happened to me—and my mother knew it.[15]

Mom and Dad had been concerned about David all along. He still had trouble falling asleep and when he did, nightmares about the robbers in Kayes would wake him. He was so terrified he couldn't sleep unless he climbed in bed with them. For my mother, just months from having nearly died of hepatitis, sleep deprived, worried about David, in conflict with the mission leaders who continued to affirm our abuser, my outburst of rage was the last straw. She quit functioning at home, wouldn't leave the house and spiraled into a deep depression that would not go away.

Dr. Roger Troup, the oldest son of Pastor Troup, was also home on furlough from his work at the SIM Hospital in Lagos, Nigeria. He came to the house and made his diagnosis: a complete nervous breakdown. He

---

[15] *"Not surprisingly [anger] is one of the strongest feelings which many children have about their sexual assault. Children may feel anger against the perpetrator and also against others who they feel failed to protect them."*
The Effects of Childhood Sexual Assault - Psychological Effects. South Eastern CASA. www.secasa.com.au/pages/the-effects-of-childhood-sexual-abuse

prescribed anti-depressants and sleeping pills and started regular counseling sessions with her in the evening after we children went to bed.

Our little house on Winston Street had two bedrooms, one for Mom and Dad and one for my brothers. I slept in a small room separated from the living room by folding accordion doors. My bed was right next to that flimsy partition through which I could hear everything: Mom crying softly, Dad asking questions, and mostly Dr. Troup's voice. In one session, sandwiched between his opening scripture reading and his closing prayer, he explained to my parents in clinical terms what sometimes happened to children who had experienced pedophilia, molestation, bestiality, incest, and rape—all with specific examples.

Overhearing these counseling sessions taking place around our dining room table was traumatic. It was upsetting to learn that what had happened to me was really serious. It was upsetting to think that what happened to me was making my mother so sad she had to talk to a doctor. Plus, I was scared to death that if they knew I was awake, I'd be in trouble. I would lie perfectly still, barely breathing until, at last, the chairs would push back from the table, the side door would open, Dr. Roger would say goodnight, the lights would go out and Mom and Dad would go to bed. When their bedroom door closed I could breathe, turn over and finally fall asleep.

Another thing weighed on me. If Dr. Roger thought this was so serious, maybe I should tell about Robert. One evening when Mom and I passed each other in the hall, I stopped her and said, "I have to tell you something." I stared at the print on her cotton dress and spoke, just above a whisper, "Robert did things to me too." She leaned back slowly against the wall and when she did not respond, I looked up at her face and added softly, "I just wanted to tell you." She said something about him being gone and that we wouldn't talk about it now. In her deep depression, it may not even have registered, but I was relieved I had told and equally relieved that questions about it never followed.

After my explosion, people may have looked around to see if there were pieces of me splattered across the landscape, but they didn't see any. Everyone, including me, was too busy picking up the pieces of my mother.[16] During Mom's worst days, Dad relied on me to help around the house and I had little time or emotional energy to think about myself. Gradually my fears

---

[16] *"Where there is mental illness, children, ... especially the oldest girl, often find that they are the 'little adults' in the family ... responsible for meeting their parents' emotional needs rather than the other way around."*
Kendall-Tackett, Kathleen. The Long Shadow: Adult Survivors of Childhood Abuse. www.vetmed.wsu.edu/docs/librariesprovider16/default-document-library/the-long-shadow-adult-survivors-of-childhood-abuse.pdf?sfvrsn=0

and anger nestled deep inside me and crystalized into a vow: I would do all I could do and be the best I could be so I would never, ever cause my parents trouble again. That vow became the bedrock of my internal landscape, deep beneath all the paths that lay before me, underscoring who I was and what I did for the rest of my life.[17]

During that time, Dr. Troup never blamed my mother's breakdown on a spiritual problem and the leadership of Goss Memorial Church stood with my parents about the severity of what had happened to David and me. And thus, while our world was falling apart, the other foundations of my life held: my childlike faith in a God who loved me and the support of godly people who cared.

Thank God for mornings and for school. I loved Grade 5, partly because it was so ridiculously easy and partly because of Mr. Griffin. The first day of class he held up his right hand and showed us the thick scars running the length of his palm up to where his index finger and thumb should have been. They had been blown off in a gun accident during the war. I had never had a male teacher and I loved the light-hearted way he handled the class and taught us. It was also a running joke in class that he usually called me Darlene instead of Dianne because of my last name, Darr.

Every Tuesday, instead of walking home with David, I'd go to my friend Elaine's house and, after dinner, her mom took us to Goss for Pioneer Girls® where she was one of the leaders. There I also forged friendships with Marcia, Neenah, Lillian and Carol. They had no idea what I was going through, nor could they relate to the places I had lived, nor to the things I had known far, far away. But they included me and have remained in touch all my life, providing a little cove where I anchored then and anchor still and feel somewhat like I belong.

Two other things happened that year that impacted me. One was the stomach aches that sometimes made me miss school. Mom eventually took me to see Dr. Widemeyer who found nothing wrong. "Does she like school?" he asked my mother.

I was insulted and didn't even wait for her to respond. "I love school," I shot back. Mom verified that I liked my teacher, that I had friends and that my grades were good. We were told to wait and see. I thought about that appointment a lot. I knew being upset could cause you to be so sad you needed help from a doctor, but it was scary to think that being upset could

---

[17] *"The need for absolute excellence can become a means of dealing with fear and anxiety created by ongoing trauma."*
Hollowood, Tia. (Healthy Place, March 7, 2018). Complex PTSD and Perfectionism. www.healthyplace.com/blogs/traumaptsdblog/2018/03/complex-ptsd-and-perfectionism

make you physically sick and it was even scarier that a doctor could accuse you of that even when he didn't know you.

The other thing was a birthday party I was invited to attend. The boy lived only a few blocks from us, but Dad drove me there. The party started upstairs with snacks and birthday cake and then we went downstairs to the basement to play games. After Pin-the-Tail-on-the-Donkey, the birthday boy had us sit in a circle on the floor and produced a bottle. When I asked what the game was they told me I'd figure it out. The first time the bottle pointed to a girl and the boy who had spun it got up and kissed her, I turned cold. I stood up, walked upstairs and asked the boy's mother if I could please call home. Dad came and got me and was surprised to learn that 10-year-olds were playing kissing games and assured me that it was okay that I wanted to leave.

The following Monday, when Mr. Griffin stood in front of the class to give the announcements, I was shocked that I was part of them. "And, I understand that Dianne went to a party on Saturday and didn't want to play one of the games." While the boys involved snickered, someone asked what he meant. "Spin the Bottle," Mr. Griffin said and the whole class laughed. I blushed, sat stone still and stared at my desk. I didn't care. If they knew the reason why I did what I did, they wouldn't be laughing.

One day some of us stayed late after school to work on a project and Mr. Griffin walked us to the bottom of the steps. "I'd better not take the shortcut across the tracks," I said. I didn't have to explain why because all the teachers knew the stories about kids walking alone being chased by a man and the rumor that another child walking alone had seen a man exposing himself there.

"I can drive you home," he offered. I had no reason to suspect him of any ulterior motives, but I declined his offer. A puzzled look crossed his face, like he was thinking too much about why I had refused but then he said, "Okay. I'll walk you to the edge of the woods and wait till you get through."

At the edge of the path, I thanked him and ran. It was dark for a short distance through the woods but there was open sky where it crossed the Belt Line. Just beyond the tracks was an open clearing and a ball field where there was no reason to be afraid. That brought me to the edge of our neighborhood, another seven blocks from home, which gave me enough time to think about what had just happened. I concluded that preventing bad things from happening might involve being embarrassed by your teacher in front of your classmates and walking home when you could have a ride, but a little girl had to do what a little girl had to do.[18]

Mom got better over time and, to any casual observer, we were just another American family living on a typical American street. We even had pets. There was a female cat, who ended up with a litter of kittens, and also a kitten we rescued next to a corn field when we were returning from one of our trips to a supporting church. A few weeks after bringing it home, we took another weekend trip and friends watched the cats for us. While we were gone, the mother cat died, which was traumatic for us kids. What was traumatic for our parents was that hundreds of flea eggs from the rescued kitten had hatched in our warm, closed up house. We spent the night at Grandma Darr's house so the insecticide bombs Dad set off in the house would kill the fleas and not us.

A missionary furlough, now called a home assignment, typically lasted just one year, but given Mom's mental breakdown and the ongoing conflict with the mission board over our abuse, we wouldn't be returning to Africa any time soon. I turned eleven in April and, after school was out, David and I went to church camp, played outside and swam in the Ohio and Erie Canal with our friends (but only when Dad was out of town). He insisted it was dangerously polluted, which it was, but when our friends knocked on the door, dressed in their swims suits, and begged us to come along, Mom would relent and let us go.

John and Rich also lucked out one time when Dad was out of town. One day, along with their five and six-year-old buddies, they were pretending to be hunters. The dog tied up in a neighbor's garage was a lion. Their plan to stalk and kill it with fire was foiled when the neighbor caught them, matches and all. She marched the culprits home, knocked on our side door and reported the details of the crime to our mother. Mom was mortified and apologized but, in typical fashion, she took it mostly in stride, unlike Dad whose reactions would have been much more explosive.

In July of 1959, Mom and Dad resigned from the mission board that continued to minimize what had happened to David and me and to affirm our abuser.[19] By late summer another mission board that worked in French West

---

[18] "… sexual or physical abuse … can profoundly affect [a child's] assumption that the world is a safe and predictable place, leaving them feeling alienated and distrustful."
Post-traumatic Stress Disorder (PTSD) Overview. (Healthy.com, March 7, 2018). www.healthyplace.com/other-info/psychiatric-disorder-definitions/post-traumatic-stress-disorder-ptsd-overview.

[19] Our parents kept all their correspondence about the abuse and their decision to leave Mission Endeavor International. The originals are archived, with the rest of their missionary papers, in the Billy Graham Center Archives in Wheaton, IL.

Africa, the Gospel Missionary Union (GMU), agreed to have them join their group. Mom and Dad sat me down and explained that Dad would have to go to the churches that supported us and explain why we were leaving one mission and joining another. I didn't like it, but I understood. Every church but one (a large church in Canton with strong ties to the mission in Dayton) agreed to send their pledged support to the new mission. The significance of this was not lost on me. It was not just my parents who believed and defended me. My resolve to do all I could do and to be all I could be would now be for them too.

When school started in September, my sixth-grade teacher was Mrs. Nolley whose no-nonsense goal was to prepare her students for junior high the following year. Her classroom management style was more structured than Mr. Griffin's, but I liked it and, for the first time since Dakar, I was academically challenged. One day at recess, when Mr. Griffin was on duty, he called me over. "Dianne," he said with a twinkle in his eye, "remember how I called you Darlene all the time last year?" I smiled at the memory. "Well, this year I have a Darlene in class and I call her Dianne!" We both laughed and I ran back to play with my friends.

The new mission board required its applicants to live at the mission for several months before being accepted. However, since my parents had already learned French and had spent a year and a half in Africa, the president of the mission, Rev. Don P. Shidler, allowed us to come for an abbreviated version of Candidate School. In the fall of 1959 we drove to Kansas City where we stayed at the GMU headquarters for two weeks. It was like going to Mrs. Troup's house to practice the piano, only 24/7. We children were warned within an inch of our lives that our behavior could make or break our return to Africa, putting us on pins and needles the whole time we were there. Even with Mrs. Shidler watching our every move, we passed muster and were accepted. A departure date was set for January of 1960.

On our drive back to Ohio, Dad stopped in Springfield, Illinois to confront the man who had never paid him, other than a deposit, for the little house in the trailer park in Greenville. He would have graduated the previous year and Dad had gotten his address from the university. It was dusk when we found the street but the house number Dad had was not on any of the houses. We watched as he knocked on door after door and talked to the people who answered. When he returned to the car, he said, "No luck. The guy in the second house told me that I am not the first person to come looking for a man by that name." He paused, "He's just a crook." Sitting in the back seat with my brothers, sensing my father's disappointment, I added another name to my list of men who called themselves Christian but whose actions told a different story.

110

Joining the new mission board meant that we children would attend Mamou Alliance Academy in Guinea as boarding students. Homeschool with the Calvert Courses had not worked out in Kayes, so sending us to Guinea where we would receive an excellent American education seemed to our parents like the right thing to do. They got the list of required clothing, linens and other supplies we'd need for attending the school and the process of packing our barrels for four years began.

Being a missionary kid whose parents were members of Goss Memorial Church was an extraordinary blessing, something I wouldn't fully appreciate until many decades later. Mom typed up and posted detailed lists on the church bulletin board of everything each of us kids would need for the next four years. For weeks, every Sunday was like Christmas. After church, we'd come home and spread out all the beautiful things that people at church, mainly the families of our peers, had bought for us.

Only one time did I get a glimpse at what I would later learn was often the norm. A woman we did not know called the house to say she was bringing over some clothing for us. She showed up at our door on Winston Street with a huge box. Mom thanked her, closed the door, took one look inside the box and was outraged. Watching her pull out one item of clothing after another in disgust and indignation was shocking because Mom rarely lost her temper.

"Who does she think she is bringing these worn out things for our kids to wear? Look at this stretched out underwear! Who does she think is going to wear this?"

"Now Anne," Dad interjected, "she meant well."

"I don't care," Mom retorted. "Would her kids wear these things? It's an insult." At that she closed up the flaps of the box, pushed it toward Dad and said, "Get it out of here."

Mom and Dad booked our passage across the Atlantic on a freighter named the *African Glade*. This time our barrels would go with us and Dad would be on hand himself to get them off the ship in Dakar and on to the train to Bamako. David and I were excited to be going back to Africa but John, who was six years old, was terrified. He had nightmares about being on the ship, especially after hearing the pastor preach about the apostle Paul being shipwrecked on one of his missionary journeys followed by his Sunday School classmates teasing him that it would happen to him too. John was also apprehensive about going away to boarding school. Time would prove that his nightmares were not just childish dreams and his apprehensions were more than childish fears. They were premonitions of things to come.

Chapter 13

Rough Seas and New Landscapes
January–March 1960

Right after Thanksgiving we flew to New York City, where our barrels had been shipped. On December 1,1959, we boarded the *African Glade*, a Farrell Lines freighter with cabins on the third deck for a dozen or so passengers. We were delighted that our shipmates included the Andersons, another missionary family with four children, whose destination was Ghana. Three times a day, we all went down a steep, narrow staircase, aptly called a

 *ladder* in shipping parlance, to the dining room to eat our meals with the captain and his first mate. The vessel was shipshape when we boarded, but we soon learned that a freighter was nothing like an ocean liner. Fumes from the smokestack and greasy dust from the diesel engines soon covered everything on deck.

On our first day at sea, something blew into Mom's eye that no one could see. Thankfully, the ship was stopping at Halifax the following day to pick up a load of wheat. The captain radioed ahead and, when we went ashore, we took a taxi to an ophthalmologist's office where the doctor removed a speck of metal from her eye. That night the ship set sail east across the North Atlantic and the very next morning, with twelve days left in our voyage and eight children on board, the galley ran out of milk. Mom was upset and Dad complained to the captain, but there was nothing that could be done about it.

It would be six days before we would arrive at the Azore Islands. We soon settled into a daily routine of watching the flying fish skim across the water, spotting whales, playing board games on deck, watching the Anderson girls sketch horses, reading or watching movies with the crew in the evenings. My days also involved something else. After breakfast every morning, John and I would crawl up into a bunk and we'd read the books his teacher had given him so he could finish the first semester of Grade 1. The curriculum at Mamou was very rigorous and Mom and Dad had been warned to make sure John was ready. He was serious about learning and made steady progress—and I take credit for all his subsequent academic accomplishments!

This routine didn't last long enough to get boring. Three days out from Halifax we sailed straight into a winter storm with gale force winds. At first it was exhilarating standing on deck, watching the bow of the ship pitching through mountainous waves, but the captain soon appeared and confined us to our cabins. "Secure everything and stay on your bunks," he said and disappeared. Dad rounded up the boys and took them to our kids' cabin. I went with Mom to hers where we clung to our bunks as the ship pitched and rolled. The thuds of a rogue suitcase, hurtling back and forth across the floor and slamming into the cabin walls, made it all the more terrifying.

Hours later, when the careening suitcase had slowed down to a crawl, the captain knocked on our door and told us we could come out because the worst was over. Later, when we were called down to the dining room to eat, the ship was still pitching so hard that I had to stop twice on the ladder because I was looking straight down at the floor. We later learned that two ships, the *George Robb* and the *Servus*, went down in that gale off the northern coast of Scotland.

A day or so later we dropped anchor in slight seas just offshore from the Azore Islands. The bustle on the main deck the next morning was interesting to watch. From our perch two decks up, we saw a barge approach and anchor right beside us. A deck hand tossed a Jacob's ladder down to the barge and then, one by one, men on the barge grabbed it and climbed on board. One unusually large swell sent a man flying way out over the barge and then crashing into the side of the ship, but he held on till the swaying slowed and then he scrambled on board.

While that was happening, the hatch opened on the main deck and a crane began hoisting large crates from the hold. It swung them effortlessly across the deck, lowered them over the side of the ship and dropped them carefully onto the barge. After the crates came the grand finale: a shiny yellow industrial vehicle.

Note the men, far below, on the right edge of the barge.

114

It slowly rose from the hold, dangling from the cables like a charm on a necklace. The arm of the crane turned ever so slowly until its precious cargo was swinging over the side of the ship. When the swaying stopped, the crane slowly lowered it toward the barge.

And then, at the exact moment that the crane released the cable, a large swell separated the barge from the ship. The vehicle hit the water with a torrential splash and disappeared.

As we stood stunned, trying to process what we had just seen, a cacophony of shouting and curses in Portuguese and English rose up from the deck. One of the men in charge looked up at us and glared, obviously not pleased that he had an audience.

"Come on, kids," one of the adults said. "We should probably go."

That uproar was not the only one that happened that day. When I learned that Dad had taken David ashore and had left me behind, I was furious. How could he? I was the oldest and got to do everything. I ran into our kids' cabin, locked the door and raged. Mom, John and Rich tried to coax me out for lunch, but I answered their pleas with shouts to leave me alone. Hours later, Dad and David came back and I still refused to open the door. Just before dinner, when Dad threatened to have the captain open the door, I relented. I thought I'd be in big trouble, but Dad just talked to me. "I didn't know this would be so upsetting to you, Dianne. I didn't take you because I knew some of the sailors would be drunk when we came back and I didn't want you to be in the boat with them."

My fury over being excluded was replaced by a wave of indignation. "Why didn't you tell me that before you left instead of sneaking off without me?" I snapped and walked away from him to the back deck where I stared out at the rolling sea and the horizon.

When I heard everyone going down to dinner, I reluctantly followed and nothing more was said about my epic tantrum. After dinner, we gathered on the deck to look out one last time at the lights of the Azores twinkling in the distance. We would weigh anchor and set out to sea again sometime during the night. As we stood watching twilight fall, we heard the shout, "Man overboard!" which sent us running pell-mell around the deck to the starboard side of the ship. We got there just in time to watch the burly first mate jump from the little boat to the landing at the base of the accommodation steps, crouch down on his knees and fish a drunken sailor out of the water by the scruff of his neck. In one motion, he dragged him to his feet, draped him over his shoulder and marched him up the steps where he disappeared from view.

After what we had witnessed and experienced on that day, it was good to have several uneventful days at sea before we docked in Dakar. It was December 14, 1959. We had been on board for two full weeks and it was several days before my legs got used to walking on solid ground. Dad stayed in Dakar to clear our barrels through customs and get them on the train bound for Bamako. Mom and us kids boarded the train for the two-day trip inland. All I remember about the train ride was lying on a narrow bunk and reading with John. Lloyd McRostie met us at the train station and took us to the GMU guest house where Marjorie had a lovely meal and a warm welcome waiting.

Dad got off the train at Mahina and somehow got to Kénieba to retrieve our household items and our Carryall. Instead of driving it to Bamako, he had to put it on the train and, when it got to Bamako, it went straight to a mechanic. "They drove the Carryall," I heard him tell Mom, "and didn't take care of it. I'm afraid there will be a lot of repairs." He was right. It had been driven through water and the back transaxle, among other things, had to be replaced at great expense. This hurt, but it was not a surprise. When mom and dad had resigned from that mission, their leaders had refused to transfer to our new mission the $4,000 that had been sent in by our churches and supporters to build us a house. Why would their missionaries on the field treat my parents any differently?

These repairs delayed us in Bamako through Christmas. With our barrels still sealed in the storeroom on the compound, we knew there would be no tree and no presents, but we took it in stride. On Christmas Day, we shared an African meal with other missionaries and African believers. It was our first ever African meal and mom was concerned. She kept warning us not to eat too much because it was very spicy. We just thought it was delicious!

When the Carryall was fixed, we took off for Sirakoro, the station about three hours from Bamako that we would call home for the next year and a half. On our way, we stopped at Mana where the mission had a Bible School and where we met more of our parents' new colleagues and the Wiens boys who would be our schoolmates at Mamou. From there we continued south on the dirt road to Bougouni, a large town on the Baoulé River, and then turned east. About forty-five minutes later we saw the little sign, Mission Protestante, and turned off the road where Helen Andres and Esther Finley came out to meet us. They had our house swept out and ready for us to move in and they hosted us for supper that night and breakfast the next morning. They continued to help with meals while we unpacked and settled in.

By now we had been on the field with our new mission board for about three weeks and, even to me as an eleven-year-old, the differences between it and our prior mission were striking. GMU's ministries had a rich legacy beginning with George Reed, who had spearheaded Protestant mission work in the French Sudan in 1919 and who later translated the New Testament into Bambara, the trade language of the region. GMU missionaries served under an elected field council responsible for a network of schools, medical dispensaries, literacy and translation teams, and national churches with their own church leaders. The field also had protocols for new missionaries, including the requirement that they learn the Bambara language. Mom and Dad had been stationed at Sirakoro because Helen and Esther would help them reach that goal.

Another difference was how the missionaries lived. Most of our parents' new colleagues had been farm kids. They knew how to be self-sufficient and how to make do with what was on hand. They shopped in the African markets and made their own bread. As if learning the Bambara language wasn't intimidating enough for our mother, there would be another learning curve for the city girl that she was: surviving on a station where access to store-bought goods and crispy loaves of French bread was non-existent. She learned how to make bread for two reasons: Dad got sick and the no-nonsense, single lady missionaries thought I was old enough to learn.

During our second week at Sirakoro, Dad woke up one morning deathly ill with a high fever. The next day, Mom and Helen drove him, moaning and groaning in the back of the Carryall, to Bamako to see the doctor. Esther was left to care for us kids and quickly seized this as an

opportunity for something else. Along with baking her own bread, baking bread for a family of six next door had gone on long enough and this was her chance to put a stop to it. After breakfast on the day Mom and Dad left, Esther said, "Dianne, you are going to help me make bread this morning. Boys, you can go back to your house and play."

When Mom and Dad rolled back into the station three days later I had two batches of bread under my belt and a recipe in my hand. "Mom," I said, all excited, "Aunt Esther taught me how to make bread!"

From then until we went to Mamou I made our bread and Mom learned from me. In later years, I saw this as one of several examples in a pattern. Mom had very little self-confidence and froze in the face of tasks she felt inadequate to tackle. This was probably why David and I had not been taught our Calvert courses in Kayes, why I was the one teaching John to read and why I was the one mixing, kneading and baking our bread.

117

Besides making the bread, I had the daily task of helping with John and Rich. After breakfast it was always, "Okay, Dianne, help the boys brush their teeth and get dressed. Then help them make their beds." They were typical little boys, mischievous and full of energy, and I was a typical big sister, impatient and rather mean. I remember grabbing their upper arms and yanking them to attention when they didn't stay focused and, worse yet, rapping them with my knuckle on their little buzz-cut heads when they defied me.

In March, Mom started packing our trunks for Mamou. First, we went out to the storage room where our barrels were kept. After checking carefully for snakes and scorpions, we'd tip a barrel till we could roll it away from the others, pry open its latch and take off the lid. As Mom pulled items out, she'd hold them up to us, making sure they were the right size and have us put them in our pile. When we were done, each of us carried our pile of clothes into the house and she checked the items against the list from Mamou. Then she and I had the tedious task of sewing name tags into every single item that went into each of our trunks. It was the beginning of the hardest, most heartrending thing she ever did.

Part IV

Mamou Academy – A Maelstrom of Memories

"Boarding school teaches you that a place can be wonderful
and horrible at the same time. Looking back,
and sorting it all out, is the task of a lifetime."

Chapter 14

The Minefields of Mamou
Spring, Summer, Fall 1960
Grade 6 Ends, Grade 7 Begins

Mom and Dad wanted to meet our teachers and dorm parents at Mamou, so in late March of 1960, our Carryall joined two other vehicles full of GMU missionary kids heading out of Bamako on that 400-mile trek. We took the route that crossed into Guinea not far from Siguiri where the road turned due south. We crossed the Tinkisso River by ferry and then the Niger River at Niandankoro. We reached the city of Kankan by nightfall and spent the night at the Christian & Missionary Alliance compound there.

On that first day of our journey, as we had traveled farther and farther away from the edge of the Sahara, we started noticing slight differences in the landscape. But, when we left Kankan on the second day of our trip, the contrast became more dramatic by the mile. The dirt road took us up into the dense forest of the Fouta Djallon Mountains and over flimsy bridges that crossed rushing streams created by heavy, almost year-round rainfall. Those torrential streams fed rivers so large that not even the Sahara could desiccate them. Some of them we had known before: the Falémé where Dad had made bricks at Kénieba, the Sénégal by whose banks we had lived in Kayes and the mighty Niger, ever flowing away but always there, a sight that never ceased to impress every time we drove into Bamako.

By late afternoon we were driving through the town of Mamou and then up a high hill where we turned down a long, curving driveway lined with mango trees. We stopped in a large, flat open area which was the center of campus. Behind us, wide steps cut through a stone wall and led to a three-room classroom building. In front of us was the Foyer, the large dormitory with its long wings at right angles to each other. That year the girls' rooms were to the right by the kitchen and the boys' rooms were to the left by the nurse's quarters. Where the wings met, there were the living room, dining room, pantry and house parents' quarters. From the Carryall, we were looking at the back of the Foyer. The front, which was entered only occasionally, was flanked by two terraces and overlooked the town of Mamou, a banana plantation and three prominent hills whose names—Monkey Rock, Camel's Hump and Sugar Loaf—were passed down to us by the MKs who had named them long before we were even born.

Our parents met the house parents, Larry and Grace Wright, and our teachers. They saw our rooms and met our roommates. They had supper with us and spent the night in the dorm. Long after my roommate, Marcia Tschetter, was asleep, long after the hurricane lanterns were lit and placed down the hall, long after the generator was turned off, I lay awake thinking about school the next day. After breakfast the next morning, our parents hugged us goodbye and left. Years later mother told us, "When we drove down the long driveway away from you and the dorm, Dad was crying so hard he had to stop the car to wipe the tears from his eyes."

From Mamou, they drove up to Dalaba to spend a few days at their mission's vacation cottage. While there, Mom and Dad allowed Richie to choose a female puppy which he named Watkins after the missionaries who lived in Dalaba year-round. On their trip back home, they drove through Mamou but strict rules prohibited them from stopping to see us. After all, a second, unnecessary round of good-byes would just disrupt the routine of the school and might upset the children. It would be almost nine months before we saw them again.

There were things I liked about dorm life. I didn't have to help nearly as much as I did at home and I especially liked being with the other girls in the dorm. I shared a room with Marcia Tschetter. Two other sixth grade girls, Margi Timyan and Pauline Arnold, shared a room close to us. The oldest girls in the dorm were Margi's ninth grade sister Judy, and two tenth graders, Pauline's sister Faith and Shary Kroeker. These girls welcomed me in and taught me the ropes which included three systems that I needed to learn to survive: the bells, the groups and the inspections.

A large hand bell in the dorm and another one in the school building rang at regular intervals from sunrise till after dark: a bell to get up, a bell to start reading your Bible, a bell to stop reading your Bible and for the younger kids' inspection, a first bell for breakfast, a late bell for breakfast, a bell for school to start, a late bell for school, a bell to start recess and one to end it, a bell for lunch, a late bell for lunch, a bell to end lunch, a bell to be in our beds for noon rest, a bell to get up from noon rest and go back to school, another late bell for school, a first shower bell for the Little Kids, a second shower bell for the Middle Kids, a third shower bell for the Big Kids, a supper bell, a late bell for supper, a first bell for Little Kids' devotions and bedtime, a second bell for the Middle Kids' devotions and bedtime, a third bell for the Big Kids devotions and bedtime—and probably some I forgot. If a child was not where he or she was supposed to be as soon as the bell rang, there was a price to pay. The fact that six-year-old children learned to navigate that system is a testament to human survival.

The second system was easy enough to learn. It was how the 50 or more children in the dorm were divided. The Little Kids were in Grades 1, 2 and 3. The Middle Kids were in Grades 4, 5 and 6. The Big Kids were in Grades 7, 8, 9 and 10. Those groups did not mingle. David learned that the hard way when he tried to help John, who was barely seven, with his shower the first day we were there. Grace Wright yanked him away and said, "You will not help your brother. He has to learn how to do it by himself." The only time children from one group could mingle with children from the other was when letters from home were handed out after lunch. Little family groups gathered in the living room where an older child in the family would read that week's letter to their younger siblings. It was wonderful to sit on the couch with my brothers and picture what mom and dad were doing back home. But we dared not linger there together or we'd be scolded for taking too long. Avoiding the radar of the dorm parents was right up there with the survival skill of obeying the bells, so we read the letters quickly and scattered back to our rooms for noon rest.

The third system was inspection, which had two parts. Physical inspection took place for the Little Kids and the Middle Kids between the end of morning devotions and the first breakfast bell. I was a Middle Kid when I first got to Mamou, so I was included in this ritual. We lined up on the front veranda in front of the school nurse, Miss Adam. She was always seated, putting her at eye level with the Little Kids but at waist level with my group. One by one, she'd look each of us over, up and down. Then she'd have us turn to see if our bows were neatly tied and centered on our waists and if the boys' shirts were properly tucked in. Some days she had us bend over to check our hair or to look into our ears. Other days she'd look in our mouths to check our teeth. But every single day she took each child's hands in hers, checked their fingernails and then turned their hands over to look at their palms. I can still feel my hands, cupped in hers. I can see the top of her head, bent over her task. I can feel myself holding my breath until it was over and I could walk away.

Room inspection took place every day after we left the dorm for the classroom building. Bedspreads had to be perfectly flat with hospital corners—a wrinkle would get you a swat. Everything had to be put away. A sock under your bed would get you a swat too. I learned to back out of my room, giving it a careful 360° inspection, before heading to school. The same impossible standards applied to the six-year-olds as they did to the older children. After lunch, we found out if we had passed. It was the most terrifying part of our day. I remember getting a knot in my stomach halfway through my meal, just thinking about what would happen when Aunt Grace rang the little bell by her plate. When she did, the dining room was instantly silent. Then she would pick up a piece of paper and start reading a list of names. We had no choice but to watch the line of children forming beside her. When she finished, she would dismiss the rest of us for noon rest. Those of us who had escaped the line walked silently past the sad souls who had not, casting sympathetic glances their way, treading softly and silently, our hearts still beating in fear. We knew that only a few of them would get reprimands. Most of them would go to Uncle Larry's room to be strapped with his belt.

The second or third week we were at Mamou, I was surprised to hear David's name called at the end of lunch. I risked my life, but I waited for him, out of sight on the veranda near the head of the boys' hall, to see why. When he joined me he explained, "Sometimes I wet my bed and Aunt Grace said that if I keep it up, she'll have to send Mom and Dad a bill for washing my sheets."

I was stunned. "Don't worry about it, David," I said. "Mom and Dad won't care one bit if they have to pay extra for your sheets. Now hurry up. We can't get caught." I circled around the dorm parents' apartment, peeked around the corner to see if anyone was in the entry to the dining room, listened for adult voices in the pantry and made a dash down the hall to my room. Only then did tears well up in my eyes, partly because I was upset for my brother but, more than that, because I felt helpless and trapped. How could Grace humiliate David publicly like that? And why did she think that shaming and threatening him would help? I lay in my bed with the weight of that inside me, like stone.

Around that same time, on April 9th, I turned twelve. On that day Grace Wright called me down to the pantry before lunch. As I walked in I heard her say to Ruth Shenk, "I looked. There wasn't anything for her." Then she turned to me and asked if my mom had sent birthday presents for us.

"No," I said. "I don't think she knew she was supposed to do that. But it's okay," I continued. "I got a lot of nice things for coming to school." In my next letter home, I told Mom to send presents for Rich and David when Rich came to join us in August.

Climate dictated the academic calendar at Mamou. We went home during the winter months when the West African climate was at its coolest, and thus less likely to kill small children. We returned to Mamou before the rains, which could make the roads impassable. Because of this, the first semester of each grade started in early August and ended in late November. We went home for three months and returned in March to finish the second semester of the grade we were in. When it ended in late July, there was a two-week break during which time kids going on furlough left and kids returning from North America came back.

Mamou prided itself on its rigorous academics based on the New York State Board of Regents. David and I adjusted rather seamlessly to our last semester as fifth and sixth graders. His teacher was Miss Hamilton who taught Grades 3, 4 and 5 in one room. My teachers were Miss Nichols and Miss Sather who taught the students in Grade 6 through 10. John, however, landed in Miss Wormley's Grade 1 and 2 classroom and it was traumatic. He came crying hysterically to me the first day of school. He had been humiliated for not knowing how to spell the word *horse*. Fortunately, he was very smart and quickly learned how to cope. It would be years before the stories of cruelty in that classroom would be documented.[20] And sadly, they would also include what happened to our little brother Richie who, when he was still only five years old, joined John in the hell that was Miss Wormley's classroom.

In late July, my classmates and I turned in all our Grade 6 textbooks, closed our desks and left our classroom behind for two weeks. We said goodbye to the children who were going to the States for a year of furlough and to Faith and Shary who had finished Grade 10 and were returning to the U.S. for good. The dorm parents and teachers left campus for a break and we had substitute house parents. Fewer bells controlled us and there was plenty of time to play inside and out. August was the rainiest time of the year, so when it rained for hours, so heavily that we couldn't see twenty feet into the school yard, the veranda became our playground where we roller skated for hours. At night, the din of the rain on the tin roof lulled us to sleep. And, all that time, David, John and I were excitedly counting down the days to when our little brother Richie would join us.

When that day came and went and Richie didn't arrive, I was concerned. I lay awake long after the generator went off and then I heard a truck coming down the driveway and I knew he was there. I jumped out of bed, threw on my robe and ran down the hall. I waited by the door till the truck stopped and the doors opened. Then I flew out the door and scooped him up in my arms. Grace immediately reprimanded me and told me to go back to bed. I ignored her, knelt down in front of him and said, "Johnny is asleep, but you will sleep in his room tonight. I will see you in the morning." I gave him another hug, stood up and walked back into the dorm. The next morning, after a brief, joyful reunion with David and John, there was a grim warning from John: "Richie, it's bad here. It's really bad."

Richie wasn't the only new student to arrive. Kids returning from furlough in the U.S. were also joining our ranks. The children I remember most clearly were the Burns kids. Judie Burns was the oldest and would be rooming with Judy Timyan, my classmate Margi's sister. I remember standing in the curtained doorway of their room, watching Judie unpack. She

---

[20] Stearns, Dunn, et al. (November 15, 1997). Independent Commission of Inquiry Regarding Mamou Alliance Academy.

was a 10th grader, so she seemed very grown up to me and her clothes were all so beautiful and up to date. She laid outfit after outfit on her bed and at one point said, "Aunt Grace had better not say I can't wear these! My mother says they are just fine." Bravado like that shocked me and, even though I knew she was nowhere near, I instinctively looked behind me to see if Grace had overheard. However, what impressed me most was the framed picture of a very handsome boy which Judie positioned carefully on her dresser. "This is my boyfriend," she declared. "We are going steady."

Judie's brother Stanley was in my class. He was not only cute with his blond hair and blue eyes but he was as smart as a whip. The other seventh grade boys in my class could have cared less about girls, except Andy Eadelman, who lived off campus in the Villa, the dorm where the Conservative Baptist kids lived. But Stanley took a liking to me and by mid-semester I had a boyfriend. It wasn't complicated. We wrote each other notes, talked together at recess and sat by each other in the Rapide, the school passenger van, when we went on outings.

There were also staff additions after the break. The school principal, Mr. Emary, had returned from furlough. He and his wife Marsha and their children Darla, John and Dawn lived in the house down the driveway. Darla was in Grade 8, a year ahead of me. Mrs. Emary taught all the school music classes and gave trumpet and piano lessons. She taught from the Thompson® piano books which I found harder than the Schaum® books I had used with Joyce Simms in Akron, but Mrs. Emary soon figured out where my skill level was and then added hymns to my repertoire.

When classes started again, I was a Big Kid in Grade 7 with the same teachers. David was still a Middle Kid in Grade 6. John, in second grade and Rich in first grade were Little Kids. As a Big Kid, I had a new responsibility every morning. After I got dressed and tidied my own room, I was to make sure that my assigned Little Sister, Joyce McKinney, was ready for Miss Adam's inspection. Every morning, between devotions and breakfast, I'd check that her little hands and face were clean, I'd tie the bow of her dress and help her brush her long, honey-brown, waist-length hair. One morning, halfway through the semester, I found her crying.

"Look," she sobbed. "During the night, someone cut my hair." I had her stand up straight and tall, and sure enough, a good six inches had disappeared. It wouldn't be the last time I saw a child cry for the same reason.

One 12-year old girl was told that her beautiful, wavy hair was making her vain and it was summarily cropped short. I can see her still, crying softly, on her way back into the dorm.

That semester a confrontation did occur with Grace Wright about inappropriate clothing, but it didn't involve Judie Burns. It involved me. My

127

name was called after lunch one day and Grace told me that my sundresses with two-inch straps were too revealing for me to wear. I had worn them every week since I had arrived in March, so I was puzzled. I argued that if I couldn't wear them, I'd have only 4 other school outfits to wear, but that didn't change her mind. On Sunday, when I wrote my obligatory letter home, I included a paragraph about this new turn of events, including how upset I was and the fact that it didn't make sense to me.

That's when I had the privilege of a one-on-one session with Grace Wright. During noon rest, on the day after I wrote that letter, the curtain over the doorway to my room parted and there she stood. She sat on my bed, explained to me that my exposed shoulders in those dresses could cause the Muslim men who worked on campus to have lustful thoughts. Furthermore, my letter would upset my parents and that would interfere with them reaching souls for Christ and I didn't want Africans going to hell on my conscience, did I? When she was done, she produced a large eraser and made me erase everything I had written about the sundresses. When I was done, she took the edited letter and walked out. To be treated unfairly is one thing but to be silenced goes way beyond unfair and there was nothing I could do about it but turn my head toward the wall so Marcia wouldn't see me cry.

A highlight of that semester was when Miss Sather offered to teach sewing classes for any girl who wanted to learn and Marcia and I signed up. This would be no simple project. It would involve learning how to cut fabric from a pattern, how to use a sewing machine and how to put in a zipper. First, Miss Sather took us to buy fabric at a store in Mamou. We picked out the same print but in two different colors—blue to match Marcia's eyes and pink to complement my brown. Then, twice a week after school, we met Miss Sather in the little building half way down the driveway and she taught us to sew. It was a wonderful gift that I have used my whole life.

Trips to town were rare but there were special events every month like picnics on the terrace outside the dorm, yearly Halloween Parties, outings to swim in nearby waterfalls, hikes up Camel's Hump and one especially daunting hike up Sugar Loaf where an entire party of kids got separated from the adults and ended up on a road alone after dark.

One memorable outing was when the Wrights took the Big Kids to Dalaba for a weekend retreat. Missionaries often vacationed there in March or April to avoid the worst of the hot season in the hotter parts of West Africa. My peers talked about Dalaba all the time, so I was excited to finally see that wonderful place.

We left after school on Friday and arrived in the late afternoon. We were all standing around waiting to be called in for supper when Stanley asked me, "Have you seen the puppies?" He disappeared into a hut right next to where our group was standing and I followed. Bales of straw were piled in

128

the middle of the hut, leaving just enough room for one person to walk between them and the walls. I followed Stanley around to the back of the hut and there, nestled between the wall and the straw, a mother dog was nursing her pups. We looked at them for a minute, I turned around, Stanley followed me out and we walked right into Larry Wright. That wouldn't have been so bad except that, inside the hut, we hadn't heard the call to dinner and when we walked out, our schoolmates were gone. It looked really bad and we knew it.

When Larry found his voice, he asked why we were in there. "Stanley found some puppies and wanted to show me. Other kids went in before us," I answered as nonchalantly as possible. He looked at us a long time, hemmed and hawed, and finally told us not to go in there together again. When Stanley and I walked into the Big House for supper with Larry, Grace had no reason to be suspicious. If she didn't find out what Larry had condoned, we would all be fine and, since Stanley and I were scared speechless, that was not about to happen!

After breakfast the next morning, we were given free time with the directive that we were all to stay together. The logical place to do that was up in the cinnamon tree whose dark green canopy and wide, inviting branches had charmed MKs for generations. We climbed up the tree, found comfortable spots, nibbled on cinnamon leaves and talked. Then the kids showed me how to "chew sticks." Two kids would strip a twig of its leaves, put the ends between their teeth and then see who could gobble up the most inches. After a while, Stanley challenged me to a match. I climbed up to where he was perched, he found a suitable twig and the contest began. When our noses touched, we stopped, and instead of taking the twig from between us to measure who had won, he took it away, leaned forward and kissed me. I looked down to see who was watching, but instead I saw our classmates scrambling to the ground far below. No one was looking up, so I leaned toward him and he kissed me again. "Don't tell," I whispered followed by, "Oh, no! They didn't wait for us!" We scrambled down, hit the ground and took off running. Half way across the terrace I glanced back, sure that Larry Wright was coming after us, but the morning mist shrouded the Big House and I knew we were safe.

When people talk about their first kiss, I never share. Who would believe that one morning when I was twelve, in one of the most beautiful places in Africa, while the morning mist hung heavy over the top of a mountain, inside the dark green canopy of an ancient cinnamon tree, a sweet boy with bright blue eyes kissed a brown-eyed girl and that girl was me? It even seems magical to me as I recall it and I take that as a gift, a sweet moment nestled halfway between the trauma that came before and the aftereffects of that trauma that were to come.

The last big event of the Mamou school year was the annual Thanksgiving Banquet to which Big Kids were allowed to invite a date. I remember that my corsage was pretty and that I had a lovely time sitting next to Stanley, but that celebration paled in comparison to my excitement about going home. In early December, during the last week of the semester, we started packing our trunks and finally the last school bell rang, the last bedtime bell rang, the last breakfast bell rang and we were going home.

Chapter 15

Sirakoro: Sad and Sweet
December 1960–March 1961

When school closed, Miss Sather accompanied the Darr and Tschetter kids to Kankan on the train. Our dads met us there and drove us back to Sirakoro. Everything seemed the same: the thick brown dust, the little villages, the rivers to cross by ferry. But things were not the same. In the months while we were at school, the federation that Mali had forged with Senegal had dissolved and Mali had severed its ties with France. Its name had changed from the Federation of Mali to the Republic of Mali and what that meant no one knew, but it wouldn't take long to find out.

When we rolled onto the station at Sirakoro, Mom and Angie were waiting by the house. I saw Mom lower her head into her hands and I knew she was crying. We jumped out of the back of the Land Rover and hugged her, jumping up and down with joy. Mom always told it this way, "Angie told me not to cry when I saw you kids, but I couldn't help it. I was so happy you were home."

While everyone was standing around outside, Mom said to me, "Come here, Dianne. I have something to show you." She led me to my room which had been completely redone. A little desk was set up as a vanity, complete with a mirror behind it on the wall. Best yet, there were dainty curtains at the windows which she had stitched for me by hand. I had never had a pretty room of my own. I knew it was a gift of love, created for me while she counted and cried down the days, until we would be home again.

The Tschetters stayed for supper before driving to their station at Tyefala, farther east down the road. Before they left, Dad and Ed went out and took a look at Watkins, Richie's pet dog, who was tied up at the edge of the station. On our trip home, Dad had told us that Watkins had scuffled with a rabid dog a few nights before and we wouldn't be allowed to go near her. What he didn't tell us was that Esther and Helen, the other missionaries on the station, were urging him to put her down. Dad wanted Ed's opinion before making his final decision and Ed agreed with the women: it was just too risky to keep her.

After breakfast the next morning, on our very first day home, Dad told us what had been decided about Watkins. He went into his bedroom, came out with his shotgun and called to our African helper, Wojuma, to get the shovel. They walked off into the bush behind the station and a few minutes later we heard the shot. We all started to cry and we were still sobbing in the living room when Dad got back to the house. As he took off his hat, he exploded, "It's bad enough that I have to shoot the dog and now I come back to a house full of blubbering people." I went to my room and tried to stifle my cries. David, John and Rich went to their room and cried into their pillows. I was old enough to know that Dad wasn't really mad at us. He was just upset by what he had to do.

Shortly afterward, a missionary couple named the Stewarts stopped at our station. They raised Springer Spaniels and, after hearing what happened to Watkins, they gave us a puppy to keep. We named him Blackie and the next time we went to Bamako, Blackie went to the vet. Dad had learned his lesson. From then on, all our dogs were vaccinated against rabies.

My brothers and I sometimes broke the monotony of life on the station by going for walks along the path that ran behind it. There was a place, just beyond the path, where people from the village made sacrifices to the evil spirits. We had been told not to go near it so, of course, that is where we really wanted to go. When our courage finally got as strong as our curiosity, we left the path to look. The sacred spot was pretty disappointing. There were just some rocks with blood on them. It reminded us, though, of why our parents were there. Some people in the village were Christians and they were no longer afraid of the spirits or the harm they could do.

At Christmas, the missionaries and the Christians planned a program for the whole village. As night fell on Christmas Eve, people gathered and seated themselves on blankets on the ground in front of a large bonfire that would be our light. The church leader greeted the people, the African Christians and missionaries sang a song and then Dad, whose Bambara was passable now, led in prayer. After another song, one of the church leaders who knew how to read held a flashlight and began to read the story of the nativity from Matthew and Luke. While he read, Christians acted out the story of Jesus' birth complete with real live sheep, a donkey, Mary, Joseph and a sweet Baby Jesus.

A Christian girl around my age and I were part of the program. We stood out of sight, just inside the entry to the thatched-roofed church and, when we got our cue, we sang a song from the Bambara hymnbook about the star and the wise men. While we waited together in our little nook for the pageant to finish, I looked up at the pitch-black sky splashed with brilliant stars and then over at the animals and the Holy Family, softly lit by the dying fire. No Christmas since has compared to the magic of that pure, simple Christmas the year I was twelve.

By January we had settled into the daily routine of living on the station. John and Rich played outside with their slingshots. David and I helped Mom with the cooking and the baking. There were books to read and puzzles to put together. Sometimes we had game night with Helen Andres and Esther Finley who still lived next door. Once in a while we went along with Dad on his runs to Bougouni to buy groceries, to pick up the mail and to buy a loaf of crispy French bread if the bakery had any left when he got there. One day, right after Christmas, he came home with a package addressed to me. It was a Christmas present from Stanley Burns, a handcrafted leather change purse, typical of those sold in west-African, open-air markets. Dad was not pleased and wanted to know why a boy would be sending his 12-year old daughter a present.

"He's just a boy in my class who likes me, I guess." I responded as guardedly and calmly as possible. "How do I know why he sent me a present?" I didn't think it was necessary, at this point, to admit that I liked Stanley too, that he kissed me in the cinnamon tree and that I was his date to the Thanksgiving Banquet. I glanced at David who knew Stanley was my boyfriend, but he didn't give anything away and Dad didn't ask him. I got a lecture about being careful around boys and that was the end of that.

One Sunday afternoon we got a big surprise—there at our gate was the Tschetter's Land Rover! They had come to spend the day. While our parents visited around the table, the seven of us kids had fun just being together. When we went outside, Judy walked us over to a circular spot in the yard, marked with stones. "That's where I was born," she said. At our puzzled looks she continued, "This circle is where a hut stood that was a medical dispensary. Arloene Skiff, a missionary midwife, delivered me here."

At that Marcia said, "Yeah, and you almost died there too!" She described how Judy had been small at birth and, on top of that, had gotten whooping cough and malaria. It was sobering to think that she could have died in that spot but it would not have been unusual. Life was risky for babies and children in the French Sudan and, in Bamako, there were graves of missionary children to prove it.

When we went back inside the house where our parents were having an afternoon coffee break, it got even better. "Can Dianne come home with us, please?" the sisters begged. Our parents talked it over, made arrangements for how and when I would get back home and I went to spend a few days at Tyefala. I remember being in awe of their pump organ which we all took turns playing. How fun it was to be with friends and not at Mamou!

Our mud block house at Sirakoro and the circle of stones
marking where the maternity hut once stood.

And then, vacation was over and we were packing for Mamou again.
But this year would be different. When Mom and Dad had learned that
Mamou had a two-week break between semesters, they decided to tough out
the hot season in Mali and risk driving into Guinea during the rainy season so
they could spend that time with us. "Sixteen weeks," I told myself. "In just
sixteen weeks we will see them again."

Chapter 16

Nightmares and Pleasant Dreams at Mamou
Spring, Summer, Fall 1961
Grade 7 Ends, Grade 8 Begins

In March of 1961, we traveled in a little caravan with other MKs back to Mamou. Other than the new classroom building for Grades 1 through 4 and the beginning of a chapel building, everything was the same as it had been when we left. We had the same dorm parents, the same teachers and the same routine from breakfast through the school day. And, after school until the shower bells rang, there was a significant amount of free time with another shorter period of free time after supper.

During that free time, the kids in each group played together. There was a sandbox for the little kids. There was a piano in the living room for those of us who knew how to play. We took turns walking around the yard or veranda on stilts and roller skating on the veranda. Best yet, on clear days, if an adult was there to supervise and there was clean water in the pool, we got to swim. One day as I was sauntering back to the Foyer after school, a little first grader came flying out the door and bounded over the steps, his bathrobe flying out behind him. In excitement to be the first one in the pool, he had forgotten one important thing: his swim trunks.

One thing that it took me awhile to notice was that the teachers never came to the Foyer and the dorm parents never went to the classrooms. The adults in charge of the children on the top of that hill were as divided from each other as the three groups of kids were in the Foyer and what they didn't know, they could never tell. One day I was caught where those adult worlds collided and, of all my memories of Mamou, it is the worst.

The day it happened, I was on my way from my room to help in the pantry before lunch. At the screen door by the pantry I heard sobs and there was Gloria Powell coming in the door, all alone. I knelt down to ask her what was wrong and, between sobs, she said, "Miss Wormley had me stay after school." My hands were on her shoulders and I was looking right into her face. And then I saw. There were scratches on her neck, dripping blood, and the collar on the left side of her dress was ripped from its seam.

I was a girl myself, barely thirteen, but I knew that somehow, I had to help Gloria without implicating Miss Wormley. I went to the pantry door and said, "Aunt Grace, come look." When she stepped into the hall I pointed to Gloria's scratches and torn collar, watching to make sure she took note. I looked at her calmly and said, "It's only Tuesday and we're not allowed to change our school clothes until tomorrow. What should we do?"

The adults in my world far away would have swept that child into their arms, washed her wounds, dried her tears and then marched up the hill to the teacher's house to give Miss Wormley a piece of their minds. I knew better than to expect that here, but I expected at least a crumb of sympathy for this bleeding little girl crying in front of us. Instead, Grace's eyes narrowed warily, she stiffened ever so slightly, looked at me with eyes of steel and said, "Help her change," then turned and walked away. If I had grown up as a Little Kid at Mamou, I would have known that a bleeding child was just a guilty child who had gotten what they deserved. But at that time, I only knew what was before my eyes, and it shocked me to the core.

My brothers, whom I only interacted with when we read our letters from home, did not escape. The doors to our rooms were covered only by curtains, so it was easy for the dorm parents to hear what was going on. If they caught John and Richie whispering at noon rest, they were strapped right then and there. Sometimes, in the middle of the night, Richie would crawl into bed with John. If they were caught, they were strapped. Sometimes Rich would risk it. However, a couple of times when he was sleeping with John, he wet the bed—another reason to get in trouble. When that happened, those little first and second graders would switch their heavy mattresses in the middle of the night so only one, and not both of them, would be in trouble the next day. Other nights if they woke to wet pajamas and sheets, they invented ingenious ways to make sure they were dry by morning. Neither of them had wet the bed at home for years.

Their classroom was worse. Miss Wormley screamed so loudly at Richie one day that we heard her rage in our classroom at the other end of the building. John, Richie and their classmates were routinely berated, slapped and picked up by their ears. Worst of all, they watched as their classmates were forced to urinate at their desks because Miss Wormley ignored their pleas to go to the bathroom.

One evening after supper, John and Rich came to talk to me. I knew something was wrong because they never left their play to talk to a Big Kid. John told me that, the night before, an older boy came into his room, went to his roommate's bed, took his roommate's hand and pressed it on his groin. Then he came to John's bed and did the same thing. Tattling wasn't my first option since it meant talking to an adult, so I told them both, "If he steps inside your room again, sit up and tell him that the next time he comes into your room you will tell your sister." It stopped. Unfortunately, even during free time when the adults weren't ready to pounce, the older children were.

The rigid bell system and the rules, brutally enforced by the adults, and the children taking their frustrations out on each other were only part of the trauma. Infusing and fueling it all were the Christian doctrines that kept us in line. My faith tradition did not believe that God demoted people from saved to hell-bound sinner every time they did something wrong, but that was the theology of the group that ran the school. We were reminded often of our wickedness, of our constant responsibility to ask God to forgive our wickedness, and of our duty to serve a holy God with all our little beings and in every little thing we did.

To keep us saturated in all things spiritual, our daily lives included all of the following: starting each day with our own Bible reading and prayer, prayer before breakfast and a devotional reading afterwards, prayer at school before morning and afternoon classes, daily classroom devotions, a long prayer before lunch for missionaries serving around the world, prayer before supper, evening devotions led by the dorm parents and, to cap it all off, two church services on Sunday where children were encouraged to come forward, confess their sins of the week and get their hearts right with God—again.

In the spring of 1961, the heat under this spiritual pot in which we simmered was turned up and I was no longer sure of my standing with God. The catalyst for this, not just at Mamou, but across all of Christian fundamentalism, was the election of John F. Kennedy the previous fall. At the time, many Protestants and Catholics mutually excluded each other as heaven bound. However, Conservative Protestants went so far as to identify Rome with the Anti-Christ. Kennedy's election, coupled with the march of atheistic communism across the globe and the threat of nuclear war pointed to just one thing: The Second Coming of Christ was at hand. That doctrine, added to the brew of the others, terrified me.

The adults at Mamou could not impeach Kennedy, nor stop the advance of communism nor end the Cold War, but one thing they could do was warn the children in their charge about the end of the world and make sure they were right with Jesus when it happened. The devotions and chapel messages homed in on that 24/7 and destroyed my childlike faith in a God who loved and cared for me and replaced it with sheer terror. Was I wicked? Of course I was! Weren't we all? Was I saved? I used to think I was, but what if I wasn't? Was I perfect? Of course not, especially by the indicators by which we were judged all day long. Therefore, when Jesus came back, I would not be one of the children meeting him in the clouds. I could think of nothing else and I could not sleep. One night, long after the generator went out, I was so upset that I ran down the hall and knocked on Ruth Shenk's door. Through my tears I told her what was bothering me. She listened to me, prayed with me and sent me back to bed. Getting my fears out in the open helped a little, but the thought of the Rapture scared the love of God out of me for years.

Thankfully, my countdown to our parents' arrival was getting shorter. Halfway through the semester, Mom and Dad verified in a letter that they were coming to be with us during the two-week break between the school years. And, to make it even better, their colleagues, the Neudorfs were coming too. When our parents arrived at the town of Mamou, they drove right past their children, who had not seen them for fifteen weeks, and kept going higher into the mountains to Dalaba because Mamou even had rules for the parents. They settled into Dalaba and waited for Friday afternoon when they were allowed to come to get us. During that week I remember thinking, "They are right here, just up the road!" After that weekend, there was one week left in the semester and then we had two wonderful weeks with them at Dalaba. It was so much fun to be a family. We went on a few outings with the Neudorfs, including one to Piké Falls, as seen below. Mom and Dad enjoyed the cool mountain air and we just relaxed. Two weeks later, when they dropped me off at Mamou to start Grade 8, I started counting the weeks again. There were sixteen until we would be going home.

There were significant changes when we got back to Mamou. A new classroom building was ready for the lower grades and, in the dorm, the halls had been flipped. The boys' hall was now by the kitchen and the girls' hall was by the nurse's quarters. We also had new house parents, Fordy and Rosalys Tyler. Rosalys could be stern (which I attributed to her constant headaches), but I didn't find her cruel. Fordy was approachable and would joke around with us. By the end of their first week there, I wouldn't say the Foyer was floating, but it certainly felt lighter.

With the younger students in the new classroom building, Grades 5 through 10 had room to spread out in the original building. Miss Sather and Miss Nichols were still my teachers and they were as different as night and day. Miss Nichols wore very thick glasses because she was almost blind, but her sense of hearing was astonishing. We couldn't even wiggle in our desks without her knowing it. We nicknamed her Snicks and she hated it. Raising our hand and saying, "Miss Nichols" would set her off. "Don't call me that!" she would shriek. We learned to pause a long time between the word Miss and the word Nichols to avoid her rage.

Miss Sather, on the other hand, was cool. She had a hump back, the result of having had polio as a child, but she was lively and energetic. One day when she and Miss [pause] Nichols switched classes, we locked the doors. Miss Sather showed up, tried the door, went to the open window, pushed aside some books that were on the windowsill, hiked up her skirt, crawled over and calmly said, "Okay, students, get out your math books." Another time we ran and hid behind the swimming pool. It took her awhile to find us and when she did, we all laughed and went back to class.

During our short recess breaks the boys would sometimes turn over the stones that were on the ground below the verandas and look for scorpions. One day they found a very large one. We girls watched while one boy stepped on it with his leather shoe (thick enough that the stinger couldn't penetrate it) and another boy cut off its stinger with his pocket knife. This six inch black beauty was then deposited in the teacher's desk drawer. I think it was right after that that Miss Nichols had a nervous breakdown.

Large mango trees lined a beautiful path between the classroom building and the teachers' house which sat at the top of the hill overlooking the campus. We were never told that something was wrong, but seeing Miss Nichols walking down the path, holding on to the mango trees gave us a clue. It was during that time that she singled me out as her assistant. At first, she asked me to bring things to her at her desk from another part of the room or from the small storage room behind our classroom. Then she had me run notes to other teachers. Then she started asking me to go up to her house to get things. The teachers' house was strictly off limits to us, so it was pretty eerie going up the long path all alone, opening the screen door to a silent house, going in and tiptoeing around till I found what she needed. It took less than a week for my classmates to start calling me her pet and that was a problem I did not need. One day when she asked me to run an errand I said,

"I'm not quite finished with these problems. Could you ask someone else?" She may have been blind and slightly bizarre, but I have to give her credit for catching on and asking various students to help after that.

I remember very little about the subjects I studied except for a private lesson from Miss Nichols, with all my classmates listening, about the proper use of apostrophes and one memorable music class at Mrs. Emary's house. Once a week my class would take the path through the orange trees to the principal's house where folding chairs were set up in the living room, so close together that there was no room on either side of the rows. We would move or fold up the chairs to find a seat, Mrs. Emary would pass out the singing books, give us a few directions, turn and sit down at the piano with her back to us and start playing and singing. We'd join in and that was it—which was pretty fun until the day Stanley, who was sitting behind me, decided to poke me in the back. The first time I flinched but kept singing; the second time I turned my head and mouthed the words, "Stop it!" The third time, two things happened. I saw white and then I heard Mrs. Emary's voice yelling, "Dianne, what are you doing?" I looked up and found myself turned around, kneeling on my chair, my fists pounding Stanley with all my might. With nowhere to go, he was hunched over, his arms up over his head, trying to protect himself from my fury.

Everyone but me was dismissed to go the Foyer for lunch. Mrs. Emary asked me for an explanation of what had happened, but made me wait for Mr. Emary to come home to determine my punishment. I had never, ever been in trouble at Mamou or anywhere for that matter. I sat waiting for him at their kitchen table and watched Mrs. Emary prepare lunch like any mom would do. It struck me how normal it all seemed when right down the driveway scores of kids were living in a dormitory. Mr. Emary came in, sat down and asked me to explain what had happened. I told him, making sure to add that if I could have moved away, I would have, but I was trapped in the middle seat. And, if I could have told the teacher, I would have, but that was impossible because her back was turned to us. I was not punished and I don't remember if Stanley got in trouble or not. I do remember trembling as I walked alone down the driveway to the dorm. When I stepped into the dining room, the tables fell silent and all eyes were on me. I was a girl and a Big Kid, which afforded me a bit of protection from bodily harm, and Mr. Emary was no Miss Wormley, but everyone had held their breath until they were sure one of their own had survived.

Before the semester ended, a very important thing happened. When Mom had packed my trunk for school that spring, I was just weeks away from turning thirteen. Along with my requisite birthday present, which Mom now knew to include, she had tucked in a sanitary belt and sanitary pads and showed me how to use them. During the fall of 1961, it happened. I told my friends and they welcomed me into the sisterhood of the burning pads. Once a month one of the older girls would tiptoe into my room after lights out and say, "Get your pads." We would glide quietly past the flickering lanterns in the hall, out the door to the front veranda and into the kitchen. One of the girls would use the lifter to remove the lid of the wood-burning stove and we'd dump them in on top of the still-burning embers inside.

One day Rosalys called all us older girls together after lunch and said, "When you burn your pads, leave the lid off for a few minutes and make sure they catch fire and start burning. The cooks weren't happy when they added wood to the fire today and some of the pads hadn't burned." And that was all the license we needed to turn a five-minute chore into a monthly party.

The first night we followed this new directive, we tried to look inside the stove to see if the pads were burning, but the heat was so intense we couldn't look long enough to tell. We had no idea how long to wait, so we stood around whispering in the dark for about five minutes until someone finally said, "We'd better go back to bed. We'll get in trouble for being here so long."

"Don't worry," another girl shot back. "If we get caught, we have the perfect excuse: Aunt Rosalys told us to make sure they burned!" With that she grabbed the poker and gave the pads a vigorous stir, sending up a flurry of sparks almost to the ceiling. We all started to laugh, holding our hands over our mouths to stifle the sound. I can still see us standing in that dark kitchen in our bathrobes, taking turns making the sparks fly and laughing till we cried.

There were two other occasions that semester when I left my room during the night. The first time, the moonlight called me. Sleep had eluded me, so I went to the bathroom just for something to do. When I came back to the hall I turned left instead of right as though pulled by some force stronger than me. I walked past the flickering lanterns and the long, dancing shadows they cast on the walls and stopped at the living room door. The beams of a full tropical moon lit the living room and dining room like magic. The moon was halfway to the horizon, so it shone brightest in the pantry and it pulled me there. I stood, just inside the door, letting the light shine directly on me and then, out of the corner of my eye, Stanley was there too, just inside the door to the boys' hall.

"It's beautiful, isn't it? I just had to see," I whispered.

"Me too."

"Why are you here?" I asked.

"I knew you'd come."

"Oh." I wondered how that could be, but standing in the pantry in the middle of the night was not a good place to start a whispering discussion so I walked closer to the window that looked out over the terrace below, still in awe of it all. I turned back to him and whispered, "I have to go. We could get caught."

"Don't worry. They're asleep," he answered confidently, nodding toward the dorm parents' quarters beyond the doorway where he was standing.

The moonlight was like a magnet so I turned toward it again, so mesmerized that for a minute I didn't notice anything else around me. And then reality hit: I was in the pantry, right around the corner from the dorm parents' quarters. I turned to face Stanley and whispered, "I'd better go."

He stepped forward and took both my hands in his. "I'm glad you came," he whispered.

"Me too," I replied and slipped my fingers away and was gone.

I never asked Stanley if his forays to the pantry included mid-night snacks, but the more I thought about it, the more I presumed they did. And, if the boys could get away with it, why not the girls? I didn't share that little conjecture with anyone because, in a place like that, secrets were best not told. But one night, when my friend Margi and I couldn't sleep because we were hungry, I decided to suggest we venture to the pantry for a snack. There was little moon that night, so we felt our way through the living room and dining room, found the cookie tin in the kitchen and tried to contain our giggles when it was harder to open without making a sound than we had anticipated. We ate three cookies each, closed the tin and started back across the dining room. As we passed the last table, one of us bumped a chair and the noise literally echoed in the room. We knew that to go toward the hall would mean being caught if the dorm parents came looking. We scrambled behind the couch where we crouched for a good five minutes, just to be sure, and then we flew down the hall to our room.

At the end of the semester there was another Thanksgiving Banquet, another week of packing up our things and then we were going back home to Mali. This time we would be living in Nonkon, north of Bamako, to oversee the ministries of Nick and Esther Kroeker and Louise Jantzen who were in the States on furlough. Sirakoro, like all my homes, had just been another stop on the way to another house down another road.

Chapter 17

Nonkon: Lessons Learned
December 1961–March 1962

After caravanning back to Bamako, our family drove up the Bamako escarpment and turned north toward our new home at Nonkon. Both homes on the station had cement block walls with better doors and windows but that didn't compensate for the lack of a toilet in the bathroom—even though there was running water for the sink and shower in the bathroom and for the kitchen sink. It's not like I had never used an outhouse before. We had one in Kénieba and it didn't even have real walls. But this one was on the edge of the compound, it was known to harbor snakes and I was expected to be a big girl and go there all by myself. This certainly did not help my propensity to constipation. And, having menstrual periods to contend with, made it all the worse.

The rest of the station comprised another missionary house where Louise Jantzen and various other single lady missionaries had lived over the years, a storage building, a mud-walled, thatched-roof church and a clinic which treated a dozen or so patients three mornings a week. Patients walked in or came on bicycles from the surrounding villages, some from as far away as 30 miles. Louise Jantzen, the nurse who ran the clinic, had learned from experience that it was best to keep the clinic open even when she was on furlough because, by the time word of mouth spread that the clinic was closed, she would be back. Besides, it wasn't that hard to identify malaria, dysentery and tetanus or to treat leg ulcers, burns and snake bites. Several weeks of hands-on training prepared my parents to take over for the year she would be gone.

While we were at school, mom had helped dad at the clinic. Once we got home, that role fell to me. After breakfast Mom would stay with the boys and Dad and I would walk across the compound to the clinic where patients were already waiting. One by one dad would ask them for their symptoms and then tell me what pills to give them. Most often it was malaria medication. We kept a stack of magazine pages, each torn into four squares, on the counter. I would take one of them, put a malaria pill and an aspirin tablet in the middle of it and fold it tightly into a small square. I would make four little packets and then turn to the patient and say in Bambara, "Take one packet now, take one when the sun goes down, take one tomorrow when the sun comes up, take one tomorrow when the sun goes down. Do not take them all at once. It will make you sick. Do not give them to anyone else. It will make them sick. Come back for more in two days." And then I would hold out my hand, they would pay me the equivalent of two cents, we would exchange the customary departing greetings and they would walk away.

Dad would treat the patients with leg ulcers last because tending to them took more time. First I watched, then I helped and then he let me do it by myself. I sprinkled sulfa powder carefully into the oozing ulcer, covered it with a gauze square and then wrapped it with ace bandaging—changing the bandaging only if it was filthy, had bled through or was stretched out too much to stay in place. When the last patient had gone, we'd tidy up the clinic, Dad would put any used needles and syringes into a little tin box and we'd walk back home. After lunch, mom would carefully put the tin and its contents in a rack, lower everything into a pot of boiling water and let it boil for ten minutes.

One afternoon a grey-haired woman came to the house and spoke to dad on the porch. I was surprised when he started walking toward the clinic because, unless it was a dire emergency like a snake bite, he never opened it in the afternoon. He returned with a little bundle for her, she thanked him, they exchanged greetings and she left. I asked him why he had made an exception for her. He explained, "That was Ba Koro Ba, the most respected matriarch of the village, who helps women deliver their babies. Louise Jantzen told us to expect her. It took Louise years to convince her to stop using the traditional concoction of mud, cow manure and ashes for covering a newborn's umbilical cord. The packet I gave her has gauze squares, a little bottle of iodine and Vaseline®. Newborns in Nonkon rarely die from tetanus now and women are coming from other villages for the packets too."

Shortly after settling in to our vacation routine, all of us kids got sick. We ran very high fevers and were so weak we could barely move. We were too sick to travel, so dad drove in to Bamako alone, described our symptoms to the doctor and returned with vials of medicine to treat us. Now the needles Mom was sterilizing for the clinic were used to give shots to us. I remember lying in my bed so weak I could barely move, drifting in and out of sleep, waking up drenched in sweat.

When we recovered and gained back our strength, Dad had a surprise for us. His sister, our Aunt Mary Jane, had sent money to get us something special for vacation. With it he bought two donkeys for us to ride. David, the animal lover in the family, took over with their feeding and their care and it was fun to ride them around the compound and even down the road. One donkey was docile, but the other one was uncooperative and would buck when John and Rich tried to ride her, sometimes sending them flying. I remember Dad watching this and saying, "I'll show her!" At that time, he

144

weighed at least 200 pounds. He walked over, got on her back and rode her around the compound a few times. She never bucked again.

Unfortunately, the donkeys had another habit that was not so easily fixed. They sometimes broke through the wire fence at night and we'd wake to find one or both of them gone. Our yard man would go looking for them and usually found them not far from the station. One morning he found one donkey dead, killed by hyenas. We kids walked out to find the carcass and I was surprised that it was not far beyond our fence, much too close to home.

Another scare happened to me one Sunday morning. After the church service, I decided to see if I could walk back to the house in 100 steps or less. I started off on a straight line to the back porch, taking strides as long as my 13-year old legs would allow. As I neared the house I looked down to judge the distance between me and the back steps and that's when I saw it: a snake, slithering around the edge of a flower pot, right next to where I was headed. I froze mid-stride, my right arm still in the air, balancing on the toes of my right foot, trying not to fall forward. I kept my eye on the snake and then very, very slowly I backed up about 10 feet, turned and ran. "Sa! Sa!" I screamed. And then, "There's a snake! There's a snake!" Before I got half way back to the church, men dashed past me and when I turned around one of them had killed it with a machete. It was a very poisonous viper and much too close to our house.

When they first moved to Nonkon, Mom and Dad had hired a young man named Thaddée to help around the house. He was only 13-years-old, but old enough to help with what the two of them needed. When we four kids swelled the household to six, they were determined not to overwork him. If the chores weren't done when it was time for him to go home, David and I picked up the slack. I complained one day and was roundly reprimanded, "You are old enough to work and it won't kill you." Thaddée grew up to become a leader of the church, fluent in French and seminary educated. I recently sent him a picture of him sitting with Dad on the steps by our house at Nonkon and he sent this warm reply, "Thank you for this picture. The Darrs were like parents to me."

Helping Thaddée was one thing. Being my little brothers' helper, on the other hand, was starting to get on my nerves. I had gotten pretty used to looking out just for myself at Mamou and I chafed every morning when Mom would say, "Help the boys make their beds and clean up their room." I didn't want to confront her about it, but I also knew it wasn't fair. One morning I spoke up. "David is older than I was when I had to take care of my room by myself. I don't think it's fair that I have to keep my room clean and help with theirs too."

I braced for a lecture about sassing her, but it didn't come. She agreed with me and, from then on, the boys cleaned their room and I cleaned mine.

The Field Council had not appointed Dad to Nonkon just to run the clinic. Nonkon and the surrounding villages had a sizable group of Christians and they had outgrown their little mud church. Dad's job was to supervise the making of blocks for their new building. Sometimes we kids would ride out with him to the worksite where several of the men from the congregation measured dirt and cement and mixed it with water. When the consistency was right, a small shovelful was put into the rectangular box of a yellow machine. Another man would push down hard on a lever, water would be forced out of the box and the pressure would shape the mixture into a dense brick. When the lever came back up, the brick would be pushed out and another man would carefully lift it and place it on the ground to dry. Making one brick at a time was tedious work, but it was the dry season and, with no farming to be done, the men were free to do it. The fact that the bricks could be made on site and consisted mostly of readily available clay made them a fraction of the cost of cement block and thus something the church could afford.

It is the memory of that clay that taught me a lesson about life that I have never forgotten. Part of the work crew included Kako who had leprosy. Before treatment had put him into remission, the disease had taken all of his fingers down to the knuckle on both hands. In spite of that, he had insisted on being part of the block-making crew. He sat by a pile of dirt which contained hard lumps of clay in various sizes. He held his daba, the traditional Malian

146

hoe, between his palms and pounded those clumps of clay to powder and then used the blade to rake the fine powder to the side. From there it would be sifted and mixed with the cement. I remember thinking, "If you believe in something, you help make it happen." And Kako's cheerful labor made me ashamed that I had complained about doing the dishes so Thaddée could go home.

Like most missionaries, we traveled in to Bamako about once a month for supplies: groceries, kerosene, gasoline, supplies for the clinic. We'd pack our suitcases the night before and after breakfast, while Mom packed a lunch for the trip, Dad would give last minute instructions to the yard man for being in charge while we were gone. On one of those trips to town our family's normal, calm, happy-go-lucky way of interacting erupted into a melée of epic proportions.

As I remember the incident, it started when a well-dressed man in flowing white robes stormed onto the compound and demanded to speak to our father. He pointed to the roof and then at John and Rich who, just seconds before the man's arrival, had appeared nonchalantly on the veranda. Dad did not even ask for their side of the story. He apologized profusely to the gentleman, pointed John and Rich toward the door to the living room, and took off his belt as he followed in behind them. Inside he began swinging his belt and yelling, "We came to Africa to tell these people about Jesus and you are throwing rocks at them from the roof?" He was furious. John and Rich were screaming. Mom and I were crying. And then, like a bolt of lightning, Blackie flew right through the screen door, took one leap and bit Dad in the stomach. Dad turned the belt on the dog and then ran out to wash his wound. Later that day, Dad left to buy a roll of new screen and, when he returned, he calmly fixed the door. [21]

I understood Dad's anger. We were strangers in a Muslim land with visas that could be revoked on a whim. But, like David and me whispering in the pew and Richie falling under the train, I also knew what triggered his anger. If there was one thing that Dad would not tolerate, it was being embarrassed by his family.

Back at Nonkon, one night near the end of our vacation, Mom and Dad told us to stay put after dinner. Mom went to their room and returned with a little package, a special gift for my fourteenth birthday. I opened it and there was a beautiful watch. I had written my parents from Mamou telling them that I was the only girl in my class who didn't have one, but I had completely forgotten about it. When they got my letter, they wrote to a missionary who

---

[21] My brothers remember Blackie biting Dad when they were in trouble for disturbing Mom's noon rest, but we all agree that the rock-throwing incident occurred as I describe it here.

was finishing up his French language training in Switzerland. He had bought the watch for them and had brought it to Mali for me. I turned it over, read "18K" and smiled. I not only had a watch, I had the prettiest, daintiest one I had ever seen.

Before we knew it, it was time to go back to school and the packing began. I lamented the fact that I wouldn't have a new dress for my eighth-grade graduation, but Mom suggested I set aside my nice white dress and not wear it until July and then it would seem special. I agreed, we closed the trunk, and we were off to Mamou again.

An incident, nothing short of miraculous, happened on that trip. The trucks in our caravan stopped under a bridge where a fast-flowing river cascaded through a rocky channel. It was a nice break from riding over the bumpy, dusty roads. Mom knelt on the edge of the rocks, took off her glasses and bent over the rushing stream to splash water on her face. When she turned to put her glasses back on, they were gone. "Oh, no, my glasses!" she shouted. Angie Tschetter instinctively reached into the water and the glasses floated right into her hands.

Chapter 18

Deviations from Normal at Mamou
Spring, Summer, Fall 1962
Grade 8 Ends–Grade 9 Begins

When we returned to Mamou in the spring of 1962, the Tylers were still our dorm parents. I presumed I'd be rooming with one of my classmates, Margi or Pauline, or maybe one of David's seventh grade classmates in the grade below me. I was surprised when Rosalys Tyler told me to unpack in the nice big room at the end of the hall where her daughter Janice, two years younger than me, had already set up residence.

Pauline and Margi's room was next to mine and as they were unpacking, they came and got me, "Come look at our dresses for graduation! Aren't they pretty? Our moms let us pick out matching fabric at the market and they sewed them for us!" My heart sank. My white dress, though pretty enough, was nothing compared to the beautiful creations draped over their beds. They asked me what I had brought to wear and I told them it was my white dress. What felt okay back in Nonkon when I put that dress in my trunk suddenly didn't feel so good. So, in my next letter home, I told Mom about my classmates' beautiful dresses and asked her if she could somehow get me a new one. Our letters took two weeks to get to Mali and our parents' replies took two weeks to get back so it was a month before I got my response. Mom had written her sister Sue in Ohio, but she had no idea if there would be time for the letter to get to her and for the dress to get to me.

I eventually learned why I was rooming with a Middle Kid. Janice had not wanted to room with any of her classmates so her mother let her choose her roommate and she picked me. Because I was a Big Kid, our light was out when I got back to the room after evening devotions, meaning I had to get ready for bed in the dark. One night I caught Janice reading in bed. She had pushed the curtain away from the door frame allowing light from the hall to stream onto her bunk. When I confronted her about it, she replied, "Mother says I can do it." And do it she did, every single night.

Although the extreme discipline measures had abated under the Tylers, the daily routine had not changed. Meals, like everything else, were regulated. Little Kids and Middle Kids sat at tables with an adult at the head. Some Big Kids also sat at the head of a table and were in charge of the Middle and Little Kids sitting with them. We were assigned to a different table every month and even the Big Kids had to rotate from being at the head of a table back to sitting with an adult.

Rules at meals were straight from Emily Post and were especially enforced at Miss Adam's table:

- Sit up straight and, after grace, place your napkin on your lap.
- Use your spoon to get soup from the back of the bowl, away from you. Don't slurp.
- Pass a dish of food by reaching for it across your body with your right hand and then switching it to your left hand to pass it to the person on your right.
- Don't butter your whole slice of bread. Put a pat of butter on your plate, butter a smaller area of the bread, put your knife down, eat the bite, repeat.
- Cut one bite of meat at a time, lay your knife across the top of your plate, eat the bite, repeat.
- Never touch your food with your fingers or your bread. Use the back of your knife.
- And, above all, eat everything on your plate even if you have to gag it down.

Concentrating on how I was eating took up so much of my energy that I have sketchy memories of what I was eating. I remember breakfasts of oatmeal, cream of wheat or cinnamon toast. There were bananas, always bananas, and sometimes orange wedges. Our main meal was at lunch. I remember small pieces of beef in gravy over noodles, curry with little bits of meat over rice, spaghetti with meat sauce and green beans with buttered bread crumbs. Sometimes we had salad. The cook and his helpers left mid-afternoon, so supper was soup or a sandwich or something else the dormitory supervisors could easily serve. To round off this lighter meal we had dessert of pudding, Jello®, cake or a cookie.

We had mangoes for dessert when they were in season, but we didn't eat them at the table. We would be excused to the porch where bright enamel bowls of peeled mangoes balanced on the veranda wall. We would take one and lean over the edge of the veranda so the juices would not drip on our clothes. Wet towels were handy to wipe the juice dripping from our fingers and sometimes all the way down to our elbows.

Milk was not served at the table either. It was served like medicine on the veranda after breakfast. I hated the stuff. It was powder from a can, mixed with water and I never had to drink it at home. However, Miss Adam presided over this dosing ritual every day so I gagged my little glass down, foamy top and all.

After supper, we had free time to play outside. At 7:30 a bell would ring and children in Grades 1 through 3 would run to the dorm, get dressed in their pajamas and go to the living room for their devotions led by one of the house parents. A half hour later, the bell would ring again and children in Grades 4 through 6 would repeat that process. Thirty minutes after that, the Grades 7 through 10 kids went into the dorm straight to devotions and got ready for bed afterwards.

Devotions didn't deviate. We sang a chorus, a dorm parent read from the Bible or a devotional book, we shared our prayer requests, several children prayed and then the dorm parent said a final prayer. However, that spring, devotions turned bizarre. Miss Adam went all mystical on us. She rambled about a man named Richard Loveless and her decision to follow God's call to Africa over her desire to be his wife. He had given her a ring with a very large pearl. Every night, as she meandered through the Song of Solomon, read passages about the Bride of Christ or the parable of the Pearl of Great Price, she gazed at that ring on her left ring finger and caressed it lovingly with the fingers of her right hand. I don't know if anyone else was inspired or blessed, but it made me uncomfortable and I thought she might be going crazy.

However, when I needed her, Miss Adam took care of me. Although I had been going on and off since the previous fall to burn my sanitary pads with my peers, my periods had never settled into a regular pattern. Early in the semester I had pretty heavy bleeding for several days and it took more than a week to taper off, but I didn't know what was normal and what wasn't, so I didn't tell anyone. The next month, after my period had lasted a week, instead of tapering off, the flow became so heavy that I bled all the way through a pad from after school until supper. One of the girls told me that sometimes her mom would put two pads on at a time, so I did that. After supper, we were outside and I started feeling weak. I went in to check and in under an hour, I had bled straight through both pads. My friend agreed this wasn't normal and she went with me to find Miss Adam.

That is how I came to sleep in Miss Adam's bed. First, she took me to her bathroom to see what I was talking about. She kept her composure, but I could tell she was surprised at what she saw. She asked my friend to go for my pajamas and clean panties. While I changed, she layered towels in the middle of her bed and told me to lie down flat on my back and not to move all night. She slept in the infirmary right next door. I don't know how I fell asleep, or how I managed to stay on my back all night, but I remember her waking me very early and asking how I was.

I said I thought I was okay, but when I sat up, the back of my pajama top was sticky and wet. She helped me stand up and there, where I had been lying, everything was soaked, bright red. She helped me to the bathroom and waited inside the door. I felt a blood clot the size of my palm slide from inside me, followed by a gush of blood. Too weak to shower, I held on to the sink as Miss Adam washed and dried my body, wrapped me in her robe, and helped me back to her bed. She left and came back with a breakfast tray and clean pajamas from my room. I sat up on the bed just long enough to change and eat and then lay back down, once again trying not to move.

Later that morning Miss Adam came back with vials of Vitamin K from the pharmacy in town, hoping it would help clot my blood and stop the bleeding. The injection hurt but, worse than that, it gave me a strong metallic taste in my mouth. The next morning, I tried eating grapefruit during the injection. It didn't take away the strange taste, but it was a distraction.

After school, the girls in my class brought me my books and explained my assignments. The next day they told me that the boys were asking what was wrong with me, but they didn't tell them. When the girls left, I sat stone still on the edge of Miss Adam's bed feeling helpless and embarrassed. I stared at the light filtering through the curtains across from me and gradually everything but the light and the weight of my books on my lap faded away.[22]

If a vitamin K deficiency was the problem, three shots would have made a difference in my bleeding. When I woke with no change on the fourth day of my ordeal, Miss Adam took me to see the French doctor in town. I remember his surprise when I was able to answer his questions in French. I also remember the serious look on his face when he explained to Miss Adam that he had to give me a shot of testosterone. After driving back to campus, I was exhausted and glad to lie back down, but I couldn't drift off to sleep right away. I kept picturing the concern on the doctor's face and, for the first time since it had all started, I was afraid.

What is wrong with me? Why is this happening? What if it doesn't stop? Will it happen again? Is this because I was molested?[23] Will I grow a mustache? If I do, will it go away? I eventually dozed off and woke to Miss Adam bringing me my lunch and asking how I was feeling. I said I didn't know, but I thought I was okay. By bedtime the bleeding had slowed down

---

[22] *"When people are dissociating they disconnect from their surroundings, which can stop the trauma memories and lower fear, anxiety and shame."* What is Dissociation and What to do About It? https://depts.washington.edu/ University of Washington, 2012

[23] Kaliray, Pavan and Drife, James. Childhood Sexual Abuse and Subsequent Gynaelogical Conditions. https://obgyn.onlinelibrary.wiley.com/doi/pdf/ 10.1576/toag.6.4.209.27017

and by the next evening it had stopped. The boys were quiet around me for the first day I was back in class, and I found out later that Mr. Emary had told them. I kept my eyes down and tried to be as invisible as possible. During that traumatic time, it never occurred to me that my parents were missing. It was just the way things were.

A few weeks later, just before the semester ended, Rosalys called my name after lunch. I stood in line, wracking my brain over what I could have done wrong, but instead of being in trouble she told me to come to her apartment after school for a package. It was from my Aunt Sue in Akron and inside was my graduation dress. As I opened it I thought, "What if it doesn't fit? What if I don't like it?" but it was beautiful, soft yellow perfection.

Most of our parents were in attendance for our Eighth Grade Graduation and my dad was the speaker, but the only thing I remember about the ceremony was our class singing, from memory, the hymn *Praise to the Lord, the Almighty*. It made an impression on me because the tune was so lovely and all four verses were an affirmation of God's love and care with not one word about sin, condemnation or The Second Coming. And I remember something else: feeling pretty and very, very grateful in my beautiful dress, flanked by Pauline and Margi in theirs.

Retouched by Chuck Jarrell

One year before, in the summer of 1961, our parents and the Neudorfs had come to Guinea to spend the between-the-school-year break with their children. In the summer of 1962, every cabin at Dalaba was booked and Mamou shut down for two weeks. A few parents could not make it, but arrangements were made for their children to stay with families who had kids their age. Both of my worlds—life with my family and life with my peers—came together for two magical weeks of heaven on earth.

You drive up to Dalaba, not just because it is 30 miles north of Mamou, but because its elevation is 4068 feet above sea level compared to

that of Mamou at 2362 feet. As the city with the highest elevation in the Fouta Djalon mountains, it became a retreat during the hot season for the French colonists and other expatriates who dubbed it "The Switzerland of Africa." One reason for the nickname was the climate. The daily temperatures in Dalaba were 10 to 15 degrees cooler than those in Mali during the day and much cooler at night. The other reason for the nickname was the stunning beauty of the place with its lush tropical vegetation, glorious mountain vistas and many waterfalls, from thousands of little cascading beauties to the awe-inspiring Ditinn Falls which plummets 393 feet in a single cascade to a pool below.

Over the years, missionaries had built cottages on three different terraces which were connected by a lane that zigzagged its way up the side of a mountain on the outskirts of Dalaba. After breakfast each morning, we kids would start gathering, one sibling group at a time, on the lowest terrace near the Big House at the bottom of the hill and we would run and play till lunch, making up what we would do as the hours unfolded before us. We'd go back home for lunch and noon rest and then play together again. After supper, our parents played games with us, read us stories and tucked us into bed where we snuggled down under heavy quilts to keep out the mountain chill. No bells. No rules. No fear.

During our two weeks at Dalaba there were afternoon volleyball games where parents and kids played together and there were a few organized outings: a picnic at The Pines, a potluck supper and an excursion to Dittinn Falls. We wore our bathing suits under our clothes, hoping to swim in the pool below the falls, but a bloated lion, floating in the water not far from shore, nixed that idea. It had fallen in upstream and crashed over the falls to its death. I shuddered to think there could be lions in the forest above the cottages where we slept or near the spring where we hiked every day.

Almost every day someone would suggest hiking to the spring. Big Kids, Middle Kids, and Little Kids would set off up the mountain to the spring where a cement catchment had been built to supply water to the cottages. Alongside the pipe that ran down the mountain from the catch to the cottages, there was a steep dirt path that led through the forest to the spring. Every hike was an adventure with the Big Kids watching out for snakes and making sure the Little Kids stayed with the group and helping them over the slippery places. When we got to the spring, we'd try to identify the insects we saw, or spot the birds we could hear in the canopy above us, or talk about water tables and gravity and the ingenuity of this simple but effective water system. But mostly we just stood quietly, amazed at the sight of the water, unadulterated and pure, bubbling out of the rock and gurgling in a never-ceasing stream into the catch below. Before we left, we would carefully remove any leaves or branches from the catch and stand there in the green, damp embrace of the rainforest before heading back to the clearing below and home.

Besides our wonderful vacation with our family and friends, there was something else that all the kids in my class were thankful for. Back at Mamou our trunks were packed and upon our return we would be moving to the Villa at the bottom of the hill. The Conservative Baptists, who had used the Villa for their dormitory for several years, had opened their own school in Bouaké, Ivory Coast. The Villa would now be the Mamou high school dorm and my parents would be our dorm parents. Frankly, I wasn't thrilled. I knew what the kids thought of the children of the dorm parents and I was bound and determined not to be one of them.

The boys included Dan Parelius, David Adams, Don Ratzloff, Jimmy McKinney, Lynn Miley and Stan Burns who lived in two rooms downstairs. The girls were Edith Rupp, Pauline Arnold, Marcia Tschetter, Margi Timyan and me. We lived in two rooms on the second floor next to my parents' room. Our routines were pretty simple. We'd get up in the morning and get ready for school and then Dad would drive us up the hill to the Foyer in the

Rapide for breakfast and morning classes. After lunch, we'd go back to the Villa for noon rest. We could read or study, sit up on our beds, and whisper without fearing for our lives. Then Dad would drive us back for afternoon classes. Unless it was raining, we walked back to the Villa when school was out for the afternoon.

Oh, what freedom it was to stroll down that path after school, passing the huts of the Fulani family that lived near the campus, looking out over the banana plantation in the valley to our right, seeing the town of Mamou in the valley straight ahead with Sugar Loaf Mountain on the far horizon behind it, laughing and talking with our friends. Mom and Dad didn't care when we got there and didn't question us about whom we were walking with or what we had been doing. We settled into a happy, relaxed routine that was nothing short of lovely.

School that year finally started to be interesting and challenging. I remember struggling at times in Algebra I and being amazed, during our study of the book of Romans, that the Bible was more complicated than the stories in it that I knew by heart. There were twelve students in the high school room, ten in my Grade 9 class and two in Grade 10—Edith and Mr. Emary's daughter, Darla. How Mr. Emary taught all subjects for both grades, I don't know, but I learned a lot under his teaching and looked forward to school every day.

And then, once again, it was early December and time to return to Mali. The Kroekers and Louise Jantzen had returned to Nonkon, so we were not needed there. Field Council had stationed Mom and Dad in Bamako where Mom would be the mission bookkeeper and where Dad would help with the bookstore ministry. Our home would be in the original house on the GMU property bought by George Reed in the early 1920s.

How different life was in Bamako from what life had been like at Sirakoro and Nonkon! Our house had electricity and indoor plumbing. There were stores where we could buy French canned goods and cheeses, bakeries with French bread and market places with eggs, meat and fresh vegetables in abundance. But there was something even better than that about living in Bamako. We got to see our friends.

Every two or three weeks a missionary family would come to town for supplies or for business. Families always stayed in the guest houses a few blocks from where we lived so it was fun to walk back and forth along the quiet streets between the mission properties, laughing and joking with our MK peers: Mary Kroeker, the Neudorf kids, the Schumacher boys, the Tschetter girls and the Wiens boys. Sometimes we would walk down to the Niger River at dusk and marvel at the sight of the new bridge spanning the river, its street lights strung bright across the evening sky. From where we stood we could also see the American flag, fluttering in the evening breeze, over the American Ambassador's residence. It was a startling reminder of our other homeland far, far away.

Living in Bamako for three months brought into clear focus the effects of the bold stand for complete independence that Mali had made two years before. Goods from the Communist Block were in abundance in the shops and many of the expatriates we met around town weren't French. They spoke to each other in Russian or Chinese and they certainly didn't make eye contact with us when we passed them in the street.

Chapter 19

Last Days at Mamou
Spring, 1963
End of Grade 9

Since Mom and Dad had to be back at the Villa a week before the students arrived, our trip to Mamou in the spring of 1963 was not in a caravan with other MKs. Our family travelled alone into Guinea, spent the night in Kankan and the next morning started the ascent into the mountains. When we were about halfway to Mamou, Dad pulled off the road near a lovely waterfall. "Who wants to get in the water?" Dad asked.

"You can't be serious!" Mom said, "We don't have our bathing suits."

"That's what underwear is for! Come on, kids, put your clothes in the car. It will be fun."

"What if someone sees us?" I asked.

"Like who?" he responded with a laugh. My brothers had already stripped down to their underpants and in a minute Mom, Dad and I were following them down a steep path to a pool at the base of the falls where we all climbed in. From that vantage point we could see Tinkisso Falls straight on, framed on the sides by the rainforest and above it by white clouds drifting across a bright blue sky.

The water was freezing, so we didn't stay long. Just as we were ready to climb out, Dad said, "Kids. Don't move. Look up to the left." We froze and watched as a troop of baboons nonchalantly crossed the falls, totally unaware of their audience far below. The memory of that scene still evokes wonder in me even today.

Dorm life at the Villa and school life on the hill picked up right where they had left off the previous December. During that semester, I had roomed with Marcia and Edith in the larger bedroom at the front of the Villa and Margi had roomed with Pauline in the smaller bedroom on the side of the house. This semester we switched so that I roomed with Pauline in the smaller room. I remember her being my roommate because on Saturdays I would negotiate with her to do the tidying of our little desk under the window if she'd let me do the cleaning.

Even though we lived off campus, we still had our music lessons at Mrs. Emary's house after school and we practiced on the piano in the Foyer. David, who had taken accordion lessons on our furlough, had switched to taking piano lessons from Mrs. Emary and had quickly caught up to me. One evening after supper, standing in front of the Emary's house, I overheard her discussing our lessons with our mother. "Dianne can play," she said, "but David has a natural ability that is impressive." I felt a pang of jealousy, but it was a good lesson to learn. I was the big sister, but that didn't make me the best at everything.

It was that semester that Lynn Miley wrote me a note asking if I would be his girlfriend. Stanley and I had parted ways the year before and I was intrigued by the quiet, intelligent boy who had joined our class the previous fall. I said yes. After school, when our group was out of sight of the main campus, Lynn and I would fall in beside each other and lag a little bit behind so we could walk together and talk. He was thoughtful and kind and loved a good conversation. We discussed what we were studying in school and I learned about his family. His parents were Freewill Baptist Missionaries and his dad served as a doctor at a mission hospital in northern Ivory Coast. He offered to teach me chess, but although I enjoyed his company, I never got the hang of it.

During that semester, the older students went on a day trip to the capital city of Conakry on the coast. I don't remember what we did that day, but I do remember the 160-mile trip back to Mamou. Since it was dark, the adults made the boys sit on the benches on one side of the Rapide and the girls sat on the other side, separated by a huge pile of supplies. As the night wore on, we lay our heads across our arms on the pile in front of us and tried to sleep. Just after I dozed off, someone touched my hand. I was sure it wasn't Lynn because he was sitting behind the driver and I was sitting further back. I looked up, ready to snap at whoever thought this was funny, and saw that it was Lynn who had unobtrusively switched places until he was across from me. I smiled, put my head back down on my arm and let him take my hand in his. I thought it was clever and rather romantic that he found a way to be near me as we wound our way through the darkness, thousands of feet up into the mountains and back to the Villa at Mamou.

One moonlit night, right after lights out, Pauline heard a voice at our window. It was Lynn asking to talk to me. I climbed out of bed and went to the window. "What are you doing and how did you get up here? You are going to fall and break your neck!" It was simple, he explained. He had climbed the ladder to the flat roof over the laundry room, had dropped down to the narrow ledge that ran around the building between the lower and upper floors and, by holding on to the branches of a small tree that grew there, he had walked along the ledge until he could hold onto our window sill. There was barely any moonlight, so I couldn't see what he was describing, but since he didn't crash to the ground before my very eyes, I decided he wasn't in mortal danger. He explained that he just wanted to talk to me all alone. I told him I was glad to be alone with him too. After a few minutes, we said good night. I heard a rustle of leaves and a little scraping sound as he clambered up to the flat roof and then I knew he was safe. I lay back in bed feeling like Juliet and wondering if my Romeo would be back another night.

On a brighter moonlit night, a week or so later, another boy came to the window. "Psst. Pauline. Dianne. A bunch of us are up on the flat roof. Go get Margi and you guys come up too." It sounded daring and the moonlight called, so we slipped on our clothes, tiptoed past my parents' door, crept down the stairs, went outside and scampered up the ladder. Once we got to the flat roof, the boys scooted over to make room for us and we sat around and talked. It was one of those nights when the moon was so bright we could have read a book. When I wondered about Lynn, one of the boys replied, "He's sleeping." They had probably assumed that their shy, serious, analytical classmate wouldn't have joined them on a lark even if they had asked.

The following Monday morning, Mr. Emary made a remark during our classroom devotions about the deeds of darkness that sent a chill down my spine. It wasn't just his remark, it was about how he paused and looked intently at us while he said it. I tensed a bit and wondered if he noticed. At our morning break, others said they had noticed it too and we all admitted that we were nervous. We tossed around theories about how he would know. We ruled out Edith Rupp telling her classmate Darla Emary because Edith had been sleeping and no one had told her. Was Mr. Emary outside the Villa in the moonlight and saw us? Was he psychic? We all agreed on one thing: Mr. Emary was shrewd. If he was watching our reactions so he could follow up on a hunch, our job would be to act as though nothing happened. In the end, nothing came of it but that ended Lynn's visits at the window and we never joined the boys on the roof again.

My years at Mamou were at an end. When I had arrived, three and a half years before, I was finishing elementary school. Now I had one year of high school under my belt and was ready to start Grade 10 back in the States. Remembering my years at Mamou is complicated. My eyes well up with tears when I long for just one more glimpse of the beauty that surrounded us there. My heart warms and I smile when I think of my classmates and the adventures we shared. But deeper than that are the scars, branded on my soul, that took half a lifetime to acknowledge and that will never completely heal this side of heaven.[24]

[24] Lamaison, Rosemary. (June 2, 2015). Boarding School Syndrome: The Symptoms and Long-term Psychological Effects. https://www.ibbclaims.co.uk/site/blog/sexual-and-physical-abuse-claims/child-abuse-at-boarding-schools/boarding-school-syndrome.

During my very last night at the Villa, I was awakened by someone tapping my left shoulder. I opened my eyes and saw Lynn kneeling by my bed. I raised up on my right elbow and whispered into his ear, "Why are you here? If Pauline wakes up . . ."

"I know, but I had to say goodbye," he whispered. And then, ever the gentleman, he asked, "May I kiss you?"

I hesitated. "Okay," I replied, "but not on the lips." I leaned toward him and he gently kissed me on the cheek, brushing the left side of my mouth. Then I put my hand on his shoulder and leaned my face against his and he drew me close. I was glad he was there, but terrified at the same time. "You've got to go. I'll miss you. Be sure to write."

"I'll miss you too and I will," he promised and then he slipped away. I lay back down, flat on my back, and stared at the ceiling while tears trickled down my face and then I turned and sobbed into my pillow for so long that I worried my mother would find it soaking wet the next morning and wonder why.

As I matured into a young woman, what had been done to me in Dakar and Kénieba came into horrific focus. Worries about the effects of my abuse sometimes gnawed at me, but they rarely lingered. After all, a little kiss, gently offered and sweetly accepted, reminded me that I really was a normal girl who had been loved by a normal boy and, surely, my abuse would not be the only thing to define me.

Part V

The Girl Survived but the Body Remembered

"The body remembers – and will tell its tale."
Donna Jackson Nakazawa, *Childhood Disrupted*

Chapter 20

Mamou Girl in America
Summer 1963–Summer 1964
Grade 10

Our trip back to the U.S. for furlough in 1963 would be the last time we traveled between Africa and Ohio as a family because, before our next furlough, David and I would be in college in the States. Mom and Dad saved and planned ahead so that we could stop in Europe en route to the States. Darla Emary was finishing Grade 10 and needed to travel home at the same time, so it was agreed that she would join our adventure.

On July 23, 1963, we flew from Conakry to Zurich, Switzerland. Other than seeing the lake, I don't remember much about the day we spent there. I do, however, remember piling into our rented Volkswagen bus the next day and setting off over the Alps. It was a memorable day because Mom was terrified. We crossed a high mountain pass where the road had just been cleared from an avalanche and where little guardrails were the only thing keeping us from going over cliffs that dropped thousands of feet below. She shrieked at every turn and we laughed at her until she started to cry. We kept quiet after that and, on the long way down the other side of the mountain, I remember pondering her reaction and came to the conclusion that just because it wasn't my reaction, it had been unkind of me to make fun of hers.

The next day Dad aimed the Volkswagen north toward Germany with just a road map as a guide. I was sure we were on roads that no other tourist had ever traveled, winding past little farms, holding our breath in anticipation of the stench of the silage, stopping for bread and lunch meat and picnicking along the road. Whether Dad had planned it or whether it was happenstance, we ended up in the town of Singen at dusk. On the main street, we stopped in front of an old, stone building that looked like a hotel and waited while Dad went in to see if they had any rooms. He came out a few minutes later and said, "I got us three rooms, but it wasn't easy." And then with a laugh he added, "No one speaks English or French in there, so I had to use sign language!" This verified my observation that tourists had never been to that part of Germany. We laughed and tumbled out of our little bus.

By now it was dark. We carried our suitcases up the steps to our rooms—one room for Mom and Dad; one for David, John and Rich; and one for Darla and me—and then we went down to the hotel restaurant for dinner.

The menu was in German and only German. We tried to order water in English and French to no avail. Dad, in desperation, launched into Bambara which had us laughing hysterically. We finally just pointed at the menu and waited. Other than the raw hamburger topped with a raw egg, we ate what they brought us and went to bed.

When we checked out the next morning, a man was waiting for us at the desk. He spoke a bit of English and offered to take us on a tour of Hohentwiel, the massive castle and fortress sitting high above the town. As we explored those ruins, it was sobering to think that lords and ladies had lived there in power and glory for a thousand years but now it was nothing but crumbling mortar and stone. From there we drove to Neufchâtel, a Swiss city on the border of France, where we spent a few days with GMU missionaries who were studying French before heading to ministries in Morocco or Mali.

My period had started in Zurich and by the time we got to Neufchâtel, I was bleeding badly. I had not had any severe bleeding since my testosterone injection the year before, but my periods had not been regular either. I told mom what was happening and she said we'd wait to see a doctor at the American Hospital in Paris if it didn't stop. During our short flight from Switzerland to Paris, Mom kept turning around in her seat to check on me and the worry on her face told me that I looked as pale and weak as I felt. We took a cab from the airport to our hotel and checked into our rooms. While Dad explained to Darla and the boys that they would need to stay at the hotel alone for a few hours, Mom helped me change and wash up and put my bloody clothes to soak in the bathroom sink. In less than an hour we were in another cab, rushing through the streets of Paris to the American Hospital.

Once again, I found myself explaining my bleeding to a doctor. I was relieved when he said I didn't need another testosterone shot. It was 1963 and there was a new way to help women who had my problem: birth control pills. Dad took the prescription to a pharmacy and I started taking the little pills that would be a blessing and a hidden curse for me in the years to come.[25] The doctor told my parents that I should rest for the next couple of days and they needed to take me to a gynecologist when we got to the States. So, while Dad took the other kids sightseeing in Paris, Mom stayed with me in the hotel. I was too weak to even care. All that mattered to me was that two days later, on our last day in France, I was well enough to take the train to Crosne for a joyous reunion with the Duquesne family.

---

[25] *"Decidual casts may be linked to taking oral contraceptives"* Nunes, Rodrigo and Pissetti, Viviane. Membranous Dysmenorrhea – Case Report. (Warning: graphic is gruesome) https://clinmedjournals.org/articles/ogcr/ogcr-2-042.pdf

Our next stop was Amsterdam where I remember two things. We toured the Anne Frank house and afterward, when we had all but given up finding a restaurant for supper, we spotted a tiny Chinese restaurant below street level where the lively owner danced around exclaiming, "Por chop! Por chop!" which proved to be the only English words he knew. We went to The Hague where we saw the Peace Palace, the home of the International Court of Justice, and also visited Madurodam. As we were strolling through the fascinating miniature city there, Dad recognized a couple he knew and we gathered round to visit. It was a small world that day in more ways than one!

Our next stop was London where we saw the requisite tourist attractions: the changing of the guard at Buckingham Palace, Madame Toussaud's Wax Museum, Big Ben, London Bridge and Westminster Abbey. From England, we crossed the Atlantic on the *S.S. Rotterdam* to New York City. It was fun to be on deck while the tug boats came alongside to guide us into New York Harbor. As the Statue of Liberty came into view, oohs and aahs rippled across the deck. When I realized my parents were silent, I looked up to see tears streaming down their faces and my eyes welled up too. I had never realized how much they missed their homeland.

There was another reason Mom was teary eyed. A year before, her dad had suffered a stroke and she knew he was dying. We flew from New York City to Akron and went straight to Grandma Koehl's house where Grandpa lay in a hospital bed in the tiny dining room. He reached up for her hand and said *my little herzen.* She was *his little heart* and he had waited almost a year for her to come home. We saw him again the next day and then he was gone. I had only a few memories of him but one has remained: following him down the narrow cellar steps where he'd give us kids pretzel sticks and ginger ale before pouring himself a beer. He didn't say much, but we could tell he loved us.

Once again, we found ourselves living in Mrs. Carlisle's house on Kenmore Boulevard, right around the corner from Goss Church and Heminger Elementary School where John enrolled in Grade 5 and Rich enrolled in Grade 4. It was a short walk to Kenmore High School where David would be a freshman and I would be a sophomore. I was anxious about going to school. I had no idea how American teenagers acted and was sure everyone would know I was an alien. One thing that helped, though, was the warm welcome our peers gave us at church. Their mothers organized a shower for David and me where we each got several stylish outfits. At least outwardly it would look like we fit in.

I was extremely nervous the first day of school, so much so that I did not want to walk down the Boulevard lest David and I run into other kids. We crossed the street and cut down an alley and approached the large, imposing building as bravely as we could. There were 1,200 students streaming through the doors and bustling through the halls, clanging their lockers and shouting happy greetings to their friends. My little high school classroom with a dozen students, in a tropical forest far away, might as well have been on another planet.

I adjusted. It took a while to learn how to get to class on time, especially when I had to rush through the basement hallway in the old building to get to my next class in the new building. One by one kids recognized me, "Aren't you Dianne who was in Mr. Griffin's class at Highland Park?" They seemed genuinely glad to see me and I gradually started to feel like I didn't need to be invisible. But even if I had wanted to hide, Mr. Ratkovich, Dad's football coach, turned the spotlight on me one day in history class and blew my cover wide open. After taking attendance, he strode down the row where I sat, planted both of his palms on my desk, leaned down so close to my face that I could smell the smoke of his last cigar and blustered, "Are you Dick Darr's daughter?"

"Yes," I answered, wanting to crawl under my desk.

"Well, I've been waiting for one of his kids to show up in my classroom for years. I had a couple of other Darrs in class and found out they were your cousins. When did you get back from Africa?" At the word Africa, heads turned and every eye in the room was on me.

"In August," I replied.

He turned and walked back up to his desk, "Class, I need to tell you about Dick Darr. He was one of the finest football players I ever coached," and then he proceeded to tell my Dad's life story starting with the city championship he helped win, going on to his stint in the Navy, followed by his college career, and ending with his missionary work in Africa. He finished with, "Tell him to come up here and see me!" and then he went to the board and launched into our history lesson for the day. When I told Dad about it after school, he threw back his head and laughed. I assured him that it had not been funny to me at all.

Underneath, however, it was cool to have a connection to my parents' high school days by being in Mr. Ratkovitch's class. It was also cool to find myself sitting next to my cousin, Fred Darr, in a study hall. About once a week the study hall supervisor would look up at us and bark, "Okay, you two cousins, knock it off or I'll separate you."

Mme Steward's French II class was absurdly easy, but like everyone else, my age locked me into the master schedule. We opened class every Monday with the Lord's Prayer in French and sang the French National

Anthem every Friday. Geometry was hard, but Mr. Green was a wonderful teacher and I understood it better than ninth grade Algebra. Miss Ross, my English teacher, walked with a crutch but she was spritely and witty and inspired my love of literature. My gym teacher, Miss Cutrone, probably taught close to 150 girls every day, but grading us certainly didn't take much of her time. If you were a cheerleader, you got an A. If you stood out athletically, you got a B. If you barely participated, you got a D. Everyone else got a C, including me, who had never had a C in her life.

One unit came along where I did stand out, but not in a way that earned me a B. Dancing was part of the gym curriculum; however, dancing was considered sinful in Evangelical circles. I told Mom and Dad about it and Dad said, "No problem." He sat down at the table and wrote a note that read, "Dear Miss Cutrone, Please excuse Dianne from dancing class. Sincerely, Rev. Dick L. Darr." When I asked him why he didn't give a reason, he told me that it was none of her business.

The first day of dancing class, Miss Cutrone was seated, as usual, on a bleacher. I handed her the note, she glanced at it, looked up at me and said, "Why?" I froze. She glanced down at the cryptic note again, saw Dad's signature for the first time and said, "Okay. Just sit in the bleachers." I learned two things from this experience. First, when you have a legitimate request, make it short and to the point. Secondly, when dancing involves tenth grade boys and girls in gym class, sinful and sensuous is not how you'd describe it.

Later that fall, Mom made an appointment for me with a gynecologist at the Akron Clinic. Mom didn't drive, so Dad drove us to the doctor's office across town. When my name was called, Dad turned to me and said, "Wait here a minute." As if on cue, they both stood up, went into the doctor's office, and closed the door. I knew they were in there telling the doctor what Don had done to me. I was stunned. A year and a half before, as I lay bleeding in Miss Adam's bed, I had worried that my abuse was linked to what was happening to me and now that closed door in front of me meant it was true. I stared at the wall across the room, my body turned to stone and everything except the weight of the magazine in my hands faded away.[26]

I vaguely remember my parents coming back and sitting down beside me, but my surroundings were still like a white cloud. Then a nurse called my name and I snapped back to reality. She took me to an examination room and told me to undress and put on a gown, open in the front. She left briefly and when she came back she positioned me on the table, my legs spread wide

---

[26] *"The whole world may ... seem to be disappearing ... or going white or totally blank."* Handelman, Mark. Trauma and Dissociation. http://psychotherapy-nyc.com/blog/2012/09/04/trauma-and-dissociation

so the doctor could do what he had to do. For any girl of 15, it would have been a harrowing experience. However, worse than that were the words, drumming in my ears, "He knows. He knows."

After sitting down and adjusting his light, the doctor said, "This will feel cold and might hurt a little."

"Of course, it will hurt," I wanted to scream, "but that's not the problem. The problem is that you know and that my parents are sitting out there worried about me. Won't this ever end?" But I had forsworn hysteria five years before, so I just lay there, perfectly still, until it was over.[27]

After I got dressed, the doctor motioned us into his office. He had found nothing wrong, but he ordered a chest X-ray and he set up an appointment for me with an endocrinologist which took place on December 26, 1963. The endocrinologist asked me all kinds of questions and drew blood. Everything came back normal except that my blood sugar was elevated. He ordered a glucose tolerance test and it came out fine. "It was probably just the candy you ate on Christmas day," he joked when we went for our last appointment. He reassured me that many women have irregular periods until after the birth of their first child. If I had heavy bleeding again, a round or two of birth control pills would always stop it and get me back on track. And with that, we thought the issues with my bleeding were over.

Drama of another sort, however, was just around the corner. One winter afternoon, Mom and Dad were sitting on the couch waiting for me as I came in the door after school. "Take your coat off and sit down," Dad said. He had a letter in his hand and proceeded to tell me that there had been trouble at Mamou and I was being accused of being a part of it. The dorm parents at the Villa had caught Stanley with a girl one night and he had been expelled. During the investigation into the incident, a student had confessed about our moonlight soirée on the roof and had accused me of instigating it.

Being accused of organizing an innocent gathering on the roof in moonlight as bright as day was the least of my worries. I was trembling, but tried not to show it. "Pauline, Margi and I joined the boys on the roof one night. It was bright moonlight and we sat around and talked. It was not my idea."

"Was Lynn there?" Dad asked pointedly. Lynn and I had been writing back and forth, so he knew that I really liked him.

---

[27] *"Intrusive thoughts, flashbacks, dissociation, body memories, and feelings of intense vulnerability were experienced during pelvic examinations."*
Watson, Victoria S. Retraumatization of Sexual Trauma in Women's Reproductive Health Care. (University of Tennessee, Knoxville, Honors Thesis, Spring 2016). https://trace.tennessee.edu/cgi/viewcontent.cgi?referer=https://www.google.com/&ht tpsredir=1&article=2983&context=utk_chanhonoproj,

"No. The boys said he was sleeping." I continued calmly. "This is not hard to figure out. I am the only one who is not there, so they are blaming me."

"Were boys coming up to the girls' rooms at night?" he asked. I was terrified that the letter on his lap said more.

"No one ever said anything to me about that," I replied truthfully, trying not to let my composure reveal the waves of panic sloshing around inside me. I barely breathed until Dad folded up the letter and launched into a speech about being disappointed in me but that he believed me. I climbed the steps to my room, literally shaking. I had not lied, but I had surely dodged the whole truth. Oh, how I wished I could talk to Lynn! But the only thing I could do was wait and bank on what I knew: still waters run deep and if anyone could keep a clandestine kiss a secret, it would be Lynn.

Around that same time, another serious matter of discussion was taking place at our house. Would I stay behind in America for my last two years of high school and first two years of college or would I finish Grade 11 and Grade 12 by correspondence on the station with my parents in Mali? Mom and Dad were very clear about the pros and cons. No other MK in all of West Africa in recent memory had taken high school courses by correspondence. The general consensus was that it was best for MKs to integrate back into North American culture when they were 16 years old and so they could have access to courses that would prepare them for college. I argued that no amount of normal American teenage experiences or courses like chemistry could make up for me being separated from my family for four years.

Before making our final decision, we contacted the University of Nebraska High School Extension School and asked for information about their program. The packet they sent us explained that a qualified person had to sponsor me, supervise my studies and administer my tests. Dad's degree in education qualified him for that. To graduate I would need two years of high school math and one year of high school science, which I already had. We liked what we saw and decided that I would go back to Mali with the family and, after one year of studying alone on the station, David would join me when I would be in Grade 12 and he would be in Grade 11.

Lynn and I wrote to each other regularly during the fall, but his letters gradually tapered off. At Christmas, he wrote to tell me that he had a new girlfriend and wouldn't be writing to me anymore. He also told me that he would be taking correspondence courses for his junior and senior years of high school. That made me smile. I wouldn't be the only MK high schooler studying on a mission station in West Africa after all.

171

In April of 1964 Mom had a birthday party for my 16th birthday. My aunts and cousins came and there was a beautiful cake. One gift I remember was from Aunt Sue. It was my very own Samsonite vanity case. When someone joked, "Sweet sixteen and never been kissed, right, Dianne?" I blushed and replied, "No one will ever know." And no one ever did, because we never heard from Mamou again.

As our departure date neared, the supplies for our next term began streaming into our house from our Goss family and Dad began packing those lovely things into the steel barrels in the basement. Besides the barrels of household supplies and clothing, there would be two very special crates heading for Africa: one contained a new Singer treadle sewing machine and the other contained a brand-new pump organ. During our year home, David and I had continued our piano lessons with Joyce Simms and her extended family had all pitched in to buy the organ for us.

In June, we visited our nearby supporting churches one last time. Between the morning and evening services at Atwater Baptist Church, we had dinner at Pastor Douglas' house. After the meal, I remember standing at the kitchen sink with Susan while I washed the dishes and she dried and put them away. When we finished, she whisked me off to her room where she closed the door and started lamenting, "Dianne, I don't know what to do. I just don't know what to do."

She grabbed her yearbook and proceeded to show me the pictures of two boys. One was Bud who had been her steady boyfriend until he had gone off last fall to Bob Jones. After Christmas, she had started to date Denny but they weren't going steady. She still liked Bud, but he had been in church that morning, home for the summer from Bob Jones, and had not even spoken to her. She was sure he had found out about Denny and she was extremely upset over her dilemma. I thought it odd that she would be pouring her heart out to me, but maybe she just needed to talk to someone who was not involved in the situation. And what better person than me who was literally going to be leaving the country within a few weeks? Over the next two years I wondered how that story ended, little knowing how important that scenario would be to me.

Around that same time, our new vehicle, a four-wheel drive Jeep®
pickup truck, was being built at the Jeep plant in Toledo. When it was
finished, Aunt Peggy drove Dad to Toledo to get it and men from the church
helped load it with our barrels. Dad and David drove it to the dock in New
York City where it was loaded onto a ship bound for Abidjan, Côte d'Ivoire.
On July 4, 1964, our family flew to New York City where we all boarded a
plane on a night flight to Lisbon, Portugal. On our seven-hour layover there
we got a hotel room, pulled the dark curtains and crashed. That afternoon we
flew across the Sahara Desert to Bamako and we were home.

Chapter 21

Studies and Survival on the Savanna
Summer 1964 – Summer 1965
Grade 11

Once again, we were at the GMU compound in Bamako. We settled into the left half of the GMU guesthouse where three bedrooms and a bathroom were perfect for our family. A large common area ran down the middle of the house from the front porch to the back veranda, comprising a living area with couches, armchairs and book cases, a dining area and, next to it, a large, communal kitchen. It would be our home for the next few weeks while Alan McCleod drove Dad to Abidjan, 700 miles away, to fetch our Jeep and supplies.

Mom and us kids would be alone for over a week. However, the Tschetter family lived next door, the Dibida market was within walking distance and Malian women arrived every afternoon with fresh vegetables, beautifully arranged in large enamel basins bobbing on their heads. We knew we'd be fine—which we were, until the night I woke in the predawn hours with a dull, throbbing pain in my lower right side that would not go away. I was pretty sure it was appendicitis, but I knew better than to wake Mom. If we kids had been taught one thing, it was never, ever to disturb our mother's sleep. Plus, I knew no doctor would see me until at least 9:00 o'clock in the morning.

I lay on my back and waited for the dawn. When it was just light enough to see, I woke Mom with the news. She questioned me, but I was adamant, "No, Mom, we can't wait. I've already waited for hours and it's not going away. Uncle Ed has to take me to the doctor." She got up, got dressed and went to tell the Tschetters. Then she woke the boys, made sure they were dressed and fed, and we were off to the doctor's office. He had me lie on my back and pushed my right knee up to my chest. When I screamed, he had a diagnosis.

From there we drove through the streets of Bamako and up the escarpment north of the city to Point G, the national hospital. Ed dropped us off at the surgery area and promised to return in the afternoon. We waited a long time and then a tall, handsome French surgeon, dripping with sweat, appeared. "I'm sorry," he said in French, "a patient needed brain surgery and it took longer than expected." He looked exhausted, but I figured a brain surgeon could perform an appendectomy in his sleep, so I didn't worry. He asked a few questions, gave some directions to a nurse, and disappeared.

Before an orderly wheeled me away, Mom held my hands in hers and prayed. Her halting phrases betrayed not only her awkwardness in that role but her fear as well. While she prayed, I thought of Dad, in another country far away, unaware of what was happening to me. I prayed that I wouldn't die before seeing him again.

I was still in my shorty pajamas. The orderly had me remove the bottoms and proceeded to shave me with a very dull razor. I lay there wincing, wondering how many others had been shaved with that razor and hoping it had been disinfected in between. When that ordeal was over, I was whisked into the operating room and then, before I knew it, I was waking up in an old metal frame bed still wearing my pajama top. My mother was hovering over me, asking how I felt. "I'm okay," I assured her.

"Your surgery went well and your appendix hadn't burst." She handed me something and continued, "Look. They gave it to us to keep!" There was my appendix floating in alcohol in a little glass bottle.

"We're on the second floor of the maternity ward and everyone who comes in looks around for a baby. When they don't see one, they ask if your baby died. I'm trying to explain to them that you just had an operation!" I started to laugh until I realized that laughing hurt. She continued by pointing to an enamel bowl on the floor by the door, "They brought rice and mutton gravy for your supper, but you can't eat that."

The nurse appeared and agreed with Mom that I shouldn't eat solid food. Ed and Angie came to check on us and brought Mom something to eat. Mom told them she couldn't leave me alone that night, so they arranged with the nurse to bring in a cot. The anesthesia was still wearing off, so I slept well that night but the next morning the reality of my surroundings came into focus and it wasn't just my bed with its lumpy mattress and torn sheet that troubled me.

A nurse came in mid-morning to change my IV needle. When she fiddled with the valve and the dripping refused to start, she pulled the needle out and looked at it. Aghast, I saw that the slanted hole at the tip of the needle was caked with dried blood. I knew from helping Dad in the clinic at Nonkon that the needle had been sterilized and the dried blood would probably not contaminate mine, but it had been in my vein for at least a minute. I had lived in Africa long enough to know that there was more than one disease out there that was deadly. "Please, God," I prayed, "please don't let this kill me."

The doctor made rounds and verified that I should not eat solid food and that Mom should stay with me. "Your surgery went well," he told me, "But look," he said, picking up the little bottle, "see how long your appendix is and how thick? You have been suffering from chronic appendicitis for some time." I remembered my unexplained stomach aches that Dr. Wedemeyer blamed on me not liking school, and felt vindicated. The surgeon then turned to Mom and continued, "Normally we keep appendectomy patients for four or five days, but if she tolerates liquids and has a good night, she'll recover better if you take her home tomorrow."

Later that morning Selma and Earl Gripp showed up with a sandwich for Mom and a thermos of chicken noodle soup for me. If all went well, one more IV needle change would be my last. Unfortunately, it didn't go smoothly either. The nurse tried and tried to get the needle into my vein. Finally, she held it up to the light and I saw that the tip was bent at a 90° angle. "That wasn't fun," I said to myself, "but at least it doesn't have the potential to kill me." And I prayed that all I would be taking with me from Point G was my appendix, floating in a little bottle, and nothing more.

I went back to the Guest House, weak but fine. A few days later, Dad was opening the gate to the compound and there was our shiny new Jeep. While I recuperated, Dad, David, John and Rich drove out to Sanankoro, our new station, with our furniture and barrels. When they returned, the boys left for Mamou and Dad loaded the truck with our last load of supplies. Mom and I climbed into the cab and we were off to our new home. The rains had begun, so we knew that isolated places in the road would be covered in water, but we were counting on our four-wheel drive vehicle to take us through.

We crossed the Niger and took the left road at the fork and headed east. An hour and a half later we drove into the station at Warsala where Henry and Hazel Neudorf and Garnet and Carrie McRostie met us and welcomed us in for a cup of tea and a piece of cake. Right beyond the mission station we turned south at Fana toward the town of Dioila where we crossed the Baoulé River by a barge attached to a cable which allowed the force of the current to push us across. We stopped at the post office, Dad filled up the gas tank and by late afternoon we were driving on the last isolated stretch of dirt road leading us to our new home.

We almost made it without incident. In several places, where water was covering the road, Dad got out, waded in and located the shallowest place to drive through. And then we came to a place where a small pond covered the road. Dad walked through it, found the shallowest place, put the Jeep into four-wheel drive and started driving. Right in the middle, the back right tire sank into a hole and we were stuck. Miraculously, within minutes, a group of five or six men came walking down the road. They assessed the

177

situation, rolled up their pants, waded into the water and positioned themselves around the back right bumper and fender. When Dad put the Jeep in gear, they lifted it with all their might and we drove to dry ground. Dad gave the oldest among them a nice tip and we drove off with no idea how much further we had to go and what the terrain would be like ahead. Fifteen minutes later, as daylight began to fade, we crested a slope and saw the buildings of the mission station below.

Katherine and Elsie had dinner waiting for us, so we made no attempt to unpack the truck, with the exception of the crate of beautiful white chickens which Dad had bought from an Israeli group in Bamako, experimenting on improving the poultry stock of the country. To our delight, there were three large eggs in the crate. They were not, however, harbingers of things to come. That long trip, and especially the part when their crate upended during our watery mishap, had traumatized them so much that we didn't see another egg for weeks.

Elsie Winsinger and Katherine Kroeker had been stationed at Sanankoro for years. Elsie ran the mission clinic that sat just outside the fence behind our house. Katherine was on the mission translation team, and was working on translating the Old Testament into Bambara. During the winter months, Katherine and Elsie taught at the Girls School whose dormitory and classroom building were on the station. Along with Bible lessons, girls between the ages of 12 and 16 were taught how to read, how to do simple math and how to sew. In a country with a literacy rate of less than ten percent, Christian families saw the benefit of improving their daughters' lives and young pastors saw the advantage of marrying girls who could help in their ministries. The school was growing and needed a new classroom building, so one of Dad's main tasks in the coming months would be making blocks like he had made for the church in Nonkon.

After we settled in, Dad set up a desk in my room. I organized my textbooks and study guides, made myself a schedule and began my studies. I kept my written assignments until the end of each unit and then studied for the unit test which Dad kept in a file in his room. The assignments and the test went into a manila envelope, which went into a burlap bag, which got picked up each Wednesday by the market truck, which took it to the post office in Dioila. From there it went to the post office in Bamako, by airplane to Paris, by airplane across the Atlantic and then across North America to Nebraska. Six weeks or so later, a letter with feedback from a teacher would arrive verifying that the envelope with my work had made it 6,000 miles across the globe.

My classes were easy, except for my Typing I class. It wasn't because the course was hard, but because perfectionism is a curse. One day, when Dad was timing me, I lost it because my word count per minute wasn't high enough for an A. When I was so frustrated that I was crying, Dad shouted, "Dianne, control your emotions!" That outburst brought Mom to my door who calmly assured me that a break was all I needed. Sure enough, when I tried again the next morning, I did just fine. However, that was not the end of my perfectionism that has plagued me all my days.[28]

As a 16-year old, I was aware for the first time of what it took to live on a mission station far out in the bush. We had no electricity and no direct way to communicate with the outside world. One day a week a little plane flew far overhead coming from, and going to, who knew where. Every Tuesday night, a market truck drove by on its way from Dioila to the market town of Massigui and tossed our bag of mail by the front gate of the station. By noon the next day we put it back there with any mail going out. In spite of our isolation, three things kept us connected to the outside world. We listened to the BBC news every evening on our shortwave radio and, in those weekly bags of mail, we got the *Readers Digest*, *Time Magazine* and the *National Geographic*—outdated by a month to be sure, but a window into the world beyond the savanna, nonetheless. Most importantly, there were Aunt Betty's aerogrammes from Akron, neatly typed, single spaced, from edge to edge. No one but mother was allowed to open them and I could tell that reading them transported her back to Akron and the ones she loved.

During the day, the station was a busy place. First thing in the morning, our two employees would show up for work. Meme helped Mom in the house. He manned the kerosene stove in the outside kitchen and the kerosene refrigerator in our inside kitchen. He carried hot water to the washing machine on wash days, kept our water filters clean and did many of the household tasks such as food prep, dishes, sweeping and mopping that were brutal in the heat.

Sédu was our yard man. Each morning he pulled water up from the well and pumped it up to the large container above our house with a Japy® hand pump. This provided running water for our bathroom and a small sink in our inside kitchen. He also brought buckets of water into the outside kitchen for cooking, washing dishes and for the buckets where sandstone tubes filtered our drinking water.

---

[28] Jantz, Gregory. (Nov. 19, 2018). Why Abused Children May Strive for Perfection. Psychology Today.

During the rainy season, Sédu worked extra hours to keep the compound free from grass. Snakes were not likely to cross an open area, so Sedu would start clearing on one side of the station and, by the time he got to the other side, he'd start on the first side all over again.

I really wasn't bored or lonely on the station. On Monday mornings, I helped Mom do the laundry. While we ate breakfast Meme got large pots of boiling on the kerosene stove in the outside kitchen and grated the washing soap that looked like cheese. While Mom and I sorted the clothes, Dad put gasoline in the thunderous Briggs and Stratton® motor that ran our Maytag® wringer

washer. Then Mom and I would do load after load, starting with the sheets, followed by the whites, the colors and the darks, calling for Meme to add water and soap as needed. My favorite part was folding the sopping wet clothes just so and feeding them carefully through the wringer. From there they'd drop into the rinse tub where I'd swish them around to get out the soap. Then I'd swivel the wringer around and put the clothes through it again, being careful that they landed in a basket below. Once there was a full basket, Mom and I hung the clothes on the clothesline. The last thing we did was wrest Dad's khaki pants onto a tight wire frame, making sure the frame creased them right down the middle of each leg. Then Meme would hang them on the highest part of the line. Wrinkle-free fabric did not exist and drying them on the frames saved us a lot of time ironing them with our flaming hot kerosene iron.

Two mornings a week I helped Mom mix and knead the bread, but once it was in the bowl to rise, I hit my books for the rest of the morning. After lunch and noon rest I studied until my lessons were done. That left time for sewing, playing the pump organ, writing letters or working on the paint-by-number pictures I had brought from America. Mom and I made dinner together and at dusk we would sit on the little veranda out back and watch

Dad light the Coleman® lantern. I can still see him pumping pressure into the kerosene container and then carefully lighting the silk mantle with a match. Once back in the house, Dad placed it in the living room and Mom would light two hurricane lamps, one for the bathroom and her room and the other for my room. When the globes got smoky, she'd wipe them clean and trim the kerosene-soaked wicks with a razor blade.

The rains subsided in October and soon the roads were dry enough for us to travel again. In early November, we went to Bamako for the Annual GMU Field Conference which included several days of business meetings with all the missionaries from all the stations. The women had a schedule for preparing and cleaning up after the meals and I was delighted that they had included me. During the business meetings, I stayed in my room and studied, read or wrote letters. It was nice to gather round the tables for meals and to join the worship services each evening after being isolated at Sanankoro for months.

After the conference, we returned to Sanankoro where final preparations for the Girls School term went into full swing. Elsie and Katherine worked on the curriculum and school materials and Dad coordinated the preparations of the buildings, transportation for the girls and bringing in supplies. Mom and I were busy with preparations of another sort. In just a few weeks, the boys would be coming home!

We arrived in Bamako a couple of days earlier than the other parents coming to meet their kids so Dad could purchase supplies for the Girls School. That put us alone in the Guest House except for one other couple, whose conversation after lunch with the field director and his wife I happened to overhear.

"They are going to regret their decision to have Dianne here," one of the men said.

"I think you're right," said the other.

"She'll be a misfit when she gets back to the States," chimed in one of the wives. "We're so glad our daughter is where she is. She's getting a good education and, from her letters, she's having fun and fitting right in."

"I agree," the other woman said. "But you can't tell Dick Darr anything. But I feel bad that Dianne will be the one to suffer the consequences."

I was so stunned I could barely breathe. What would happen if they stepped into the common living area, saw me sitting there reading a book, and realized I had heard every word? I closed my book, stood up as quietly as possible and tiptoed to my room. I thought these people were my parents' friends. Just last month everyone had been so nice to me at the conference and now they were saying things like this behind my back?

181

When I told Mom and Dad about it, they weren't surprised, knowing all along that their decision to bring me back to Mali for Grade 11 was frowned upon. "Don't worry," Dad said, "They have no idea what you're studying or how much fun we're having, do they? You'll be fine!" I smiled but, underneath, I was worried. Would I really be an uneducated misfit when I got back to the States? And, along with being worried, I was angry. I vowed right then and there to prove them wrong.

Two days later we had a happy reunion with David, John and Rich and we headed back to Sanankoro. Stopping at Warsala for tea and treats was even more fun now that the Neudorf kids were home. The dry season had shrunk the Baoulé and slowed its flow so the cable no longer worked to carry the barge across the river. Instead, men used long bamboo poles to push it across to the opposite bank. We checked the post office for mail, filled the truck up with gas, and bounced back to Sanankoro on dry ground. And finally, all six of us were home.

With the boys at home, I spent more time helping Mom in the kitchen, but I didn't mind. I still had time to finish up my lessons before the end of the semester. Once the girls arrived for school, we enjoyed the hustle and bustle of having them on the station and we were in for a real treat when they put on their annual Christmas pageant complete with a donkey, sheep and a real live baby Jesus. It was magical sitting under the stars with believers from villages near and far, watching the girls act out the nativity story and hearing them sing. The only reminder we had of Christmas in Ohio was our little silver Christmas tree tucked into the corner of our living room and, under it, eight little presents—two each—that Mom had saved and wrapped for us.

In January, despite the activity on the station and at our house, I had to start meeting the deadlines of my second semester of Grade 11. I learned to close my door, block everything out and concentrate on studying until lunchtime. I wanted to get a good start while Girls School was in session because, when it was over, we'd be going into Bamako for supplies and a little break. Elsie and Katherine would also be going on a month of vacation at that time.

Our trip to Bamako was rather uneventful because, as I remember it, none of our MK friends were in town that week. The eventful part came when we got back home and were met by one of the church leaders. "Sedu told us you would be home this evening. We know the clinic is closed this month because Miss Elsie is gone, but a couple came from far. They are waiting at the clinic."

Dad turned to us and said, "Boys, unload the truck while your mom starts supper and Dianne, you come with me." We turned and went out the narrow gate behind our house and found a little family of three waiting for us.

The man explained, "My wife was weak from diarrhea and fainted into her cooking fire. Her milk has dried up and our child has no nourishment."

Dad opened the clinic and asked the woman to come in. When she unwrapped the shawl from her upper body, I gasped. Her right breast and chest were covered with second and third-degree burns. Dad assessed the situation and then reached for the large container of sulfa powder. "First we have to remove the charred skin because the burned area is starting to get infected. As I pull off the pieces with the forceps, sprinkle those areas with this powder." Some of the pieces bled when he tugged at them, and when I winced, the woman gave me a quizzical look. She was wondering, I supposed, why a young woman my age didn't know that pain was never to be expressed.

When all the infected places were treated, Dad reached for a square tin box filled with layers of gauze saturated in A & D Ointment®. "This will be the most challenging part of all and here's where I'll really need your help. We have to cover her breast with these pieces of gauze and figure out how to keep them in place. We'll work together, but I want you to be the one to touch her, not me." I took a deep breath, and we began. There were a finite number of those eight inch squares and we had to make them last, so we cut them into the sizes and shapes we needed as we went along. When everything was covered, we used rolls of plain gauze until her burned breast was securely wrapped. At that point, I suggested that we continue the plain gauze up around her neck to make a sling to hold everything in place. Covering the burns on her upper chest was easier because there was healthy skin next to the burned area where we could put adhesive tape. The sling idea worked and now all we could do was wait.

"I'll give her some pills to treat her dysentery and some aspirin to help with her pain. You run to the house and wash your hands with lots of soap. Tell mom we need powdered milk and filtered water for the baby."

Back at the house, Mom was busy making supper and I could see that the truck had been unloaded. After I washed my hands, the boys gathered round and I gave everyone a summary of what had happened and told Mom about the baby. "Could you tell how old he is?" she asked. I had to think a minute and then said it was hard to tell, but probably less than a year because I didn't think he was walking. She got down our tin of powdered milk and started to read the label. "Well, it's not formula, but it's all we have for now." She got out a smaller tin and measured two bottles worth of powder into it, handed it to me along with a pitcher of filtered water and I was off to the clinic again.

When I got there, the woman was clutching her little packets of tablets so all we needed were the glass baby bottles which Dad found on the top shelf of the dispensary. I showed the mother how to measure the water into the bottle, add the milk powder, screw on the nipple, and shake it till the powder dissolved. I told her to rinse the bottles very well after each use and told her husband to come back tomorrow for more powder and water. When Dad got home after walking them to the guest hut he said, "We need to pray for them, kids. I'm more worried about the baby than I am about the mother. If he won't take the bottle or if the milk doesn't agree with him, I'll have to take them to Bamako tomorrow."

The baby took the bottle, the mother's burns slowly healed and her milk came back. The day they returned to their village, they came onto the compound to say goodbye. The little boy's cheeks, peeking out from the cloth that tied him to his mother's back, were nice and plump. I will never forget how the young mother took my hands in hers and thanked me, her eyes shining bright and then brimming with tears. My Bambara limited me to the customary, "No problem" but I hope that my eyes, brimming with tears as well, conveyed to her that it had been my honor to help her.

February flew by and in March it was time to open the barrels, find new clothes for the boys and start packing their trunks for Mamou. It was the end of March, 1965. David was finishing Grade 10, John was finishing Grade 6 and Rich was finishing Grade 5. We took them to Bamako and our last words were, "See you in four months at Dalaba!" and they were gone.

Back at Sanankoro, the hot season was upon us. With no electricity for fans, it was brutal, but I settled back into the calm routine I had followed in the fall. One day, to break the monotony, I went with Dad to Dioila. As Dad flipped through our mail at the post office, he handed a letter to me. It was from Lynn, my classmate at Mamou, telling me about the courses he was taking and about his life on his station in the Ivory Coast. I had good news to share in my letter back to him. Come September, David's classmate Mary Kroeker would be coming to live at Sanankoro with her Aunt Katherine and would study with us. Writing back and forth to Lynn and looking forward to David and Mary's company that coming fall made me feel less alone, less weird.

A month or so later, another letter made me happy again. The first paragraph read, "You have been named an Honorable Mention Student in your division among high school students enrolled at the University of Nebraska Extension Division in the Annual Certificate of Award Competition." Included with the letter was an alphabetical list of all the outstanding students studying overseas. I flipped to page two and smiled when I saw that Lynn's name was there too.

Retouched by Chuck Jarrell

After I finished my last units of Grade 11 in June, Mom and I began preparing for our four-week vacation in Dalaba with the boys. We had to take all our food, including meat, which meant that for several weeks Dad ordered an extra leg of beef from the market at Massigui. He butchered the meat into cuts that would fit inside a quart jar—small roasts, steaks, stew meat and hamburger. All the cuts were cooked thoroughly, put into Mason jars, covered with beef bouillon and cooked in a pressure canner for over an hour. This used an extra tank of propane, but we had no other choice. As the Guinea government had aligned itself with the Soviet Block, its economy had collapsed and the shelves in the stores in Guinea were bare.

Chapter 22

The Last Year I Called Africa Home
Summer 1965–Summer 1966
Grade 12

All my trips to and from Mamou had been in the dry season. How different it was when the elephant grass was high and the rivers were wide and wild! Even more strange was driving down the driveway at Mamou, knowing I was no longer a student there. Thankfully, the new house parents, the Gardners, had loosened up on the rules about parents stopping to see their kids. We saw the boys briefly, told them we'd be back on Friday, and drove up to Dalaba to settle in.

This time Mom and Dad had rented a smaller house on the highest level of the vacation site. Coming out of the over-100 degree temperatures of Mali, it was like heaven to wear flannel pajamas and to curl up under a heavy quilt to sleep. The menus Mom and I had planned worked out well with only one mishap. We had bought a nice round of cheese in Bamako and kept it on the back porch, along with our eggs, to keep them cool. A dog found the cheese and left nothing but the rind!

During the month we were there, David, John and Rich came for two weekends and then two full weeks. I enjoyed being with David's classmates who were just one year behind me, but it had been two full years since I had seen them, so it was not the same as when I had been at Dalaba with my peers. When we left, oh joy, David was in the truck with us!

When we got back to Sanankoro, we still had a few weeks of summer vacation left before Mary arrived. The new classroom building had been built that spring and David and I decided we would create a real classroom in it for our studies. We chose the end classroom because it was close to our house and because it had ventilation on three sides. We set up three desks—two on one side for David and Mary who would be taking Grade 11 courses and one on the other side for me. In early September, Mary's parents brought her to the station and she settled in with her Aunt Katharine. When they left, we began our routine that would last until the girls arrived for Girls School.

Each morning after breakfast, the three of us met in the classroom until lunch. David and Mary studied their subjects at the same time, and I was jealous that they could discuss their assignments with each other. We all shared a typewriter, so I did my typing lessons first and they did theirs after

 me. I empathized with them on their timed assignments but, unlike me, they never freaked out when their work wasn't perfect! That fall, three sets of manila envelopes left the station on their way to Nebraska and it was wonderful for me to have schoolmates once again.

We had barely settled into a nice routine when it was abruptly interrupted. One day I was struck with agonizing abdominal pain and considerable bleeding. At one point, I was lying on the area rug in our living room, writhing in pain. I finally passed a large mass that was definitely not a blood clot. Without hesitation or deliberation, Dad said to Mom, "Put it in a bottle with alcohol. We're going to the mission hospital at Ferke."

It would be a 300-mile trip, starting on the road in front of our station that, in places, was little more than a dirt path. When we reached the main road, we turned east to Sikasso where we spent the night with missionaries. The next morning, we drove south across the Côte d'Ivoire border to Ferkessédougou where we got an appointment at the Conservative Baptist Mission Hospital to see Dr. Dwight Slater in a few days. We then drove on to Bouaké, a large town where we could stock up on supplies and could stay at the guest house on the campus of the Ivory Coast Academy, the Conservative Baptist school for MKs.

On the morning of my appointment, as I was waiting for Mom and Dad in the pickup, a lady approached me. "Who are you?" she asked.

"I'm Dianne Darr," I replied, taken aback by her confrontational tone.

"Why aren't you in class?" she continued.

"Oh, I'm not a student at ICA. I'm taking correspondence courses on the station with my parents in Mali."

Her inquisition continued, "What grade are you in?"

"Twelfth," I replied.

"You are not," she snapped. "You do not look anywhere old enough to be a senior in high school. You are lying."

"I am not," I snapped back. "My parents are in there, checking us out of the guest house. When they come out, ask them yourself." She waited, she asked and she was told—but she didn't apologize.

At our appointment with Dr. Slater, we explained the writhing pain I had experienced and showed him the bottle with its mysterious contents. He poured the mass onto a metal tray and stretched it out using forceps. "Look," he said, "see how it's shaped like a pear? It's a uterine cast.[29] We don't know what causes them, but instead of the lining of the womb sloughing off during a normal menstrual period, it builds up for a few months and comes out all at once." Then, looking kindly at me, he said, "It was really painful, wasn't it?" I nodded, thankful for his validation. Unfortunately, the cause was not known, but he prescribed shots of Lutogyl once a month[30] to induce normal periods until I returned to the States.

By now I had seen five doctors in four countries on three continents about my bleeding. So far, the only real cure might be the birth of a child but that wasn't likely to happen any time soon and not just because I was just seventeen. Who would want to marry me, an uneducated misfit who looked like a child? My worries about my body combined with my fears of being a freak began to carve a canyon of anxiety and despair inside me. But, thankfully, this year at least I was not alone.

David and I were gone about a week but we didn't miss any deadlines for our assignments. We did more, of course, than just study. In our free time, I kept up with my sewing and Mom and I completed a large paint-by-number project. David and I both enjoyed playing the organ and helping mom with the cooking and baking. David's love and understanding of animals evolved into him being in charge of our dog Major and of the chickens, the eggs and the baby chicks. This kept him busy several times a day and also put him at the center of two dramatic events.

When there were baby chicks, David fed them termites several times a week. He would drive down the dirt road on our motor bike, spot a termite hill, knock part of it over, put the pieces in a bucket tied to the back of the bike and come home in under an hour. But one morning, an hour came and went, and he didn't come home. We were worried. Perhaps he had fallen off the bike and was hurt. Snakes were also a real danger and, although I knew it was highly unlikely, pictures of hyenas kept flitting through my mind. When he wasn't back in an hour and a half, Dad set out in the Jeep to look for him. Within a few minutes, we heard the pickup heading back toward the station and when it came into view, there was David riding ahead of it. He had spotted the top of a termite hill a little way off the road and had walked through high elephant grass to get to it. When he turned to walk out, he had

---

[29] Silver, Natalie. What Is a Decidual Cast?, Healthline, December 19, 2019. https://www.healthline.com/health/womens-health/decidual-cast#causes
[30] Dwight M. Slater, M.D. letter to Dianne Darr, March 31, 1966.

been swallowed by a sea of grass and he couldn't see the road. He had just made his way out when he heard the Jeep approaching.

Another morning, before I was even out of bed, I heard David screaming, "Dad! There's a humongous snake in the chicken coop!" By the time I threw on my robe, Dad was rushing out the door with his shotgun. When Mom and I got to the coop, Dad was peering over the top of the door. "It's still curled up and not moving." He cautiously lifted the gun over the top of the door and took aim but, instead of shooting, he paused and said, "It's in a dead sleep, digesting the chickens it ate. If I shoot it with the shot gun, there will be little holes all over the skin and that won't look good if we get it tanned. David, run and get the pellet gun." He brought it back, dad put a pellet in it and pumped it with so many pumps that I was sure the entire thing would pop. He leaned over the door, took aim and fired. The python didn't move, but just to be on the safe side, he put another pellet into its brain.

By now Sedu had joined us. Dad sent him to the warehouse for a rake. He opened the door, prodded the snake with the handle and it barely moved. He then used the rake to pull the entire mass out into the open where it twitched slightly and then didn't move at all. Sedu stretched it out to its full 12 feet and there were no holes at all in that beautiful skin. He skinned it and cut it open to remove three young chickens. The first one it had swallowed was a slimy mass with only its beak and feet still intact, the second had just its feathers gone, and the last one looked like a wet chicken.

Sedu hung the meat over the clothesline to keep it clean. Then he stretched the skin, flesh side up, onto a very long board and tacked it down with small nails, rubbed it with coarse salt and left it to dry in the hot African sun. Later that day, when he left for home, he slung the snake meat over his shoulder and it nearly touched the ground. It would provide more protein for his extended family than they usually ate in a month. On our next trip to Bamako, the crispy skin lay in the back of the pickup. Dad took it to the tanner in Bamako and David has it to this day.

Now that the new classroom building was completed, Dad could turn his attention to visiting the little groups of believers in the villages surrounding Sanankoro. He also preached each Sunday in the little mud church that stood near the village. The men sat on the mud benches on the right and the women sat on the left. Women, wearing nothing but a skirt, often nursed their naked babies or cradled them to sleep during the service. I don't have anything against organ music, oak beams and stained-glass windows, but five decades later I sometimes look around me in church and wonder, "What is all this stuff and what does it have to do with worshiping God?"

 On Wednesday nights, we would light two kerosene lanterns that would light our way to the village where Dad would meet for Bible study and prayer with the men in one believer's hut and Mom and I would meet with the women and children in another. For some reason, this did not intimidate her, perhaps because it was scripted. She read a Bible passage in Bambara followed by a printed lesson that went with the passage. After that, several women prayed and mom closed with a final prayer. It was lovely sitting on a tiny three-legged stool, seven inches off the mud floor, watching the flickering lantern cast shadows on the wall that encircled us, listening to my mother pray.

On Friday evenings on the station, the two households took turns hosting each other in their homes. It always ended with hymn singing and prayer but before that we played board games, sat around and talked and shared a treat like cookies, cake, popcorn or fudge. The biggest treat was when we made homemade ice cream. The freezer in a kerosene refrigerator is about the size of a shoebox, but between our fridge and the two that Elsie and Katherine owned, we could save up enough ice if we planned ahead. Mary, David and I took turns cranking the ice-cream maker until the ice cream was churned. It never got really hard because the ice melted pretty fast and there was barely enough of it, but we called it soft serve and slurped it down.

When the Girls School sessions began in December, David, Mary and I set up a study area at Mary's aunt's house which was quiet all morning, had a larger living room than ours and didn't have little brothers coming in and out. Once again, the Christmas pageant was the highlight of the season. During the closing song, I stared at the ebony sky, brilliant with stars, moved by the moment but at the same time feeling a pang of sadness knowing I would never experience Christmas this way again.

It was not lost on me that some of the Bambara girls were feeling the same way. By next year, those who were 16 would be married. All the girls faced marriages that had been arranged by their male relatives when they were little girls. I tried not to think about what lay ahead for them including the high risk of death in childbirth, an infant mortality rate of 25%, and years of hard work hauling water, cutting firewood, and pounding grain. Mostly I hoped their education and their exuberant faith would carry them through whatever lay ahead.

We had put up our little Christmas tree as usual, but this year there would be no presents. Mali's alignment with the Soviet Block had led it down the same path that Guinea had followed. Mali's currency had no value and the shelves in Bamako were bare. Because of that, we were told our Christmas presents would come in February when we would travel to Burkina Faso to get supplies. But just for fun, my brothers and I wrapped an old puzzle and some of our books to put under the tree. On Christmas morning, we gathered around the tree. "Wow, the puzzle I always wanted!" someone joked and at that Mom burst into tears. She had tried to take the economic situation in the country in stride but seeing us with no presents to open on Christmas morning was too much for her. We gathered round her, assured her we were okay, and left the other packages under the tree as the props we all knew they really were.

Right before the school year ended, a man on a bicycle brought a small bundle to the Malian couple who were in charge of the Girls School dorm. They opened it and found the Bible of a girl named Nyagali who had graduated the year before. In the Bible was a note to her parents telling them that should she die, she wanted her Bible to go back to her schoolmates at the Girls School. At that news, a wailing rose up from the girls that haunts me to this day. Her Muslim husband had forbidden her to read her Bible and then, mysteriously, she had died. This made a profound impression on me and I resolved to measure any tragedy in my life by the terrible price this sweet girl had paid for her education and her faith.

That year the National Church Conference was held at Sanankoro. Missionaries and church leaders from all over southern Mali came. After one of the sessions, Dad invited all the pastors to our home for pancakes. Mom and I fried pancakes until a quadruple batch of batter was gone and the men had literally licked their plates clean. One of the missionaries was not amused, telling Dad that it was not good to set a precedent like that. Dad didn't care. Why shouldn't he host his Malian colleagues in his home?

Dad was different from many of his fellow GMU missionaries in another way. Dad owned guns and not just the shotgun that had appeared the morning of the python. He also had a .22 and a .300 Savage which he told us could drop an elephant. These were kept in his closet and we were never to go near them. One of the uses for the shotgun was to shoot chicken hawks. When the chickens in the yard started scattering and cackling in panic, someone would yell "Hawk." Dad would run into his bedroom, load the shotgun, run into the yard, aim at the circling hawk high above and fire. Every single time, the hawk dropped like a rock.

Losing a chicken would have been a shame, but being bit by a rabid dog could kill you; hence, another use for the shotgun. Dad was often asked to come to the village to shoot a rabid dog and once he shot one on the road outside our fence. One day during noon rest, our dog Major was attacked by a rabid dog right outside our front door. Round and round the two dogs went, snarling, yipping and biting at each other. Dad loaded his rifle, opened the screen door a crack and put the barrel of the gun through it. It seemed like the dogs would tangle forever, but in the one split second they separated, there was a boom and the rabid dog was lying motionless on its side. Being so close to a rabid dog, with its spit and blood splattered on my front porch, terrified me for weeks. I was sure some minuscule drop of one or the other had gotten into an invisible scratch on my skin and I was doomed.

This incident wasn't the only thing that affected me like that. One afternoon, someone called from our kitchen door where I found a man holding his young son unconscious across his arms. Dad took him to the clinic and then went for Elsie. When he got back, he asked me how close I had been to them. I assured him I had only talked to the man through the screen. "Okay. It's probably still a good idea to wash your hands. It's meningitis." Elsie treated him, but the boy died the next day. For weeks, I was terrified every time I got a headache or felt a twinge in my neck or shoulders. I understand now that fears like this are a typical symptom of people who have experienced trauma as a child.[31] Although my parents were sympathetic, I knew they thought I was being irrational and so after a while, I kept my terror to myself and just endured.

Excelling in my studies kept the terror at bay. In February, an article about me, picture and all, was featured in the University of Nebraska News, Supervised Correspondence Division Edition. In April, I once again made the list as one of the outstanding high school students of the year studying overseas. I added it to the letter from the year before and hoped it meant that I was at least halfway prepared academically for college.

I finished my last semester of high school in June and during the month of July, Mom and I spent many mornings canning meat for our trip to Dalaba. This year, because canned goods were no longer available in Bamako, we also canned carrots, tomatoes and green beans from the large garden that Dad and Sedu had planted. When David and I packed for Dalaba, we also packed to leave Mali for good. When we pulled away from the station I was saying good-bye to a place I would never see again.

---

[31] *"Risk factors for illness anxiety disorder may include: history of abuse as a child, a serious childhood illness or a parent with a serious illness."* Illness Anxiety Disorder, The Mayo Clinic. https://www.mayoclinic.org/diseases-conditions/illness-anxiety-disorder/symptoms-causes/syc-20373782

Just like the year before, our family was together at Dalaba for two weekends and two full weeks. A banquet was planned for the Grade 10 students who would be leaving Mamou to return to America. It was to be held on a Friday evening and David and I were invited. I happened to be sitting at a table across from an MK whose father was the GMU Field Director at the time. She kept referring to a missionary named Don who sometimes came to Bamako on business. She was almost giddy as she told stories about the funny things he said and did and added that she always looked forward to when he came to eat at their house. I ran through the list of names of every missionary in French West Africa and, to my knowledge, there was only one whose name was Don and that was my abuser. I literally turned cold. For the rest of the meal, the real me was floating near the ceiling watching my ice-cold body eating and talking like nothing at all was wrong.[32]

I told Dad. Dad checked. It was true.

My parents' colleagues, who had supported us in 1959, had decided that seven years was long enough for Don to suffer and it was high time that my parents forgive him. Furthermore, they argued, why should Don waste the Lord's money on a hotel room when the GMU Guest House was there for missionaries to use?

It's a long ride from the mountains of Dalaba to Bamako. It was hard sitting between my parents in the front of the pickup, listening to them strategize about what to do in light of this startling information. But in hindsight, I'm glad it happened. When I told about the abuse when I was ten, I wasn't aware of what Mom and Dad went through to champion me. At eighteen, I learned from their example that when you are wronged, you don't just react emotionally. You deliberate first and then you calmly stand up for the truth.

David and I had a few days in Bamako before it was time to board our Air France flight back to America where David would take his twelfth-grade year and where I would start college. That didn't intimidate me. What bothered me was that even though I had tried so hard to keep my vow to never upset them, I was leaving my parents to face, once again, a controversy on account of me.

---

[32] *"Symptoms of depersonalization include: Feelings that you're an outside observer of your ... body— for example, as if you were floating in air above yourself."* Depersonalization-derealizastion Disorder. https://www.mayoclinic.org/diseases-conditions/depersonalization-derealization-disorder/symptoms-causes/syc-20352911, (Mayo Foundation for Medical Education and Research (MFMER, 1998-2018).

Chapter 23

The Old World Haunts Me in My New World
Freshman Year of College in Greenville
September 1966–June 1967

David and I flew from Bamako to Paris with the Tschetters, their daughter Nancy and David Wiens who had both just finished Grade 10 at Mamou. What should have been a routine change of planes in Paris turned into a nightmare because Air France was on strike and only a few of their planes were flying. The airport was crowded with people waiting for flights and the lines were long. While David and I waited in line for our flight, Ed Tschetter came up to us and said, "We all have seats on the next plane. Good luck." And we were on our own.

When we finally reached the counter, the agent told us to wait where we could hear her if she called our names. A half hour later she motioned to us and said, "Walk down the steps, cross the tarmac, walk around the wing and go up the steps to First Class. You have the last two seats on the plane." When the stewardess showed us to our seats I sat down and burst into tears of exhaustion, relief and gratitude. First class did not disappoint. The service was wonderful and the food divine. We landed in Newark and got a flight to Akron the next day.

Aunt Shelly (our mom's youngest sister, the one in whose car I had overheard mom telling about my abuse) met us at the airport. We stayed with Aunt Shelly, Uncle Ron and Cousin Ronnie for a couple of weeks and then we went to stay with Uncle John and Aunt Fern, our dad's oldest brother and his wife. This put us closer to church and back with our cousins where we had stayed eight years before when I came down with hepatitis.

Both Shelly and Fern helped us shop for clothes and supplies for college but we soon ran out of money. I knew GMU would send us money from Mom and Dad's account, but by the time I contacted them and they sent it, it would be too late. I wrote a letter to the missions committee at Goss, asking if they could give David and me $50 each and take it out of our parents' next support check. After church the next Sunday, I was handed an envelope with $200 in it and a note saying it was their gift to us.

Mom and Dad had written to their pastor friend in Atwater, letting him know we were enrolled at Bob Jones University and asking if he could help arrange a ride for us to Greenville. Sure enough, I got a phone call from the pastor's daughter one day, inviting David and me to a bonfire at the church where we would meet some of the kids who attended BJU and make arrangements for driving down to the school. Before she hung up she said, "My boyfriend and I will come to pick you up around 5:00." I pictured the two guys Susan had pointed out in her yearbook two years before and wondered, "Will it be Denny or will it be Bud?" When she drove up, it was Denny. I was curious what had happened to Bud but, after two years, it would have been inappropriate to ask.

A few weeks later, David and I were in a car making the trip from Akron to Greenville, South Carolina, a trip we had made so often as preschoolers. But this time we were students, heading off to college with Jack Pittman, a kid from the Sunday School class at Atwater Baptist Church where we'd been asked about Tarzan years ago. I vaguely remember arriving on campus, Aunt Peggy arriving from Toccoa the next day to help us register, standing in line to schedule my classes and checking into the dorm. My three roommates were Bobbie, Cindy and Neila. Our room had two bunk beds, two closets, four dressers and a sink in the corner by the window. The bathroom was down the hall. Other than the size of the dorm, it wasn't much different from Mamou. There was daily room inspection, a strict study time after supper, a strict bedtime, and a strict wake up time. The dress code was even stricter than at Mamou. Girls wore dresses at all times other than for sports. Chapel and Sunday services were mandatory and so were meals except for breakfast, which saved me. As usual, I found it hard to fall asleep and didn't sleep well when I did. I had to be out of bed no later than 7:30 or else. To sleep until that time meant I'd miss breakfast, but it was the choice I had to make. Every morning I got a pastry from the vending machine downstairs and made do. Even so, I was sleep deprived the entire time I was there.

Two weeks or so into the school year I was so exhausted that I could not get off my bunk to go to supper. When the hall monitor found me in bed during her room check, I burst into tears and said I could not go. "You either go to supper or to the infirmary," she said firmly.

"Well," I answered, "since I don't have the strength to make it to supper, someone will have to get me to the infirmary." After a night of rest, I felt better and so they sent me back to the dorm. Two weeks later, I was back. This time I told the nurse that I had come from Africa and that's when I met Dr. John Dreisbach. He had served at the SIM hospital in Lagos, Nigeria with people from my home church, Dr. Jeanette Troup and Dr. Roger Troup, the doctor who had helped my mother during her nervous breakdown. His diagnosis was malaria, even though I had taken my antimalarial medication for the prescribed amount of time after returning to the U.S. I stayed in the infirmary for a couple of days to rest and to allow the antimalarial medicine to take effect and then I bravely walked back to the dorm, hoping I would have the strength to make it through the semester.

I was barely back on my feet when an unexpected aftershock from my abuse hit me. I was reading a letter from Mom and Dad while walking back to the dorm. However, instead of the normal chit-chat about life at Sanankoro, this letter included a synopsis of a meeting that had taken place with the Gospel Missionary Union field council, a Mission Endeavor International missionary from Mali, a MEI administrator who had flown in from the States, Don who had abused David and me, and Dad. I stopped walking when I read, "Don had been telling missionaries you seduced him, but at the meeting he signed a full confession admitting that he was solely responsible for molesting David and you."

My thoughts reeled. "They let him stay at the guesthouse because he blamed me and they believed him." I had to step off the sidewalk because everything around me had disappeared except for the letter in my hands, a tiny patch of blue sky directly over my head and a little circle of grass around my feet. Rooted there, between heaven and earth, another thought hit me like lightning. "What if Robert were alive and accused me of the same thing?" At that I felt myself disappearing too until a second bolt jolted me back to the green patch around my feet: "Fire fell. He's dead."

Half a lifetime ago, when I was still a child, I had thought this was over. However, in the years since, I had come to understand the depravity of what had been done to my body. Now, as an eighteen-year old, reading that my abuser had been attacking my reputation too was utterly shocking.[33] The injustice of it all fell into my soul with a thud and I knew the weight of it would be there until the day I died. However, simultaneously, my spirit rose up with great resolve that in spite of that soul-crushing weight, I would continue to fulfill my vows: never to upset my parents, to prove my naysayers wrong, and to carry life's sorrows unflinchingly.

When the circle of grass around my feet grew large enough to include the sidewalk, I stepped onto it, squared my shoulders, stared at the doorway to the dorm and forced my feet to take me there. It helped that I could share the letter with David and express my outrage at what I had been accused of. We were both glad there was finally a confession, but we agreed that the GMU missionaries had betrayed us and that Don may have signed a confession but, if he had been truly repentant for his actions, he wouldn't

---

[33] *A hallmark trait of child sexual abusers is to blame others for their actions, most often their victims. They typically fail to take responsibility for committing abuse. On the contrary, they see themselves as victims.*
Scott, Halee Gray. (June 16, 2014). To Publish a Predator. Christianity Today.

have spread lies about me to cover them up and it wouldn't have taken a showdown to get him to confess.

It also helped that our mom's sister Peggy lived less than two hours away. Peggy's husband Julian was the director of the music department at Toccoa Falls Bible College, just over the border into Georgia. One Friday afternoon in October she came and took David and me home with her for the weekend. It was wonderful to be off campus and to be with our cousins Greg, Tim and Peggy Lynn. Because Toccoa was a Christian and Missionary Alliance School, I knew Mamou alumni attended there, including Stanley, but I doubted that we would get to meet any of them. However, what I didn't know was that the teachers at Toccoa ate their evening meal in the student dining hall, so we did get to see them.

After dinner, Stanley walked me home. Peggy's house was small, so I was staying at the home of her in-laws, Dr. and Mrs. Bandy. It was over a little bridge that crossed the stream that ran through the campus. As we crossed the bridge, Stanley took my hand and when we got inside the house, we sat on the couch and he kissed me. A minute later we heard footsteps on the porch and when Dr. Bandy walked in to the living room I said, "Stanley and I were classmates at Mamou and he walked me home." He simply nodded and went upstairs. I stood up and once again, like on that enchanted moonlit night when we were children, I said, "I have to go." We exchanged addresses and promised to write. At the door we kissed again, and he was gone.

The following week I was shocked to get a notice in my mail box telling me to report to the Dean of Women's office. When I sat down in the chair in front of her desk, trembling, she asked me why I had gone off campus for the weekend when I knew I was not allowed. I was stunned and asked her to explain. "Any student admitted to the university with a high school transcript from a correspondence school is automatically on probation until the end of the first semester. Probation prohibits you from leaving campus for a weekend until we see your first semester grades," she intoned.

"I did everything I was supposed to do to sign out and no one mentioned that," I responded, "and no one explained that to me when I enrolled." She lowered her head to look at me over the top of her glasses. When she remained silent, I continued. "And, if you want to check with my teachers, I have As and Bs in all my classes."

"Okay. You can go now." And then, sternly, "But don't leave campus again until we take you off probation." She never got back to me and I didn't get in trouble, so either she believed me or she checked with my teachers and decided to let it slide.

My classes that semester were English Composition, History of Civilization, New Testament Survey, Speech and Minor Sports. The day we got our grades, I walked into my room to find my roommates discussing their report cards. Neila, who was a freshman like me, was worried because she had, as I remember it, two Cs and two Ds. Cindy, who was a junior, was laughing about her grades which weren't much better. Bobbie was a senior and was happy with what she had, but hoped to bring one or two of her grades up by the end of the semester. I kept quiet. Finally, Cindy said, "Come on, Dianne, you have to tell us yours too!"

"I have all As and Bs," I said quietly.

"You do not," Cindy said emphatically. "Let me see."

She grabbed my report card and stopped dead in her tracks. Neila looked at my grades over Cindy's shoulder, turned and looked at me and said, in awe, "You have an A in Biology? How did you do that?"

"I don't know," I replied sheepishly. "It's just easy." I didn't bother to explain French school, Mamou and the study skills I had acquired doing correspondence courses in Africa.

Each night after dinner, the students streamed out of the dining room and went to check their mailboxes one last time. One evening, in the middle of that throng, I found Stanley standing right in front of me. He reached for my hand and I pulled it away. "What are you doing here? You can't be here!"

"Can't we just talk?"

"No, we can't. Even people who are students here have to go to the dating parlor to talk and someone from off campus has to sign up ahead of time. How did you even get on campus?"

"I came with some other guys and we just drove in."

"You just drove in? Past the security gate?"

By now I was hyperventilating and scared out of my mind. "You have to go, Stanley, I'm sorry, but you have to go. I don't want to be in trouble. Please, please, just go."

The crowd had thinned by now and I hoped that no one was watching. Stanley was stunned and bewildered. What kind of a place was this that he couldn't talk to me? What kind of a place had me so terrified? He would soon find out. Even though he and his buddies got through the gates, someone reported them to the Dean of Men at Toccoa Falls for trespassing after dark on the BJU campus and they were in trouble. I also got called in by a BJU administrator who questioned me about the incident. Had I invited him? Did I talk to him? I told him that Stanley had simply appeared on campus, I had spoken to him very briefly and had told him to leave. Even though he seemed satisfied with my answers, I held my breath for days worrying that the Dean of Women and my interrogator would compare notes and somehow find me guilty of something worthy of shipping me out.

I fully intended to keep writing to Stanley and to see him the next time I visited Toccoa, but that would not happen. Word spread throughout the mission community in West Africa that Stanley was in trouble at Toccoa and that we were dating. I got a letter from my parents expressing their concerns and asking me not to date him. I cried and thought it terribly unfair, but my vow to never upset them again was stronger than my feelings for him and I wrote him that I couldn't see him alone again.

And then it was time to go back to Akron for Christmas break. David was flying to South Dakota to be with Judy Tschetter, his girlfriend from Mali. Jack, the fellow from Atwater who had brought David and me to school, was driving first to his fiancée's house, so he couldn't give me a ride home, but promised me a place going back to school in January. Someone offered me a ride as far as Cincinnati where Uncle John and Aunt Fern came to get me. I had not realized when I made that arrangement that Cincinnati was a four-hour drive from Akron, but they came and didn't complain about that trip or about having me, once again, in their home.

While in Akron, I reconnected with my friends at Goss, went to a Koehl family Christmas party and helped my Darr cousins decorate their Christmas tree but, in spite of all that, I was very lonely. I was upset about my parents' directive not to see Stanley, I missed David, I wanted to sit with my parents and brothers under the African stars to hear the Girls School choir and I didn't want to be in a twin bed in my younger cousin Bob's room, pretending like I didn't know he was smoking after the lights went out. If he heard me sobbing every night into my pillow, he never asked me why.

When I called Jack to find out where to meet him to return to school, I was surprised to learn that we'd be meeting at dusk and driving all night in order to arrive at BJU some time on Sunday morning. The school frowned on students driving all day on the Lord's Day and, should something happen to delay us on the road, Jack didn't want to risk arriving after the dorms were locked at night. That is how it happened that on December 31, 1966, I found myself in a cold, dark parking lot hugging Aunt Fern and Uncle John goodbye and climbing into Jack's car with three people I didn't know. As the car pulled away, I knew one year was ending and a new one was about to begin. What I didn't know was that that New Year's Eve would mark the beginning of the rest of my life.

Jack introduced me to the others in his car. His fiancée, Margie, was sitting next to him in the front seat and her warm welcome made me feel at ease. She introduced me to Rose Curry in the middle of the back seat. I recognized her right away because, alphabetically, Curry comes before Darr and we sat near each other in two lecture classes. Beside her, sitting behind

200

Jack, was Bud. I leaned forward and said hello, but I couldn't really see him in the dark. Could this be the Bud that the pastor's daughter had told me about two and a half years before? If yes, where had he been? He hadn't been at the bonfire in August nor in the car with us driving down to Greenville last fall. "Probably not him," I said to myself.

We had not driven very far when Rose dozed off and her head fell over onto my shoulder. I adjusted myself to accommodate her, but with every passing mile her body leaned heavier and heavier against mine until I was smashed against the side of the car and could barely move. At one point, I slowly heaved her back into an upright position and placed her head directly above her neck on the back of the seat, only to have her slump over onto my shoulder again. Bud noticed and we shared a chuckle over Rose's impressive ability to sleep so soundly. I knew that at some point we'd have to stop for gas, so I just resigned myself to being her mattress until then.

Rose woke up when the car stopped and while Jack got gas in the car, we three ladies went into the restroom. Out of earshot of the guys, I asked Margie, "Is Bud the guy the pastor's daughter went steady with in high school?"

"Yes," she answered, "but how did you know?"

"She told me about him and Denny just before I went back to Africa two years ago."

"Well," she continued, "Bud has not dated anyone since but whoever catches him has a keeper."

Before we got back in the car, I suggested to Rose that she might be more comfortable leaning on the side of the car to sleep instead of on me. The blank look on her face told me that she hadn't even been aware that she had been doing that, but I wasn't about to be squished the rest of the way to Greenville. She let me climb into the middle and she sat by the door and was out within minutes. Before long, Bud was holding my hand, and as the radio announcer finished counting down the seconds to midnight, Jack leaned over and kissed his girl and Bud kissed me. He proved to be a keeper and I have been his girl ever since.

That semester, since I was off academic probation, I was allowed to take a heavier load. I added French II to my class load and, for my second required semester of PE, I got a coveted spot in the Beginning Fencing class.

"Great," I remember complaining. "I get a boyfriend and this fencing mask is a disaster for my hairdo."

Besides a heavy class load, I was also learning the ropes of dating at Bob Jones University where a 6-inch rule was enforced between the boys and the girls. There were perks, however to dating Bud who was a respected senior, one of the head ushers and a room monitor for three junior high boys. For one thing, he ushered in the Concert Hall where I was assigned for

Vespers and afterwards I would wait for him while he finished up and then he would walk me back to the dorm.

One night it took him longer than usual to lock everything up. I waited as I always did on a bench just inside the front door. Just as Bud was returning to the lobby, a girl walked in to look for something she had left on her seat. Something told me I should leave and walk to the dorm alone, but Bud said, "Wait here," so I did. Sure enough, the girl turned us in as everyone in that place was taught to do if they suspected someone was breaking the rules. Once again, I was explaining myself to the Dean of Women and Bud found himself, for the first time in four years, explaining himself to the Dean of Men. Bud was a senior and in a position of trust, so the blame and the punishment fell on him. He was to be demoted to a regular usher position for the rest of the semester. I was furious. I told him if he accepted their punishment he was admitting his guilt and we weren't guilty of anything. He had a right to walk me back to the dorm and waiting for him was not a crime.

My anger over that was mild compared to how upset I was after chapel one day. The spring of 1967 was at the height of the Civil Rights Movement and Bob Jones University would have none of it.[34] The speaker that morning had lowered his voice and in words as smooth as a silk had urged us to hold firm to the truth that the Negro race was inferior to ours. He gave several examples, one of which was this, "There are Negro football players, but be assured, there will never be a Negro quarterback. They are not smart enough to lead the team." I pictured Yuba and Thaddée and Sedu and the Girls School girls and, as he continued to speak, my cheeks burned hot with indignation. I decided right then that, since I was stuck there, I would let them educate me, but I certainly wouldn't let their legalism and their bigotry contaminate my soul.

At the very end of the semester, I ended up back at the infirmary. The pain started with a dull ache in my lower back and escalated to heavy cramping. When one contraction doubled me over, I knew I had to go to the infirmary. It was on the edge of campus and I walked there alone, bending over and gasping when a contraction hit and then walking as fast as I could before the next wave doubled me over again. When the nurse asked me what was wrong, I said, "Please call Dr. Dreisbach and tell him I am passing a uterine cast. I've had one before." I was gasping in pain while she called him and when she hung up, she motioned for me to follow her to a room where she handed me a gown, pointed to a bed and then left me alone, sobbing in

---

[34] Due to its racial policies, Bob Jones University's tax-exempt status was revoked in 1976, retroactive to 1970. The case went all the way to the Supreme Court. https://www.britannica.com/event/Bob-Jones-University-v-United-States

pain. She hadn't said a word, treating me as though I were some hysterical college girl who didn't know how to cope with menstrual cramps.

Within an hour it was over. I stood up by the bed, walked to the door and called down the hall for the nurse to come and help me into the bathroom. When I sat down on the toilet and showed her the solid, pear-shaped mass lying on my blood-soak sanitary pad she gasped and froze. "Great," I thought. "She thinks I've had a miscarriage. Next she'll be calling the dean of women to report that a pregnant girl was living in the dorm and I'll be shipped before dawn."

"Call Dr. Dreisbach and ask him if he wants to see it," I said, my voice firm. I knew that his diagnosis would outrank any of her wild ideas. She scurried back to her desk and returned about five minutes later. "He doesn't need to see it," she said softly. "I brought you a clean pad. Do you need help cleaning up?"

"No, but I'm pretty shaky. Can you stand by the door till I'm done?" When I finished, she helped me across the hall to my room. Before she left I said, "I know you're supposed to leave the door open, but please close it. The light in the hall will keep me awake. And, if possible, ask the morning nurse to let me sleep." She turned off the light and closed the door. I turned over on my right side, pulled the sheet up over my shoulders, closed my eyes and passed out.

I woke the next morning in the same position I had fallen asleep to broad daylight streaming through the window and to a cheery nurse tapping me on the shoulder. "I kept your breakfast as long as I could, but they come at nine to take the trays back to the dining commons so you'd better eat. How are you feeling? I understand you went through quite an ordeal last night." I told her I felt weak but okay. While she cranked up the head of my bed so I could sit up to eat she continued, "Dr. Dreisbach was in early this morning and told me to let you sleep. He's keeping you admitted so we can monitor your bleeding. He'll be back tomorrow." Her voice was kind and caring. "Do you want to place a call to your parents?"

I told her they were in Africa and, at this point, it was unnecessary to send them a telegram. I did have her call my brother David who came for a long visit. His high school graduation was coming up and I was worried I might miss it. I told him to tell Bud who, of course, was not allowed to visit me. I was discharged in time for David's graduation and I was relieved that Bud didn't pry for details when I saw him again.

Between January and June, I had learned a lot about Bud Couts. His father was a crane operator, his mother was a church organist and taught piano lessons. His two oldest brothers had died in a car accident and he had three brothers and two sisters. One important thing I learned was that Bud's real name was George which was the name my dad had always called my future husband when he teased me about marrying a preacher. I always retorted that I hated that name and that I had been a poor missionary kid, so I wasn't about to marry a preacher. I did not intend to share Bud's real name with my parents, but David did. They thought it was hilarious and ribbed me about it in the next letter I got from home.

As the school year was winding down, Bud had informed me that his parents, his sister Sharon and his brother Norm would be driving down for his graduation and there would be room in the car for me to drive back with them. As we pulled off campus, Bud put his arm around

me and the image of myself as an uneducated misfit whose appearance was so childlike that no man would ever love me evaporated. I leaned my head back on his arm, closed my eyes and knew I was home.

Part VI

Weathering the Aftershocks

"Through many dangers, toils and snares, I have already come;
'Tis grace hath brought me safe thus far, and grace will lead me home."
John Newton, *Amazing Grace*

Chapter 24

Mountains High and Valleys Low
Summer 1967–Summer 1973
College in Akron, Marriage, Motherhood, Moving Away

Mom and Dad arranged for David and me to live with Grandma Koehl during the summer of 1967. Every day one or more of our aunts came to visit, often bringing our cousins along. David got a job at the Waterloo Restaurant washing dishes in the evening to save money for another trip to South Dakota to see Judy. Aunt Peggy came up from Toccoa for a few weeks which was lots of fun, except that we had to share a double bed and I was so nervous I'd disturb her that I didn't sleep very well.

Grandma and the aunts thought Bud was, in their words, "a doll." He had been hired at a Baptist church in Medina, 30 miles away, as their Assistant to the Pastor and Choir Director. He came every weekend to see me and some Sundays he would take me back to Medina for the evening service. On his day off, he would take me to visit his parents in Atwater, 30 miles in the opposite direction. Somewhere along the line he told me that he remembered our family visiting his church and that he and his friends had dubbed me "The Ugly Little African" which explained the boys giggling and laughing at me after Sunday School the year I was ten!

In July, David flew to South Dakota to see Judy and that trip turned our lives upside down. When David got to South Dakota, he collapsed. When he was taken to the ER, they saw he was dehydrated and underweight. Without any blood or urine tests, they hooked him up to an IV with glucose and admitted him. He would have died if a doctor had not stopped by his room to check on him one last time before going home. The smell of David's breath indicated that he was in diabetic ketoacidosis. The doctor ordered insulin and sat by his bed until David opened his eyes eight hours later.

In hindsight, it made sense. I had noticed that David would come home from work around 11:00 at night and then would sleep till noon the next day. I asked him about it, but he said it was just the hours he was working. Grandma had noticed crystals in the toilet bowl, but didn't know what they were, so she said nothing. Somehow that summer he had become a Type I diabetic and no one knew. He was 17.

Judy's parents and Nancy had to leave for Africa and Judy and her sister Marcia had to return to their jobs in Omaha. This meant that, in less than 36 hours of learning that David had nearly died, I was on a plane to Chicago with a connecting flight to Sioux Falls. Judy's uncle met me and drove me to Huron, South Dakota. Visiting hours were over at the hospital, so we went straight to Judy's Grandma Hofer's house. She welcomed me with a warm hug and a delicious Mennonite supper. The next morning, just before ten o'clock, I walked alone to the hospital, saying over and over to myself, "Be brave for David." The last I had heard he was at death's door, so what a relief it was to find him sitting up in bed. It was now just a matter of waiting until he learned how to regulate his insulin shots and until he was strong enough to fly back to Akron.

Mom and Dad met the Tschetters in Bamako to get a firsthand account of what had happened to David and immediately decided to pack up and come home. John and Rich told me that when the plane landed in New York City, Mom was literally catatonic and, at one point, unable to move or speak. The airport doctor told Dad to delay their flight to Akron and let her rest. The stress of packing up at a moment's notice, the long flight home and her anxiety about David's condition sent her, once again, over the edge. This time her condition was temporary. After a few hours of rest, they flew to Akron and, when she saw that David was okay, she was fine.

Mom and Dad rented a house in Kenmore and, after we moved in, David and I launched a campaign to persuade Mom and Dad not to send us back to Bob Jones. David, who wanted to study chemistry, argued that The University of Akron had a world-class science program. I argued that I wanted to be near Bud. Mom and Dad argued that we should attend a Christian college. David and I countered that we had spent so many years going to school away from them, why couldn't we be together as a family now that we had the chance? We won them over and, in August, we went down to The University of Akron (often referred to as Akron U.) to register.

We had expected to get the tuition rate for city residents, but the person behind the registration table didn't know what to do with two kids who said they were from Akron but who had lived in South Carolina the past year and whose parents had been living in Africa for the past three years. He called the registrar who told him to send us over to his office.

"Do you have American passports?" he asked. I thought it was an odd question but we said we did. "To get a passport, you have to have an address in one of the fifty States. What is that address?"

"It's our Dad's brother's address, 2465 Conrad Avenue in Kenmore."

"Well then, that's easy. That's an Akron address." He picked up his pen, signed our forms and we were enrolled at the city rate. Another miracle was that my credits transferred from Bob Jones which, at the time, was unaccredited. I was enrolled as a sophomore in the College of Education majoring in French and minoring in English.

I took College Algebra my first year at Akron U. The class was co-taught by two bizarre women who thought that making a craft using math would help us learn. David, in the meantime, was studying advanced math and had no idea how to help me with the most rudimentary of problems. Thankfully, John and Rich, who were in Grades 8 and 9, came to my rescue. I consider the B I got in that class one of the major accomplishments of my academic career.

My French professor, Dr. Claude Meade, grew up in England with his French mother and British father. He had a lovely Parisian accent and appreciated mine. I had a wonderful British literature professor, an inspiring writing professor and a detached grammar professor who based our entire grade on one single thing: our final exam. This totally stressed me out because, by then, I had an academic scholarship and I didn't like not knowing what my grade was. Many students failed the class, but I passed with either an A- or a B+ and, to this day, I can diagram pretty much any sentence in the English language.

Two other professors were impressive for the wrong reasons. My Psychology of Education professor smoked, chewed gum and drank coffee while he lectured all at the same time. My Tests and Measurements professor didn't show up for our first three classes. When he finally appeared on the fourth day of class, he used every 4-letter word to express his disgust at having to teach peons, the word he used to describe us. He was another professor who couldn't be bothered with grading assignments or tests during the quarter, leaving all of us wondering what our grades would be. His final exam had two questions: "What grade do you want in this course?" and "Outline all the testing for Grade 1 through Grade 12 for a school district in Ohio." When I saw question number two, I wrote down a B for question number one. And then, anger rose in me at how he had demeaned us all quarter and had taught us nothing. I scratched out the B and wrote an A in its place, made a skeleton outline for question number two, stood up, walked up to his desk, put the exam down, turned and walked out. I hoped my exit let him know that his sadistic exam didn't intimidate me. And, sure enough, I got an A.

Meanwhile, Bud and I continued to date. My parents not only approved of Bud, they loved him. He was a BJU grad, he was in the ministry and he was a wonderful person. Every Sunday he came to our house for Sunday dinner and, in the afternoon, I'd go back to Medina with him for the evening service at his church. In December of 1967, just before the Christmas Eve Candlelight service at Goss, Bud proposed. My parents' only concern was that I finish college and we promised that I would. We set our wedding date for June of the next year. Aunt Peggy made my wedding gown, Jack Pittman was Bud's best man and Marcia Tschetter was my maid of honor. Our siblings and cousins filled out the wedding party and Goss Church was packed the evening of June 14, 1968 when we got married.

Early in our courtship I had sobbed out the story of my abuse to Bud. He was very understanding and assured me it didn't matter to him. However, during our honeymoon, we learned that courtship was very different from marriage. While some research existed at the time on the effects of childhood sexual abuse in a marriage, it was unknown to me. I just knew that sex was painful, that it always came with flashbacks and that my husband was a saint. However, at least I no longer had to worry about the bleeding problems that had plagued me for the past seven years. We knew that the birth of a child would prevent me from finishing college and so I was on birth control every month, making my periods regular for the first time in my life.

Members of the church in Medina chipped in to pay for our honeymoon at Scott's Oquaga Lake House in New York and when we got home, I moved to

Bud's little apartment on the second floor of Mrs. Weltmer's house on Liberty Street in Medina. Over the next two years I attended all the church services and taught Sunday School. Each summer I helped with Vacation Bible School and was a counselor at church camp, but other than that, I kept to my studies. I managed to find a ride to Akron U every semester with other students and, in the fall of 1970, I got a ride with teachers to Wadsworth High School, where I did my student teaching under the excellent tutelage of Helen Gairing.

It was a good thing I enjoyed being a student. Bud's senior pastor was overbearing, judgmental and delighted in keeping us poor. Until Bud got a job driving school bus, which was something the pastor tried to make him quit, I cried every week because we could barely make ends meet. When the pastor left a letter on Bud's desk castigating him for things that were clearly untrue, Bud went to the chairman of the church board. His response made us realize that things would never change.

"This isn't a surprise," he said. "This is how he treated his assistants before you. When you leave, we won't let him have another one."

It came to a head in the spring of 1970 when Bud asked for vacation time in June so we could attend David and Judy's wedding in South Dakota. The date was during Vacation Bible School and the pastor was adamant that we could not be gone. The conflict ended up going to the board for a vote and they let us go. At that point, while Bud quietly started networking for another job, I quietly developed a stubborn case of colitis which landed me in the hospital. The tests the doctor ran all came back negative and his prescription was to rest over the summer. I realized that Dr. Widemyer, twelve years earlier, had been right after all: being upset can indeed make you have a stomach ache.[35]

In July of 1970, Mom, Dad and Rich returned to Mali. John, however, stayed in Akron until December so that he could play football as a high-school senior. The prior year, when John was a junior on the team, the Kenmore Cardinals had won the 1969 Akron City Championship and the coaches were hoping for a repeat performance. The team did not disappoint, winning the title again on November 26, 1970. Because much of our childhood was disconnected from our roots, it was fun to link our present to our family's past when we watched our brother play for Kenmore and when we saw John's name in the paper as a football star, just like our dad.

---

[35] Thorpe, JR. Trauma Affects Your Digestive Health in Very Real Ways. www.bustle.com/p/trauma-affects-your-digestive-health-in-very-real-ways-31764

In early December, I finished my student teaching and graduated from Akron U. When the dean announced my name, and added *magna cum laude* behind it, I was happy to walk across the stage to get my diploma but I knew I had not done it alone. Bud had supported me and never complained while I finished my degree and, every semester, my parents had made up the difference in my tuition that my scholarships didn't cover. After the ceremony, when I joined David, Judy and Bud in the lobby, elation evaded me. Mostly I felt sad that Mom and Dad were so far away.

Around that same time, after serving for three and a half years in Medina, Bud's networking paid off and he was hired at a Baptist church near Akron where he would serve as Youth and Music Director along with a Senior Pastor and a young Assistant Pastor. Ironically, in early December, just as I was finishing up my student teaching in French, the French teacher at Medina High School was drafted into the Vietnam War and I was hired to replace him. In January of 1971, I would start to commute 43 miles to Medina in the opposite direction I had commuted to Akron U over the past two and a half years.

Right after my graduation, we moved to Akron and rented a house near the church where Bud had started working. He was enjoying his new position and I was okay with mine except for the long commute. In the spring of 1971, I was hired by Cuyahoga Valley Christian Academy (CVCA) to teach French and English in the fall, shortening my commute to 27 miles. I enjoyed my new job at CVCA, but in December I developed symptoms of what I thought was a stomach bug, but they didn't go away. When a restful Christmas break didn't cure me, I wondered if I was pregnant and made an appointment with my gynecologist.

"I'm either deathly ill or I'm pregnant," I told him and he confirmed that it was the latter. When he asked me when I had my last period, it was difficult to answer. After I had gone off the pill in the fall, I had what I thought was a period and then had been spotting on and off ever since. He said this was not uncommon and assured me it would stop as the pregnancy progressed. He guessed I was due in late August or early September. I finished out the year at CVCA very obviously pregnant. At a Fourth of July gathering that summer, Bud's sister Sharon thought I was ready to have the baby any day. She threw her head back and laughed when I told her the baby wasn't due for almost two more months.

Unfortunately, the happy anticipation of having our first child was overshadowed by something dreadful that was happening at church. The Senior Pastor was spending far too much time behind closed doors with his secretary who was going through a divorce. The Assistant Pastor, the Custodian and Bud had all glimpsed him either hugging, or kissing, or touching her inappropriately. The pastor was confronted, he accused the young ministers of wanting to ruin his ministry, the board supported him and Bud was out of a job.

Bud was twenty-seven years old and, in just five years of ministry, he had been badly treated by two different pastors. These things did not come as a surprise to me. I had known since I was ten years old that, in independent Christian organizations, men in leadership answered to no one but themselves. But thankfully, as I had also learned as a child, there were good men who believed the truth. Within weeks, the Assistant Pastor was hired as an intern at a prominent church in Akron and Bud was hired as Choir Director and Public Relations Director at Cuyahoga Valley Christian Academy.

I had something else to be thankful for during that tumultuous time. Mom and Dad were coming home for good at the end of August! Gospel Missionary Union (GMU) had asked Dad to serve as Vice President of Public Affairs at their headquarters in Smithville, Missouri. Although we would be scattered across the country with David and Judy and their baby girl Kerry in Akron near us, John at Wheaton College near Chicago and Rich at Columbia Bible College in South Carolina, at least we were all on the same continent.

Other than the spotting and the morning sickness, my pregnancy had been normal. My labor and delivery, on the other hand, were not. On August 29, 1972, my water broke at home. Bud took me to the hospital around 4:00 in the afternoon and waited in the waiting area as men did in those days. Around 9:00, as the labor got intense, I was given something that took the edge off the contractions and then, around 10:30, first a nurse came in to check the baby's heartbeat, followed immediately by an intern, followed immediately by a doctor.

"Is there something wrong with my baby?" I asked.

"Yes. Your labor is hard and you're barely dilated. It's causing stress for the baby. We've called your doctor."

A half hour later my doctor appeared at the foot of my bed and said, "This girl will never have this baby. Prep her for a C-Section." Within minutes I was in the operating room and at 11:20 p.m., my baby boy was born. I woke up an hour later with Bud sitting by my bed.

"It's a boy," he said. "He is huge. He weighs 9 pounds, 6 ounces and is 22 inches long!" And then he added, "You lost so much blood, they had to give you a transfusion."

After he left and before I drifted off to sleep, all the trauma to my body flashed through my mind—the abuse, the bleeding, the casts. And, that night, a long row of clamps, from my navel to my pubic bone, proved that my body had been traumatized once more.

Worse than my old, crank-up bed and having to walk to the bathroom across the hall was that the nurses gave Robbie a bottle when he cried and then brought him to me on a four-hour schedule to nurse. They literally plopped him in my arms on top of my clamps and walked out, not even offering to raise the head of the bed or to help me position him properly. I had never heard of the La Leche League and, if they were available to coach me, no one told me. On the third day of this, I tearfully told the nurse to give me the shot to dry up my milk. After she left, I lay back down and stared at the ceiling. "I couldn't even deliver my own baby and now I can't nurse him either." And then, "Is everything in my body that makes me a woman broken?" I didn't want to curse God and die, but I cried angry, heartbroken tears and it didn't help that, because of the strict visiting hours, most of the time I was all alone.[36]

We liked the name Robbie but we gave him a formal name on his birth certificate: Robert Jason Couts. He was a darling baby boy, but by the time he was five months old, he had the dubious honor of being the second youngest baby to have tubes put in his ears at Akron Children's Hospital. Before that, it had been a long, hard winter for me with a very sick baby. Around Thanksgiving, our pediatrician lanced Rob's ear drums in his office while Bud and I held him down. When that and multiple rounds of antibiotics didn't help, he was hospitalized in January to find out what was causing the infections. As if the poor baby wasn't going through enough, I could only be with him during the day and had to leave him in the hospital at night. The infection ended up being a staph infection with drainage so thick that it pushed out the first set of tubes the surgeon put in and the surgery had to be repeated.

By the spring of 1973, that ordeal was over, but then we got another blow. Bud's job at CVCA would end in June. Even though he was enrolled in a course at Akron U on a path to be certified to teach, the state was no longer granting temporary teaching certificates. CVCA was applying for its

---

[36] *"Women with a history of sexual trauma are 12 times more likely to experience labor and delivery as traumatic than women without such history."*
Watson, Victoria S. (Spring 2016). Retraumatization of Sexual Trauma in Women's Reproductive Health Care. (University of Tennessee, Knoxville, Honors Thesis).

State Charter and one of the requirements was that all its employees be certified. Bud would be unemployed. Leads at two churches didn't work out and then something happened that changed the course of our lives and led us to a place of ministry that we loved.

In March, I read an article in Gospel Missionary Union's monthly news magazine about their ministry in the Bahamas, Windermere High School. It was a Christian high school on the island of Eleuthera for Bahamian teens, the only high school in all the Bahamian islands other than those in Nassau and Freeport. In a little box at the end of the article it said, "Needed: English Teacher, Bible Teacher, Campus Pastor, P.E. Teacher, Music Director, Youth Worker."

I looked at Bud and said, "Why don't we try this? I'll take the first one and you can do the rest." In April, we applied to GMU as missionaries and in early July we went to Smithville, Missouri for Candidate Orientation. Naturally, my parents were delighted to see us follow in their footsteps. During the next two months, we contacted individuals and visited churches to raise our support. It was heartwarming that Goss Memorial Church was the first church to have us share our vision with them. They started supporting us right away and let us stay, rent free, in a house they owned behind the church. Four other churches and a dozen or so of our friends also pledged to support us financially and by late summer we were ready to go.

On September 13, 1973. we boarded a little Missionary Flights International airplane in West Palm Beach and flew to Rock Sound, Eleuthera, Bahamas. We called that lovely island with its beautiful people home for the next 21 years, and our children still consider it home.

Chapter 25

Tropical Paradise and Stormy Seas
1973–1979
Teaching in the Bahamas, Childbirth Trauma Again

On July 10, 1973, just two months before we arrived on Eleuthera, the Bahamas had gained their independence from Britain. I had grown up in a colony, so many things like the government buildings and how the stores were stocked with goods imported from abroad felt familiar to me. I had also grown up in an undeveloped country, so settlements without electricity, including the one where the school was located, and houses without running water did not surprise me. Most importantly, the beautiful Bahamian people reminded me of the people of my childhood with their formal greetings, their sense of humor, their proverbs, their ability to read a person and to imitate them to a T, and their dignity and grace.

Our move to Eleuthera marked the beginning of my adult life. I was a wife and a mother, I had the teaching career I had always dreamed of and I felt at home.

Like my mother in Mali, I hung our clothes out to dry on a clothesline, I made all our bread and I wrote newsletters home to our supporters. Our life on Eleuthera is documented in other places, so I will not write about that in detail. However, the ripples of my childhood splashed, and sometimes crashed, on the shore of my adulthood, so they bear telling here.

First, there was the birth of our daughter. My pregnancy with Jennie was so completely different from my pregnancy with Rob that I knew I was having a girl. I was not nauseous, nor did I have any spotting. However, one evening after supper I felt really sick. I told Bud that maybe a walk would help me feel better so we took Robbie by the hand and walked down our little driveway to the road that ran along the bay where I had to turn around. Back at the house, I went to the bathroom and there was bright red blood. Bud jumped in the car, drove to the Batelco Office and had the switchboard operator call the clinic in Rock Sound. A nurse, he was told, would be on her way.

When she arrived, she gave me a shot of some kind and told me to stay downstairs on the couch, to lie perfectly still and to get up only to go to the bathroom. Flashbacks of Miss Adam giving me those same directions didn't help, but I couldn't dwell on that. Bud stayed home the next morning to watch Robbie so I could continue lying still. By that evening, the bleeding had stopped.

We knew I would have to leave the island to have a C-section and by summer we settled on going to Anniston, Alabama where Bud's brother-in-law Bob was stationed in the Army. Bud's sister Marge would take good care of me and her children, Kim and Todd, would make good playmates for Robbie in the weeks prior to and after having the baby. On our way back to the Bahamas, after being in the U.S. for Bud's Dad's funeral in July, we stopped in Anniston and I had one appointment with an obstetrician. From there we returned to Eleuthera and settled into a house in Savannah Sound which put us closer to the Windermere campus. My due date was around Christmas so, in mid-November I flew to Alabama with Robbie, who was just over two years old.

Compared to my pregnancy with Robbie, my belly looked small. One doctor wondered if my due date was later than had been calculated, so he ordered an amniocentesis to make sure. It indicated that all was well, so we proceeded with the date we had picked, December 19, 1974. This time I had a spinal block and was awake for the delivery. I couldn't see the surgery, of course, but when I saw the doctor lift his arms up and away from my body, I knew my baby had been born. And then, when the operating room fell silent, I knew something was wrong. I heard a faint cry and then saw a nurse rush from the room with a small, towel-wrapped bundle in her hands. "What's wrong? What's wrong with my baby?" I cried, lifting myself up on my elbow and turning to catch a glimpse of the nurse fleeing from the room. At that point, a white mask covered my face and everything went black.

I woke up to the doctor standing at the end of my bed. "We picked her a little green," he said. "But her lungs are fine. That's the main thing. We have her in an incubator because she weighs only 4 pounds, 4 ounces. You won't be able to take her home anytime soon, so you won't be able to nurse her. I've ordered the shot to stop your milk from coming in."

This latest devastation dredged up all the others[37] and, at night, when the nurses brought my roommate's baby in to nurse, I would get out of bed, grab a tissue to wipe my tears, and walk to the nursery window to stare at my tiny baby girl, sleeping in her incubator. In the wee morning hours of December 24, 1974, the nursery door opened and a nurse said kindly, "You haven't held her yet, have you?" I shook my head no. "Come on in," she motioned, "it's time you met your little girl." I was so grateful, but, things did not look good. Viable lungs notwithstanding, she kept losing weight.

I left the hospital later that morning to join Bud and Robbie at Marge's house. At 7:00 on Christmas morning, I called the nurse's desk for the daily report and was told that Jennie had dropped to 3 pounds, 13 ounces. The pediatrician had ordered her to be kept in the incubator, even for her feedings. I hung up, dropped my head into my hands and sobbed.

Marge and her husband did not have a car but got around instead on large Honda motorcycles. Marge had already borrowed her friend's car the day before to bring me home and was reluctant to ask her friend to borrow her car on Christmas Day. But car or no car, I had to see my baby. Somehow, I managed to climb up behind Bud on Bob's bike and we followed Marge on hers to the hospital. Every bump in the road was excruciating, but it was worth it because we got to see our baby through the window where we prayed our hearts out. The next morning when I called, her weight was the same.

On December 27th, she had gained two ounces and the next day she had gained one more. In early January, just before he had to go back to the Bahamas, Bud was allowed to go into the nursery to hold her. I see him still, cradling her tiny body in the palm of his hand, his fingertips supporting her little head, saying hello and goodbye to his baby girl.

Poor Robbie. I told him his sister was too little to come out of the hospital and that he was too little to go in to see her. What a sweet boy he

---

[37] *"Experiences that could trigger a traumatic stress reaction include ...having someone in your family (including you or your child) become seriously ill."*
Kendall-Tackett, Kathleen The Long Shadow: Adult Survivors of Childhood Abuse. www.vetmed.wsu.edu/docs/librariesprovider16/default-document-library/the-long-shadow-adult-survivors-of-childhood-abuse.pdf?sfvrsn=0

was. The day Marge and I brought her home, we put her in his arms for a minute in the back seat of a borrowed car. He would have held her all day if we had let him. We named her Jeanette after Dr. Jeanette Troup who had died of Lassa Fever in Nigeria just five years before. We gave her the middle name Lynn because the two names sounded pretty together. We called her Jennie or Jennie Lynn and, after almost losing her once before she came and fearing for her life once she got here, we are so very grateful that she came to stay.

Jennie gained weight by leaps and bounds once I brought her home and by late January the pediatrician cleared her to go home to the Bahamas. My parents drove down from Missouri to drive us down to Florida. I put a pillow in a large wicker basket and that was where Jennie slept all the way to West Palm Beach. From there we flew to Eleuthera and settled into our home in Savannah Sound where we had moved in the summer of 1974 to be closer to the school. The settlement had just gotten electricity, but we had water only in the mornings—which was a challenge for showering, flushing the toilet, washing the dishes and doing the laundry for a family of four. When I felt sorry for myself, the memory of my mother living in huts in Africa and my vow to meet life's struggles unflinchingly kicked in and I carried on.

We moved back to Tarpum Bay in the summer of 1977 when Jennie was two and a half and Robbie was five, old enough to start Grade 1 at the Little Prep Primary School in the middle of the settlement. Bud and several leaders from other churches opened a Youth Center in town and he and I both continued teaching at Windermere.

Near the end of the 1978 school year, I was interrupted one afternoon during class to take a phone call in the school office. It was Leonard Reimer from GMU headquarters telling me that Dad had just been appointed the President of GMU. When I hung up the phone I remembered how, twenty years before, Dad's spiritual life as a missionary had been questioned because he championed his kids. I wanted to laugh right out loud, but the principal was there and didn't know that story, so instead I smiled all the way back to class at the irony of it all. It was a good lesson to learn: standing for the truth may cost you, but ultimately people will respect you for holding your ground.

Around that same time, Bud and I were having on-and-off discussions about having a third child. Finally, in the spring of 1979, when Jennie was four and a half and we were packing up to return to Ohio for a year, I said, "I don't want to keep storing the crib and the high chair forever. We need to decide if we're having a third child or not. Plus, I'm not getting any younger, you know!"

Bud didn't answer for a minute and then solemnly said, "It's the sleep, Dianne. It's the sleep." Like her big brother, Jennie had serious ear infections until she was a toddler and this had meant many sleepless nights at the Couts house. His reasoning was good enough for me, and so we got rid of the crib but kept the high chair—and it was a good thing we did!

Chapter 26

Full Circles, Lasting Ripples
1979–1986
Furlough, Third Childbirth, Medical Problems Escalate

We returned to Akron in the summer of 1979 and furloughed in Mrs. Troup's house. She had broken her hip and had moved in with her daughter to recuperate. The family graciously let us rent her house for a nominal fee. It was right around the corner from Goss Memorial Church. Robbie attended Heminger School for Grade 4—where his uncles and I had attended before him—and Jennie went to pre-school. I reconnected with my childhood friends at church and took a college course to keep my Ohio teaching certification. We visited our supporting churches and our families. It was a rather routine furlough until one February morning when I sat up on the edge of my bed, felt a wave of nausea and knew I was pregnant.

This time there was ultrasound. The doctor ordered one when I started spotting as I had with Robbie. All was well with the baby. I, however, was not well at all. On top of the nausea, I was depressed and weepy. The dark winter weather didn't help—nor did the dark drapes and dark furniture that surrounded me. My perpetual exhaustion and my rising anxiety at the thought of packing up and returning to the Bahamas were overwhelming. I was also worried about where to have the baby and how to pay for our flights. In May, a couple at Goss, Gordon and Elizabeth Morgan, heard my concerns and offered to pay for Bud and me to fly to Smithville, Missouri where I could stay with my parents to have the baby. By now I was over my first trimester and that, coupled with this unexpected, generous gift, brought me back to myself.

We returned to Eleuthera in August of 1980 and, fortunately, that year was one of the few years Windermere was adequately staffed, so I was not needed as a teacher. This allowed me to pace myself as I unpacked and settled in to our home in Tarpum Bay. September in Eleuthera is sweltering hot, but two things helped: we'd brought back an area carpet and a ceiling fan for the living room. When I needed a break, I'd lie down on the carpet, my growing belly directly beneath the fan. When I cooled down, I would start unpacking again.

Robbie was now in Grade 4 and Jennie was in Grade 2. I dreaded leaving them for two months, but I bravely kissed them goodbye one October morning and boarded a plane in Rock Sound on my way to Missouri. As the plane took off, I leaned my face into the window, stared at the turquoise water beneath me and started to cry.

"They're with their father," I admonished myself. "This is nothing compared to what your mother went through." But sometimes, vows to be unflinching don't stop the tears.

I missed my children, but it was fun being home with my parents. The summer before, while we were visiting Mom and Dad, I had chosen an ob-gyn to do my C-section. His lack of a bedside manner was legendary in Smithville, but he was a good surgeon and, since I'd never see him again after the baby was born, his brusque style really didn't matter. We picked November 10, 1980 as the day for the baby's birth. I was not as huge as I had been with Robbie, nor as small as I had been with Jennie, but I was big enough that it was hard bending over to curve my spine for the spinal block. After I was wheeled into surgery, I was delighted that I could see what was happening in the reflection of the anesthesiologist's glasses. I watched as the baby was lifted from me and immediately heard a lusty cry. The doctor said, "It's a girl!" followed by "Write down the time," and then they showed me my wailing baby's little blood-covered face. The nurse said, "I'll clean her up and bring her to you after they stitch you up. You did great!"

I had been sure I was having a boy, but we had a girl's name picked out, just in case. We named our new baby Janelle, a variation of her big sister Jeanette's name, and Marie for my mother's middle name and in honor of our Bahamian friend Mrs. Marie Ingraham who was caring for Robbie and Jennie while Bud and I were gone. It took Bud a couple of days to get through to the operator in Tarpum Bay to tell Mrs. Marie that we had a healthy baby girl. At lunch that day, Mrs. Marie said to Robbie and Jennie, "I heard from your daddy today. You have a baby sister." Jennie clapped her hands and jumped for joy.

"What would you have said if I told you it was a boy?" Marie asked.

"I would have cried," Jennie replied.

On the second day of my recovery, when the nurse brought Janelle to nurse, she said, "Did you see her little dimple?" I had not noticed it but I had noticed that she was a sweet, contented baby. How wonderful it was to take her home to my parents, to have her sleep in a bassinet beside my bed and to have her nurse at my breast. The coming of this third child helped replace some of the trauma of delivering the previous two and, for that, I was grateful.

After Bud returned to the Bahamas, something happened that transported me straight back to my childhood. I had a dentist appointment one afternoon to get my back, left molar pulled. Before I left, I nursed Janelle and left her with Mom to babysit. During the extraction, the tooth broke and fragments of tooth and filling went flying. There was a flurry of activity as the dentist's assistant suctioned the socket to remove any fragments followed by the dentist prying out the other half of the tooth. When this ordeal was over, I was drained. When I got home, I told Dad I might not be able to go to the banquet that evening at the mission headquarters.

"If you don't attend, your mother won't either. You have to go. I'm counting on you," he said and I knew it was useless to argue with him or with myself.

After moving to Smithville in 1972, Mother had never adjusted to life as an empty nester nor to life in Smithville, a southern town she claimed was unfriendly. In reality, she had made few efforts to make friends, even among the missionary women at headquarters. She was under the care of a psychiatrist, who had hospitalized her and had treated her with electro-shock therapy for her suicidal depression. It's hard to say why she often refused to attend important functions with Dad, but if it was her way to hurt and upset him, it worked.

So, instead of lying down to rest, I nursed Janelle, styled my mother's hair, got myself dressed, dressed Janelle, packed a diaper bag, got in the car and went with my parents to the banquet. I could still taste blood in my mouth, I couldn't eat and I was angry. Once again, I was a traumatized ten-year old girl holding it together for her parents. Even though I was old enough to know that there was nothing heroic or noble about the motions I was going through, there would be no hysterics.

On the day Janelle was four weeks old, Mom and Dad took me to the Kansas City Airport to begin our journey home to Eleuthera. I was worried about the long flight to Miami with an infant, but when I found my seat, a lady turned to her husband and exclaimed, "Oh look, honey! We have a baby!" She didn't mind when I discreetly nursed Janelle and then she held her so I could put my seat back and rest. From Miami, I flew to Eleuthera where Robbie and Jennie met their baby sister. Jennie got to hold her first because Rob had held her when

225

we brought her home. Bud had forgotten to assemble our borrowed crib, so we emptied a dresser drawer, put a blanket in the bottom and that's where she slept her first night home.

All is well that ends well—until it isn't. A week after returning to Eleuthera I was suspicious that I had an infection. Three days later I had some cramping and, in the discharge, I was startled to see a black suture. After the doctor in Rock Sound examined me, he held up his gloved hand, dripping with pus, and exclaimed with alarm, "This is from the womb!"

"I know," I replied. "I told you I found a stitch."

When he left the examining room, I found myself staring at the ceiling, feeling like I was one with the cold metal table beneath me, unable to move. "Everything was so perfect and now my uterus is literally rotting. Will it ever stop?" I thought. Then a nurse poked her head in the door to ask if I was alright, so I calmly sat up, got dressed and went to the doctor's office. I was obviously weak and he was obviously worried but, thankfully, the one antibiotic that all the government clinics kept in stock worked and the infection went away.

The doctor in Smithville had tied my tubes, and I was relieved to finally go off birth control pills for good. Things were okay as long as I nursed Janelle, but when I weaned her in February of 1982, all my old problems returned. The gynecologist's suggestion when I was a tenth grader that having children might clear up my problems did not prove to be true for me. I either didn't have a period for months, spotted for weeks, or bled for days. My gynecologist in St. Petersburg did a D & C in 1983 to see if that would help. It didn't.

We were due to go on furlough in 1985 and I was determined to see what my options were for solving my problems which, by now, had been going on for over twenty years. When we returned to Akron in the summer of 1985, I made an appointment with the same doctor who had delivered Robbie and outlined in detail, for the first time, my entire history of excessive bleeding and my uterine casts. When I finished, he looked at me and said, "If you have one more bleeding episode, we'll do a hysterectomy."

"Really?" I answered. "Just like that?" I had been reading about the proliferation of C-sections and hysterectomies and what some experts were referring to as unnecessary. When I mentioned this he said, "You have a long history of bleeding. You don't want any more children. We both know this has gone on far too long."

Within a few weeks, I knew he was right. While Bud and I were at an Association of Christian Schools International conference in Indiana, an episode of bleeding started. By the time we left, I was lying on the floor in the back of our van, white as a sheet. When we got back to Akron, I called the doctor, he ordered something to stop the bleeding and scheduled me for surgery.

On the day of the surgery in October, Bud saw me in the recovery room after my operation, but had to leave before I was taken to my room to be home when the kids returned from school. Although my room had two beds, I was alone. Just after supper a nurse came in to check on me. "That was really something that they had to take your ovaries," she commented nonchalantly while checking my IV.

I was too stunned to speak. "Oh," she continued, "didn't anyone tell you?"

"No," I answered, "They didn't tell me. Why didn't they ask me first?"

"You'll have to ask the doctor in the morning," she replied and then changed the subject. "How is your bleeding?"

"Okay, I guess. I've only been up to the bathroom once."

"And your pain?"

"I'm fine."

When she left I picked up the phone and called Bud. "Did they tell you they took my ovaries?"

"What? No one said anything to me about that!"

"Well, the nurse was just in and mentioned it like I knew. You know this means I'm now in menopause, something I had not bargained for. I'm pretty upset," I said, trying to keep my composure.

"It'll be okay, honey. Ask the doctor about it in the morning."

"How are the kids?"

"Fine. Carol Morgan brought supper over. Our Goss Sunday School has meals coming for weeks!" he chuckled

"I know. It's such a help. Kiss the kids goodnight for me," I said.
"Goodnight."

It was not a good night. It was not a good night at all.

The next morning the doctor explained. "When I opened you up, your entire pelvic cavity was dotted with endometriosis."[38]

"That's odd," I said. "Doesn't that usually mean you have severe pain and it's hard to get pregnant? I bled a lot, but I didn't have either of those things."

"Well, the endometriosis would have continued to grow if I had left your ovaries. I could have discussed removing them with your husband but that would have meant keeping you under anesthesia longer. I decided it was best to just take them out while I was in there."

"I'm upset that now I will start menopause," I said pointedly.

"There are hormones for that. And you won't need to start them for a couple of months. You'll be fine."[39]

As he turned to leave, I wanted to tell him I would not be fine at all but instead I turned my face toward the wall and I thought about how I had gone into the operating room that day thinking I'd wake up relieved that my body would no longer traumatize me. Instead it had been traumatized again. Those thoughts triggered a scene in which I watched from the ceiling as the doctor's hands took a scalpel and neatly removed my uterus and then, in horror, I watched as his right hand reached in and ripped out my ovaries and tossed them into a trash can near my head. Tears trickling across my nose brought me back to my pillow, my bed, the wall in front of me and the hospital sounds coming through the door behind me.

My body healed and I adjusted to the hormones. But it would be a long time before the crescendo of waves that crashed over my soul that day would calm down. And sometimes, even now, there are ripples of them still.

There were joys that year too. Grandma Koehl had died in 1978, but the aunts were renting her little house and made it available to us. And so it was that we lived where my mother had grown up and where David and I had spent the summer of 1967. We were cozy in that little house at the end of a dead-end street, next to the Beltline and just down the street from eight sets of tracks that, sadly, were bringing fewer and fewer raw materials into Akron and carrying fewer and fewer tires out. Jennie went to Rimer School for Grade 5 where all the Koehl girls had attended and where I had almost

---

[38] Mapes, Diane. (July 17, 2018). Endometriosis linked to childhood abuse. Fred Hutch News Service.

[39] Zimmermann, Elizabeth. (June 7, 2017). Women with past adverse childhood experiences more likely to have ovaries removed, study shows. Mayo Clinic News Network.

infected the student body with hepatitis. Rob went to Innes Junior High for Grade 8 where his Uncle John and Uncle Rich had been students. Janelle went to pre-school at Lockwood United Methodist Church in the Portage Lakes. And, oh what joy, I went back to Africa!

Dad and Mom were scheduled to visit the Mali field in February of 1986 and invited me to go with them. Friends of theirs chipped in to buy my ticket and, as my body healed from surgery, my spirit began to hum and then sing again as I made preparations for that trip. Irene Ogg, a widow whose husband had worked at GMU headquarters, was going along too and she and I would be roommates. It amazed me how being in the familiar surroundings of Bamako brought back my French and Bambara. Unfortunately, we didn't visit any of the stations where we had lived, but we did stop at Mana on our way to see the Bible Seminary in Bougouni, near Sirakoro. Another trip took us to Segou, past the road we had taken to cross the river at Dioila on our way to Sanankoro. Segou was further north than I had ever been in Mali. As we approached the city, after driving for hours through dry, brown, dusty terrain, it was amazing to see huge flooded rice fields where the Niger had been dammed.

We had lunch with some of the church leaders in Segou who took us to a warehouse where we saw a huge pile of grain that had been imported with famine relief funds from North America. One of the leaders explained, "We have a committee that assesses which villages have the greatest need. When we deliver grain to a village, we have a ceremony at which we present bags of grain to every household whether they were Christian, Muslim or Animist. When we are asked, 'Why don't you just give grain to the Christians?' our answer is that the love of God is not just for the Christians, but for all." It was an honor to be there and to realize that, along with growth in Mali's economy, the church was thriving too.

After I returned from that trip, and as winter turned to spring, I felt a longing to stay in Ohio. I loved Eleuthera and the people there, but relationships among the teaching staff were not always easy. In spite of my tears and my reluctance to return, Bud decided we should go back because it was where we were needed. I knew that was true and, in the summer of 1986, we returned to Eleuthera where we stayed for eight more years. During that time, our children grew up and sat in our classrooms as students at Windermere High School and we have never regretted the 21 years we called Eleuthera home.

Chapter 27

All My Worlds
1986–2020

Family Matters

When we returned to Eleuthera in the summer of 1986, Rob started high school at Windermere in Grade 10. When he graduated in 1989, the year he turned 17, he spent a year living with my parents in Smithville, Missouri, picking up Grade 12 courses that would prepare him for college in America. He got straight A's in his classes, including physics and calculus, played trumpet in the jazz band and had a lead role in the school musical. But if he struggled adapting to life in America, we were too far away to know. We came home in the summer of 1990 to take him to John Brown University in Arkansas. When Bud hugged him goodbye, they both choked up. I teared up at the sight and shed a few tears as we drove away, but I did not feel the need to weep. After all, we were still in the same hemisphere and his grandparents were just four hours away.

Jennie graduated from Windermere in 1991 and that year we returned to the U.S. for our last furlough. She repeated Grade 12 at Green High School in the Akron suburb where we lived that year. She joined the band and did well in school, but she struggled too. One of her teachers told us that she sat alone every day at lunch. I remembered how I felt when I went to Kenmore High and I knew she was in that chaotic emotional crack between the life she knew in the Bahamas and the world she was supposed to know in America. We hoped her transition to college in the fall of 1992 would be easier, especially since her brother Rob would be at John Brown to help her adjust. When we left them both there before returning to Eleuthera, I don't remember crying. But, a few weeks later, when Bud, Janelle and I were back in Eleuthera, I reached for four dinner plates to set the table, and the reality that my sweet Jennie was gone caught me unaware and the tears came.

Two years later, our life on Eleuthera came to a sudden end when we had to return to the States to care for Bud's mother, Eileen. We packed up twenty-one years of living in two weeks and returned to Ohio. I knew our supporters would stand behind us for at least a year, but as we drove from Florida to Ohio, I was in a panic over how we would survive. I lamented to

Bud, "You might be able to be a rep for the mission, but we can't live in the U.S. on our support and I'll never get a teaching job. English teachers are a dime a dozen and schools usually need only one or two French teachers."

I should have been more worried about Janelle than I was about our financial situation. Like her sister before her, coming from Windermere High School with 100 kids in the entire student body to Alliance High School with an enrollment of 1,200 was not easy. One day, as we were driving down the main commercial street in town, Janelle said quietly, "Mom, sometimes I don't feel like I belong here." But she quickly made friends, played sports and had lead roles in the school musicals. By her senior year she had integrated fairly well into life in America and graduated in the top 10% of her class.

The first year we were back in the U.S., Bud represented the mission at various churches and conferences and I stayed home to care for his mom. During that year we sometimes attended First Friends Church in Alliance where Janelle went to youth group. One Sunday morning, as we sang the hymn *Spirit Song,* I started sobbing. The words, "O give Him all your tears and sadness, Give Him all your years of pain," described me and, for the first time, I cried for me, the little lamb who had been so terribly hurt four decades before.

By the summer of 1995, Eileen could no longer walk, talk or feed herself, so the family placed her in a nursing home. In 1996, I got a job teaching English in the nearby village of Minerva and Bud was hired as senior pastor of Goss Memorial Church. I had never fancied myself a pastor's wife and Bud encouraged me to continue with my career. I faithfully attended Sunday services where I smiled, kissed the babies and hugged the old ladies, but I was happy to have my own professional life, 41 miles away. I thrived teaching in a secular setting, first as a dime-a-dozen English teacher and then as Minerva's only French teacher which was exactly what I had predicted would never happen! While at Minerva, I completed my master's degree, made a good salary, insured our family and was very grateful that, despite my lack of faith, I not only got a teaching job, but I landed in a place that I loved.

Advocacy for Missionary Kids

During the early 1990s, as Mamou MKs became reacquainted and started comparing stories, it became evident that many of our former Mamou classmates were suffering from the aftereffects of the abuse we experienced there. They also learned that, for years, letters and phone calls had been made to the Christian and Missionary Alliance (C&MA), the denomination that ran the school, but these attempts to bring the abuse to light had either been ignored or minimized. The Mamou Steering Committee, whose members included my brothers David and Rich, was formed to address this issue in a more organized fashion, but although the C&MA met with the committee a couple of times, there was more stonewalling than progress.

That is how I found myself in attorney Doug Yauger's office in Pittsburgh, Pennsylvania on May 23, 1995 participating in a press conference and being coached on how to hold a public protest. There were six of us there that day: the Shellrude sisters, Marilyn and Beverly, and the Darr siblings, Dianne, David, John and Rich. After the press conference, we went to the convention center in downtown Pittsburgh where the C&MA was holding its annual conference with hundreds of attendees from every state of the union and from all over the world. We passed out flyers about MK abuse as the attendees streamed inside and faced angry accusations as people figured out what we were doing. Then, holding simple crosses, we formed a semi-circle, bowed our heads and stood without moving while the stream of attendees trickled to a halt and finally, the sidewalk was quiet in front of us.

That evening our protest was on the evening news. The next morning our story was in both Pittsburgh newspapers. Within a year, an Independent Commission of Inquiry (ICI) was formed to investigate abuse at Mamou and their final report was published in November, 1997. On the opening page it read, "Prior to and during the existence of the ICI, many people struggled with the questions about the existence, nature and extent of abuse that may have occurred at Mamou. Were children abused at Mamou? As this report will demonstrate, the answer is unequivocal. Yes, a significant number of children were seriously abused at Mamou."

The day I recounted to Mom and Dad what had happened in Pittsburgh, Dad grinned from ear to ear. They were obviously proud that all four of their children challenged the mission whose failures had done so much harm. However, they didn't just pat us on the back. They were interviewed by David Briggs for articles in the *Cleveland Plain Dealer* about abuse in mission settings and Dad wrote letters to the Independent Commission of Inquiry. In November, 1996 he traveled with us to Kansas City where we, along with the Neudorf family, confronted GMU about their policy that had mandated that their Mali missionaries send their children to Mamou and about their current policies for prevention and reporting of child abuse. In July of 1998, he wrote a letter to his now-retired Mali colleagues whose children had attended Mamou, encouraging them to reach out to their children and listen to their stories. In May, 1999, he attended the retreat in Atlanta, hosted by the C&MA, for the students and parents of those who had attended Mamou.

And then, just five years later, when Dad was 78 years old, a minor operation followed by an infection weakened his already failing heart and we had five days to say good-bye. The entire family came home in time to have him beam one last time at the little ones and to make all of us laugh. "I know the Lord will be with me," he said smiling and then, his eyes shining, "I love my family and I know they love me." His funeral was held at Goss Memorial Church and then, at the grave side, one of his fellow missionaries from Mali gave the benediction. How fitting that on a hill overlooking Kenmore, with the steeple of Goss Memorial Church plainly visible in the valley below, a prayer in the Bambara language thanked God for the life of Dick Linder Darr and asked a blessing on all of us who stood weeping there.

Sadly, Dad was gone before the story of Mamou was memorialized in the documentary *All God's Children*. Filmmakers Luci Westphall and Scott Solary interviewed the Beardslee, the Shellrude and the Darr families to recount what happened at Mamou and how each family had fought to have their stories heard and believed. Filming began in 2004 and it premiered at the Sarasota Film Festival in 2008 where the Darr kids and the Shellrude girls found themselves together once again. But this time it was on a stage to answer questions from an audience who had just watched a film that chronicled their horrors and their pain.

In 2009, Luci and I organized several screenings of *All God's Children* in Ohio. Goss Memorial Church held the first one and, after the showing, many in the audience were stunned. Articles about the film and my story ran in the *Akron Beacon Journal*, the *Canton Repository,* the *Alliance Review* and the *Minerva Leader*.

When I retired from Minerva in 2012, I became active as a member of the board of MK Safety Net, a group that was formed in 1999 to expand the pioneering work of the Mamou Steering Committee. Missionary kids who have been abused can reach out to us for affirmation and understanding, encouragement and resources as they pursue justice and healing in their lives. As part of that, I speak around the country in conferences and churches about abuse in mission settings. I am grateful for these opportunities to educate people about the effects of abuse and how organizations react when it is brought to light. However, revisiting those years over and over again is not easy.

Repercussions of a Vow Fulfilled

Something else that was not easy was caring for my mother in the years after Dad died. After a series of minor strokes in 2002, she had developed vascular dementia. When Dad died on April, 26, 2004 we knew she could not live alone. She moved in with Bud and me that fall and lived with us for eight and a half years. Over time, and through several hospitalizations and surgery for breast cancer, we hired a crew of ladies to help with her care during the week. David, John and Rich visited often and were very supportive, but her care in the evenings and the weekends, plus the overseeing of her ongoing medical conditions fell on me. I often wondered why I did it, why I could not put her in a nursing home. The answers are, of course, complex. But when I would think of how she had borne my sorrows as best as she could when I was a little girl, I knew I could not abandon her, defenseless, to the care of strangers—even though this is precisely what had happened to me.

In the spring of 2013 Mom stumbled, caught herself on the edge of the couch and slumped to the floor on her knees. Her legs broke, just above her knee replacements, and she never walked again. At that point, she needed skilled nursing care, so we placed her in a nursing home where I spent time with her every day and made sure she got the best possible care. And then, on April 28, 2014, she had a massive stroke and we were told she had just days to live. She rallied for two days while family came or called to say goodbye. Ten years and six days after our father died, she was gone.

My father was always my hero, not just because I was his little girl, but because his love was steady and strong and he championed me all my life. My relationship with my mother was not so simple. However, during the years I cared for her in my home, I learned to appreciate her for who she was: a shy, no-nonsense, witty person who loved a quiet life and simple things. Although she had suffered much, there was never any doubt that she loved her children with all her heart. It was an honor to be the daughter of Dick and Anne Darr and I have never regretted my vow to make them proud.

However, carrying that banner for a lifetime has been hard and over the decades it has taken its toll. I am ever mindful that people are watching. I worry constantly about making mistakes. And, on top of physical effects of the sexual abuse I have endured, there have been emotional ones related to that as well. I don't trust anyone completely and, when I read the symptoms of Generalized Anxiety Disorder a few years ago, it was like looking in a mirror.

Hope for the Future

The field of epigenetics would have us believe that trauma trickles down. I can look back at the lives of my grandparents and see how the ripple effects of the things they suffered impacted their offspring. I shudder to think that the trauma that happened to me could affect my children. But I also know that resilience, courage and love are also passed down and these I have known in far greater measure than all of my sorrows. This gives me hope for my children and theirs that although life may be hard, grace, as it has for me, will lead them home.

Epilogue

In May of 2015, I went to Olean, New York with my brother David and his son Jonathan to learn more about our Darr (Dörr) roots. We visited the cemetery where our great-grandparents were buried and, at the library, we unearthed a couple of articles we had never before seen. On our way out of town, we drove to the scene of the fire that killed our great-grandfather in 1910 when he thought his son, our grandfather, was trapped inside. Between two small houses there sat a lot—empty still.

The Linder family, who welcomed their sister Dora's fatherless boy into their home every summer, followed their nephew Dick's missionary career with pride. Interestingly, Dad's cousin Lloyd Linder, the one whom Dad accompanied on the milk route to town, became a much-loved Lutheran minister in Cleveland and a chaplain at the Cleveland Clinic. Linder Dairy is still in operation and Dora's legacy of hard work and no-nonsense common sense is evident in her successful grandchildren and great-grandchildren to this day.

Frank Koehl's family, if they were paying attention, learned that their disdain of Frank's wife did not hinder the success of his offspring. The eight Koehl girls married well and, of his 21 grandchildren, eight hold advanced degrees, including five at the doctoral level. His grandchildren and great-grandchildren include business executives, business owners, teachers, ministers, college professors, engineers, chemists and a medical doctor.

As for my Grandma Koehl, gentle reminders continue to ripple through time that remind me of the sorrows that made her resilient and wise. One involves finding and marking her little boy's grave in Philadelphia. Another involves our granddaughter (Annie's great-great-granddaughter) Sarah Couts, who was born on December 19, 2007. Her father's name is Robert, the name Annie gave her son on that very date almost a century before. As for me, the name Sarah—the name that another Robert, in a sinister world long ago, ascribed to me—now conjures up a lovely, bright-eyed child with sunlit hair who is a princess indeed.

Resources

Websites about and for Missionary Kids (MKs) and Third Culture Kids (TCKs):

Missionary Kids Safety Net – mksafetynet.org
Communicating Across the Boundaries of Faith & Culture (blog by Marilyn R. Gardner) – communicatingacrossboundariesblog.com
Families in Global Transition – figt.org
Interaction International – interactionintl.org
Lois Bushong, Counselor – loisbushong.com
Michèle Phoenix, Writer and MK Advocate – michelephoenix.com

Books about MKs and TCKs:

Belonging Everywhere & Nowhere: Insights into Counseling the Globally Mobile by Lois Bushong
Third Culture Kids: Growing Up Among Worlds (Third Ed.) by David Pollock, Ruth Van Reken and Michael Pollock

Documentary about Abuse at Dianne's MK Boarding School:
allgodschildrenthefilm.com

Books Explaining the Lifelong Impact of Childhood Abuse:

Childhood Disrupted: How Your Biography Becomes Your Biology and How You Can Heal by Donna Jackson Nakazawa
The Body Keeps the Score – Brain, Mind, and Body in the Healing of Trauma by Bessel Van der Kolk, M.D.
The Deepest Well: Healing the Long-Term Effects of Childhood Adversity by Dr. Nadine Burke Harris

Books about Preventing and Responding to Abuse:

How Little We Knew: Collusion and Confusion with Sexual Misconduct by
   Dee Ann Miller

*Tear Down This Wall of Silence: Dealing with Sexual Abuse in Our
   Churches* by Dale Ingraham and Rebecca Davis

*The Courage Coach: A Practical, Friendly Guide on How to Heal from
   Abuse* by Ashley Easter

This Little Light: Beyond a Baptist Preacher Predator and His Gang by
   Christa Brown

*What Is a Girl Worth?: My Story of Breaking the Silence and Exposing the
   Truth About Larry Nassar and USA Gymnastics* by Rachel Denhollander

My Body Is Private by Linda Girard (a resource for children)

Organizations Focused on Preventing and Responding to Abuse:

A Better Way: A Proactive Approach to Combating Sexual Abuse –
   abetterway.org

Adverse Childhood Experiences Connection (A social network that
   accelerates the global movement toward recognizing the impact of
   adverse childhood experiences in shaping adult behavior and health) –
   ACEsConnection.com

Diane Langberg, Ph.D., Practicing psychologist and international speaker
   working with trauma survivors, caregivers, and clergy around the world
   – dianelangberg.com

Jimmy Hinton (a minister familiar with abuse, God and the journey of
   healing for survivors) – jimmyhinton.org

GRACE (Godly Response to Abuse in the Christian Environment) –
   netgrace.org

Plan to Protect – plantoprotect.com

SNAP (Survivors Network of those Abused by Priests) – snapnetwork.org

The Courage Conference (Ending Abuse Together) –
   thecourageconference.com

The Hope of Survivors (A safe place where healing begins) –
   thehopeofsurvivors.org

About the Author

Dianne was born in 1948 in Akron, Ohio, the same city where her parents had lived their entire lives. Until she was two years old, Dianne was just like millions of children born in America after WWII. However, in the years that followed, her extraordinary childhood spanned continents and cultures and included both wonderful and traumatic experiences.

Dianne's first memories were made in Greenville, South Carolina where her father attended college for four years. Her family returned to Akron when she was six, the year she attended first grade. The next year, Dianne's parents went overseas as missionaries and, because of that, her education continued in a quaint little town near Paris, then in the West African port city of Dakar, back to school in Akron for a year and a half, followed by boarding school in the rain forest of Guinea, West Africa. Her family returned to Akron the year Dianne was a sophomore and then she finished high school on an isolated station on the savanna of Mali, West Africa.

Dianne graduated from the University of Akron and has a Master's Degree in the Art of Teaching from Marygrove College. She is a retired high school teacher whose career of teaching English and French spanned four decades and included teaching in private and public schools in the U.S. and abroad. Dianne and her husband Bud, who have been married for over fifty years, live in Akron, Ohio. They have three married children and seven grandchildren. (Their oldest granddaughter is missing from the picture.)

Drawing on her own experience of trauma and its lasting effects, and on her years as a board member of *MK Safety Net*, Dianne speaks at national conferences and in churches to raise awareness of abuse in religious settings and to encourage abuse survivors on their healing journeys.

To contact Dianne:

FaceBook Page: Dianne's Memoir

Email: diannesmemoir@yahoo.com

Made in the USA
Monee, IL
04 July 2020

35698419R00134